The Great Books Reading & Discussion Program

FOURTH SERIES · VOLUME TWO

The Great Books Foundation

A Nonprofit Educational Corporation

Designed by Don Walkoe Design, Chicago

Handmade marbled paper, photographed on cover,
courtesy of Andrews, Nelson, Whitehead.

9   8   7   6   5   4   3   2   1

Published and distributed by

The Great Books Foundation
A Nonprofit Educational Corporation
35 East Wacker Drive, Suite 2300
Chicago, IL 60601-2298

Acknowledgments

"Rameau's Nephew" from *Rameau's Nephew and Other Works* by Denis Diderot, translated by Jacques Barzun and Ralph H. Bowen. Copyright 1956 by Jacques Barzun and Ralph H. Bowen. Reprinted by permission of the publisher, Doubleday & Company, Inc.

"Medea" from *Greek Plays in Modern Translation* by Euripides, translated by Frederic Prokosch and edited by Dudley Fitts. Copyright 1947 by Frederic Prokosch. Published by The Dial Press, 1953.

"The Overcoat" from *The Diary of a Madman and Other Stories* by Nikolai Gogol, translated by Andrew R. MacAndrew. Copyright 1960 by Andrew R. MacAndrew. Reprinted by permission of the publisher, New American Library, Inc.

"Utilitarianism" by John Stuart Mill, edited by Oskar Piest. Copyright 1957 by The Bobbs-Merrill Company, Inc. Reprinted by permission of the publisher, The Bobbs-Merrill Company, Inc.

"The Misanthrope" by Molière, translated by Richard Wilbur. Copyright 1955 by Richard Wilbur. Reprinted by permission of the publisher, Harcourt Brace Jovanovich, Inc.

"Of Experience" from *The Complete Essays of Montaigne*, translated by Donald M. Frame. Copyright 1958 by the Board of Trustees of the Leland Stanford Junior University. Reprinted by permission of the publisher, Stanford University Press.

"Symposium" from *Five Dialogues by Plato*, translated by Michael Joyce. Reprinted by permission of the Executors of Michael Joyce deceased.

"The Indestructibility of Our Inner Nature" from *The World as Will and Representation* by Arthur Schopenhauer, translated by E.F.J. Payne. Copyright 1958 by The Falcon's Wing Press. Reprinted by permission of the publisher, Dover Publications, Inc.

"Caesar and Cleopatra" by Bernard Shaw. Copyright 1913, renewed 1941 by Bernard Shaw. Reprinted by permission of The Society of Authors, London.

A source note appears, together with biographical information about the author, opposite the opening page of each work in this series. Footnotes by the author are not bracketed; footnotes by GBF or a translator are [bracketed].

CONTENTS

*

JOB
Bible / *Page 1*

•

UTILITARIANISM
John Stuart Mill / *Page 33*

•

CAESAR AND CLEOPATRA
Bernard Shaw / *Page 55*

•

THE CITY OF GOD
St. Augustine / *Page 171*

•

SYMPOSIUM
Plato / *Page 213*

A selection from "The Book of Job" in *The Holy Bible,*
King James Version. Publisher: Meridian Books, The
World Publishing Co., 1964. Chapters: 1; 2; 3:1–19;
4; 5:8–19; 6:1–4, 8–14, 22–24; 7:1–7, 11–21; 8:1–
13, 20–22; 9:1–22, 32–35; 10:1–9, 18–22; 11:1–11;
12:1–5; 13:2–28; 14; 16:16–22; 17:1–4; 18:1–15, 21;
19:1–7, 21–29; 20:1–7, 27–29; 21; 22:1–7, 30; 23:1–
14; 24:1–12, 25; 25; 26:1–3; 27:1–7; 28:1–3, 10–
15, 20–28; 29:1–13; 30:16–26; 31:1–30, 35–37;
32:1–8, 11–12; 33; 34:1, 7–19, 31–37; 35; 36:1–6,
11–18; 37:14–24; 38:1–18, 37–41; 39:1–12; 40:1–19;
41:1–2, 8–11, 33–34; 42.

Job

There was a man in the land of Uz, whose name was Job; and that man was perfect and upright, and one that feared God, and eschewed evil. And there were born unto him seven sons and three daughters. His substance also was seven thousand sheep, and three thousand camels, and five hundred yoke of oxen, and five hundred she-asses, and a very great household; so that this man was the greatest of all the men of the east. And his sons went and feasted in their houses, every one his day; and sent and called for their three sisters to eat and to drink with them. And it was so, when the days of their feasting were gone about, that Job sent and sanctified them, and rose up early in the morning, and offered burnt offerings according to the number of them all: for Job said, It may be that my sons have sinned and cursed God in their hearts. Thus did Job continually.

Now there was a day when the sons of God came to present themselves before the Lord, and Satan came also among them. And the Lord said unto Satan, Whence comest thou? Then Satan answered the Lord, and said, From going to and fro in the earth, and from walking up and down in it. And the Lord said unto Satan, Hast thou considered my servant Job, that there is none like him in the earth, a perfect and an upright man, one that feareth God, and escheweth evil? Then Satan answered the Lord, and said, Doth Job fear God for nought? Hast not thou made an hedge about him, and about his house, and about all that he hath on every side? thou hast blessed the work of his hands, and his substance is increased in the land. But put forth thine hand now, and touch all that he hath, and he will curse thee to thy face. And the Lord said unto Satan, Behold, all that he hath is in thy power; only upon himself put not forth thine hand. So Satan went forth from the presence of the Lord.

And there was a day when his sons and his daughters were eating and drinking wine in their eldest brother's house: and there came a messenger unto Job, and said, The oxen were plowing, and the asses feeding beside them: and the Sabeans fell upon them, and took them away; yea, they have slain the servants with the edge of the sword; and I only am escaped alone to tell thee. While he was yet speaking, there came also another, and said, The fire of God is fallen from heaven, and hath burned up the sheep, and the servants, and consumed them; and I only am escaped alone to tell thee. While he was yet speaking, there came also another, and said, the Chaldeans made out three bands, and fell upon the camels, and have carried them away, yea, and slain the servants with the edge of the sword; and I only am escaped alone to tell thee. While he was yet speaking, there came also another, and said, Thy sons and thy daughters were eating and drinking wine in their eldest brother's house: and, behold, there came a great wind from the wilderness, and smote the four corners of the house, and it fell upon the young men, and they are dead; and I only am escaped alone to tell thee. Then Job arose, and rent his mantle, and shaved his head, and fell down upon the ground, and worshipped, and said, Naked came I out of my mother's womb, and naked shall I return thither: the Lord gave, and the Lord hath taken away; blessed be the name of the Lord. In all this Job sinned not, nor charged God foolishly.

Again there was a day when the sons of God came to present themselves before the Lord, and Satan came also among them to present himself before the Lord. And the Lord said unto Satan, From whence comest thou? And Satan answered the Lord, and said, From going to and fro in the earth, and from walking up and down in it. And the Lord said unto Satan, Hast thou considered my servant Job, that there is none like him in the earth, a perfect and an upright man, one that feareth God, and escheweth evil? and still he holdeth fast his integrity, although thou movedst me against him, to destroy him without cause. And Satan answered the Lord, and said, Skin for skin, yea, all that a man hath will he give for his life. But put forth thine hand now, and touch his bone and his flesh, and he will curse thee to thy face. And the Lord said unto Satan, Behold, he is in thine hand; but save his life.

So went Satan forth from the presence of the Lord, and smote Job with sore boils from the sole of his foot unto his crown. And he took him a potsherd to scrape himself withal; and he sat down among the ashes. Then said his wife unto him, Dost thou still retain thine integrity? curse God, and die. But he said unto her, Thou speakest as one of the foolish women speaketh. What? shall we receive good at the hand of God, and shall we not receive evil? In all this did not Job sin with his lips.

Now when Job's three friends heard of all this evil that was come upon him, they came every one from his own place; Eliphaz, the Temanite, and Bildad the Shuhite, and Zophar the Naamathite: for they had made an appointment together to come to mourn with him and to comfort him. And when they lifted up their eyes afar off, and knew him not, they lifted up their voice, and wept; and they rent every one his mantle, and sprinkled dust upon their heads toward heaven. So they sat down with him upon the ground seven days and seven nights, and none spake a word unto him: for they saw that his grief was very great.

After this opened Job his mouth, and cursed his day. And Job spake, and said, Let the day perish wherein I was born, and the night in which it was said, There is a man child conceived. Let that day be darkness; let not God regard it from above, neither let the light shine upon it. Let darkness and the shadow of death stain it; let a cloud dwell upon it; let the blackness of the day terrify it. As for that night, let darkness seize upon it; let it not be joined unto the days of the year, let it not come into the number of the months. Lo, let that night be solitary; let no joyful voice come therein. Let them curse it that curse the day, who are ready to raise up their mourning. Let the stars of the twilight thereof be dark; let it look for light, but have none; neither let it see the dawning of the day: because it shut not up the doors of my mother's womb, nor hid sorrow from mine eyes.

Why died I not from the womb? why did I not give up the ghost when I came out of the belly? Why did the knees prevent me? Or why the breasts that I should suck? For now should I have lain still and been quiet, I should have slept: then had I been at rest, with kings and counsellors of the earth, which built desolate places for themselves; or with princes that had gold, who filled their houses with silver: or as an hidden untimely birth I had not been; as infants which never saw light. There the wicked cease from troubling; and there the weary be at rest. There the prisoners rest together; they hear not the voice of the oppressor. The small and great are there; and the servant is free from his master. . . .

Then Eliphaz the Temanite answered and said, If we assay to commune with thee, wilt thou be grieved? but who can withhold himself from speaking? Behold, thou hast instructed many, and thou hast strengthened the weak hands. Thy words have upholden him that was falling, and thou hast strengthened the feeble knees. But now it is come upon thee, and thou faintest; it toucheth thee, and thou art troubled. Is not this thy fear, thy confidence, thy hope, and the uprightness of thy ways? Remember, I pray thee, who ever perished, being innocent? or where were the righteous cut off? Even as I have seen, they that plow iniquity, and sow wickedness, reap the same. By the blast of God they perish, and by the breath of his nostrils are they consumed. The roaring of the lion, and the voice of the fierce lion, and the teeth of the young lions, are broken. The old lion perisheth for lack of prey, and the stout lion's whelps are scattered abroad.

Now a thing was secretly brought to me, and mine ear received a little thereof. In thoughts from the visions of the night, when deep sleep falleth on men, fear came upon me, and trembling, which made all my bones to shake. Then a spirit passed before my face; the hair of my flesh stood up: it stood still, but I could not discern the form thereof: an image was before mine eyes, there was silence, and I heard a voice, saying, Shall mortal man be more just than God? shall a man be more pure than his maker? Behold, he put no trust in his servants; and his angels he charged with folly: how much less in them that dwell in houses of clay, whose foundation is in the dust, which are crushed before the moth? They are destroyed from morning to evening: they perish for ever without any regarding it. Doth not their excellency which is in them go away? they die, even without wisdom.

I would seek unto God, and unto God would I commit my cause: which doeth great things and unsearchable; marvellous things without number: who giveth rain upon the earth, and sendeth waters upon the fields: to set up on high those that be low; that those which mourn may be exalted to safety. He disappointeth the devices of the crafty, so that their hands cannot perform their enterprise. He taketh the wise in their own craftiness: and the counsel of the froward is carried headlong. They meet with darkness in the daytime, and grope in the noonday as in the night. But he saveth the poor from the sword, from their mouth, and from the hand of the mighty. So the poor hath hope, and iniquity stoppeth her mouth. Behold, happy is the man whom God correcteth: therefore despise not thou the chastening of the Almighty: for he maketh sore, and bindeth up: he woundeth, and his hands make whole. He shall deliver thee in six troubles: yea, in seven there shall no evil touch thee. . . .

But Job answered and said, Oh that my grief were thoroughly weighed, and my calamity laid in the balances together! For now it would be heavier than the sand of the sea: therefore my words are swallowed up. For the arrows of the Almighty are within me, the poison whereof drinketh up my spirit: the terrors of God do set themselves in array against me. . . . Oh that I might have my request; and that God would grant me the thing that I long for! Even that it would please God to destroy me; that he would let loose his hand, and cut me off! Then should I yet have comfort; yea, I would harden myself in sorrow: let him not spare; for I have not concealed the words of the Holy One. What is my strength, that I should hope? and what is mine end, that I should prolong my life? Is my strength the strength of stones? or is my flesh of brass? Is not my help in me? and is wisdom driven quite from me?

To him that is afflicted pity should be shewed from his friend; but he forsaketh the fear of the Almighty. . . . Did I say, Bring unto me? or, Give a reward for me of your substance? or, Deliver me from the enemy's hand? or, Redeem me from the hand of the mighty? Teach me, and I will hold my tongue: and cause me to understand wherein I have erred. . . .

Is there not an appointed time to man upon earth? are not his days also like the days of an hireling? As a servant earnestly desireth the shadow, and as an hireling looketh for the reward of his work: so am I made to possess months of vanity, and wearisome nights are appointed to me. When I lie down, I say, When shall I arise, and the night be gone? and I am full of tossings to and fro unto the dawning of the day. My flesh is clothed with worms and clods of dust; my skin is broken, and become loathsome. My days are swifter than a weaver's shuttle, and are spent without hope. O remember that my life is wind: mine eyes shall no more see good. . . .

Therefore I will not refrain my mouth; I will speak in the anguish of my spirit; I will complain in the bitterness of my soul. Am I a sea, or a whale, that thou settest a watch over me? When I say, My bed shall comfort me, my couch shall ease my complaint; then thou scarest me with dreams, and terrifiest me through visions: so that my soul chooseth strangling, and death rather than my life. I loathe it; I would not live always: let me alone; for my days are vanity.

What is man, that thou shouldest magnify him? and that thou shouldest set thine heart upon him? and that thou shouldest visit him every morning, and try him every moment? How long wilt thou not depart from me, nor let me alone till I swallow down my spittle? I have sinned; what shall I do unto thee, O thou preserver of men? why hast thou set me as a mark against thee, so that I am a burden to myself? And why dost thou not pardon my transgression, and take away mine iniquity? For now shall I sleep in the dust; and thou shalt seek me in the morning, but I shall not be.

Then answered Bildad the Shuhite, and said, How long wilt thou speak these things? and how long shall the words of thy mouth be like a strong wind? Doth God pervert judgment? or doth the Almighty pervert justice? If thy children have sinned against him, and he have cast them away for their transgression; if thou wouldest seek unto God betimes, and make thy supplication to the Almighty; if thou wert pure and upright; surely now he would awake for thee, and make the habitation of thy righteousness prosperous. Though thy beginning was small, yet thy latter end should greatly increase.

For enquire, I pray thee, of the former age, and prepare thyself to the search of their fathers: (For we are but of yesterday, and know nothing, because our days upon earth are a shadow:) Shall not they teach thee, and tell thee, and utter words out of their heart? Can the rush grow up without mire? can the flag grow without water? Whilst it is yet in his greenness, and not cut down, it withereth before any other herb. So are the paths of all that forget God; and the hypocrite's hope shall perish. . . .

Behold, God will not cast away a perfect man, neither will he help the evil doers: till he fill thy mouth with laughing, and thy lips with rejoicing. They that hate thee shall be clothed with shame; and the dwelling place of the wicked shall come to nought.

Then Job answered and said, I know it is so of a truth: but how should man be just with God? If he will contend with him, he cannot answer him one of a thousand. He is wise in heart, and mighty in strength: who hath hardened himself against him, and hath prospered? Which removeth the mountains, and they know not: which overturneth them in his anger. Which shaketh the earth out of her place, and the pillars thereof tremble. Which commandeth the sun, and it riseth not; and sealeth up the stars. Which alone spreadeth out the heavens, and treadeth upon the waves of the sea. Which maketh Arcturus, Orion, and Pleiades, and the chambers of the south. Which doeth great things past finding out; yea, and wonders without number. Lo, he goeth by me, and I see him not: he passeth on also, but I perceive him not. Behold, he taketh away, who can hinder him? who will say unto him, What doest thou? If God will not withdraw his anger, the proud helpers do stoop under him.

How much less shall I answer him, and choose out my words to reason with him? Whom, though I were righteous, yet would

I not answer, but I would make supplication to my judge. If I had called, and he had answered me; yet would I not believe that he had hearkened unto my voice. For he breaketh me with a tempest, and multiplieth my wounds without cause. He will not suffer me to take my breath, but filleth me with bitterness. If I speak of strength, lo, he is strong: and if of judgment, who shall set me a time to plead? If I justify myself, mine own mouth shall condemn me: if I say, I am perfect, it shall also prove me perverse. Though I were perfect, yet would I not know my soul: I would despise my life. This is one thing, therefore I said it, He destroyeth the perfect and the wicked. . . .

For he is not a man, as I am, that I should answer him, and we should come together in judgment. Neither is there any daysman betwixt us, that might lay his hand upon us both. Let him take his rod away from me, and let not his fear terrify me: then would I speak, and not fear him; but it is not so with me.

My soul is weary of my life; I will leave my complaint upon myself; I will speak in the bitterness of my soul. I will say unto God, Do not condemn me; shew me wherefore thou contendest with me. Is it good unto thee that thou shouldest oppress, that thou shouldest despise the work of thine hands, and shine upon the counsel of the wicked? Hast thou eyes of flesh? or seest thou as man seeth? Are thy days as the days of man? are thy years as man's days, that thou enquirest after mine iniquity, and searchest after my sin? Thou knowest that I am not wicked; and there is none that I can deliver out of thine hand. Thine hands have made me and fashioned me together round about; yet thou dost destroy me. Remember, I beseech thee, that thou hast made me as the clay; and wilt thou bring me into dust again? . . .

Wherefore then hast thou brought me forth out of the womb? Oh that I had given up the ghost, and no eye had seen me! I should have been as though I had not been; I should have been carried from the womb to the grave. Are not my days few? Cease then, and let me alone, that I may take comfort a little, before I go whence I shall not return, even to the land of darkness and the shadow of death; a land of darkness, as darkness itself; and of the shadow of death, without any order, and where the light is as darkness.

Then answered Zophar the Naamathite, and said, Should not the multitude of words be answered? and should a man full of talk be justified? Should thy lies make men hold their peace? and when thou mockest, shall no man make thee ashamed? For thou hast said, My doctrine is pure, and I am clean in thine eyes. But oh that God would speak, and open his lips against thee; and that he would shew thee the secrets of wisdom, that they are double to that which is! Know therefore that God exacteth of thee less than thine iniquity deserveth. Canst thou by searching find out God? canst thou find out the Almighty unto perfection? It is as high as heaven; what canst thou do? deeper than hell; what canst thou know? The measure thereof is longer than the earth, and broader than the sea. If he cut off, and shut up, or gather together, then who can hinder him? For he knoweth vain men: he seeth wickedness also; will he not then consider it? . . .

And Job answered and said, No doubt but ye are the people, and wisdom shall die with you. But I have understanding as well as you; I am not inferior to you: yea, who knoweth not such things as these? I am as one mocked of his neighbour, who calleth upon God, and he answereth him: the just upright man is laughed to scorn. He that is ready to slip with his feet is as a lamp despised in the thought of him that is at ease. . . .

What ye know, the same do I know also: I am not inferior unto you. Surely I would speak to the Almighty, and I desire to reason with God. But ye are forgers of lies, ye are all physicians of no value. O that ye would altogether hold your peace! and it should be your wisdom. Hear now my reasoning, and hearken to the pleadings of my lips. Will ye speak wickedly for God? and talk deceitfully for him? Will ye accept his person? will ye contend for God? Is it good that he should search you out? or as one man mocketh another, do ye so mock him? He will surely reprove you, if ye do secretly accept persons. Shall not his excellency make you afraid? and his dread fall upon you?

Your remembrances are like unto ashes, your bodies to bodies of clay. Hold your peace, let me alone, that I may speak, and let come on me what will. Wherefore do I take my flesh in my teeth, and put my life in mine hand? Though he slay me, yet will I trust in him: but I will maintain mine own ways before him. He also shall be my salvation: for an hypocrite shall not come before him.

Hear diligently my speech, and my declaration with your ears. Behold now, I have ordered my cause; I know that I shall be justified. Who is he that will plead with me? for now, if I hold my tongue, I shall give up the ghost. Only do now two things unto me: then will I not hide myself from thee. Withdraw thine hand far from me: and let not thy dread make me afraid. Then call thou, and I will answer: or let me speak, and answer thou me. How many are mine iniquities and sins? Make me to know my transgression and my sin. Wherefore hidest thou thy face, and holdest me for thine enemy? Wilt thou break a leaf driven to and fro? and wilt thou pursue the dry stubble? For thou writest bitter things against me, and makest me to possess the iniquities of my youth. Thou puttest my feet also in the stocks, and lookest narrowly unto all my paths; thou settest a print upon the heels of my feet. And he, as a rotten thing, consumeth, as a garment that is moth eaten.

Man that is born of a woman is of few days, and full of trouble. He cometh forth like a flower, and is cut down: he fleeth also as a shadow, and continueth not. And dost thou open thine eyes upon such an one, and bringest me into judgment with thee? Who can bring a clean thing out of an unclean? not one. Seeing his days are determined, the number of his months are with thee, thou hast appointed his bounds that he cannot pass; turn from him, that he may rest, till he shall accomplish, as an hireling, his day.

For there is hope of a tree, if it be cut down, that it will sprout again, and that the tender branch thereof will not cease. Though the root thereof wax old in the earth, and the stock thereof die in the ground; yet through the scent of water it will bud, and bring forth boughs like a plant. But man dieth, and wasteth away: yea, man giveth up the ghost, and where is he? As the waters fail from the sea, and the flood decayeth and drieth up: so man lieth down, and riseth not: till the heavens be no more, they shall not awake, nor be raised out of their sleep. O that thou wouldest hide me in the grave, that thou wouldest keep me secret, until thy wrath be past, that thou wouldest appoint me a set time, and remember me! If a man die, shall he live again? all the days of my appointed time will I wait, till my change come. Thou shalt call, and I will answer thee: thou wilt have a desire to the work of thine hands.

For now thou numberest my steps: dost thou not watch over my sin? My transgression is sealed up in a bag, and thou sewest up mine iniquity. And surely the mountain falling cometh to nought, and the rock is removed out of his place. The waters wear the stones: thou washest away the things which grow out of the dust of the earth; and thou destroyest the hope of man. Thou prevailest for ever against him, and he passeth: thou changest his countenance, and sendest him away. His sons come to honour, and he knoweth it not; and they are brought low, but he perceiveth it not of them. But his flesh upon him shall have pain, and his soul within him shall mourn.

* * *

My face is foul with weeping, and on my eyelids is the shadow of death; not for any injustice in mine hands: also my prayer is pure. O earth, cover not thou my blood, and let my cry have no place. Also now, behold, my witness is in heaven, and my record is on high. My friends scorn me: but mine eye poureth out tears unto God. O that one might plead for a man with God, as a man pleadeth for his neighbour! When a few years are come, then I shall go the way whence I shall not return.

My breath is corrupt. my days are extinct, the graves are ready for me. Are there not mockers with me? and doth not mine eye continue in their provocation? Lay down now, put me in a surety with thee; who is he that will strike hands with me? For thou hast hid their heart from understanding: therefore shalt thou not exalt them. . . .

Then answered Bildad the Shuhite, and said, How long will it be ere ye make an end of words? mark, and afterwards we will speak. Wherefore are we counted as beasts, and reputed vile in your sight? He teareth himself in his anger: shall the earth be forsaken for thee? and shall the rock be removed out of his place? Yea, the light of the wicked shall be put out, and the spark of his fire shall not shine. The light shall be dark in his tabernacle, and his candle shall be put out with him. The steps of his strength shall be straitened, and his own counsel shall cast him down.

For he is cast into a net by his own feet, and he walketh upon a snare. The gin shall take him by the heel, and the robber shall prevail against him. The snare is laid for him in the ground, and a trap for him in the way. Terrors shall make him afraid on every side, and shall drive him to his feet. His strength shall be hungerbitten, and destruction shall be ready at his side. It shall devour the strength of his skin: even the firstborn of death shall devour his strength. His confidence shall be rooted out of his tabernacle, and it shall bring him to the king of terrors. It shall dwell in his tabernacle, because it is none of his: brimstone shall be scattered upon his habitation. . . . Surely such are the dwellings of the wicked, and this is the place of him that knoweth not God.

Then Job answered and said, How long will ye vex my soul, and break me in pieces with words? These ten times have ye reproached me: ye are not ashamed that ye make yourselves strange to me. And be it indeed that I have erred, mine error remaineth with myself. If indeed ye will magnify yourselves against me, and plead against me my reproach: know now that God hath overthrown me, and hath compassed me with his net. Behold, I cry out of wrong, but I am not heard: I cry aloud, but there is no judgment. . . .

Have pity upon me, have pity upon me, O ye my friends; for the hand of God hath touched me. Why do ye persecute me as God, and are not satisfied with my flesh? Oh that my words were now written! oh that they were printed in a book! That they were graven with an iron pen and lead in the rock for ever! For I know that my redeemer liveth, and that he shall stand at the latter day upon the earth: and though after my skin worms destroy this body, yet in my flesh shall I see God: whom I shall see for myself, and mine eyes shall behold, and not another; though my reins be consumed within me. But ye should say, Why persecute we him, seeing the root of the matter is found in me? Be ye afraid of the sword: for wrath bringeth the punishments of the sword, that ye may know there is a judgment.

Then answered Zophar the Naamathite, and said, Therefore do my thoughts cause me to answer, and for this I make haste. I have heard the check of my reproach, and the spirit of my understanding causeth me to answer. Knowest thou not this of old, since man was placed upon earth, that the triumphing of the wicked is short, and the joy of the hypocrite but for a moment? Though his excellency mount up to the heavens, and his head reach unto the clouds; yet he shall perish for ever like his own dung: they which have seen him shall say, Where is he? . . .

The heaven shall reveal his iniquity; and the earth shall rise up against him. The increase of his house shall depart, and his goods shall flow away in the day of his wrath. This is the portion of a wicked man from God, and the heritage appointed unto him by God.

But Job answered and said, Hear diligently my speech, and let this be your consolation. Suffer me that I may speak; and after that I have spoken, mock on. As for me, is my complaint to man? and if it were so, why should not my spirit be troubled? Mark me, and be astonished, and lay your hand upon your mouth. Even when I remember I am afraid, and trembling taketh hold on my flesh.

Wherefore do the wicked live, become old, yea, are mighty in power? Their seed is established in their sight with them, and their offspring before their eyes. Their houses are safe from fear, neither is the rod of God upon them. Their bull gendereth, and faileth not; their cow calveth, and casteth not her calf. They send forth their little ones like a flock, and their children dance. They take the timbrel and harp, and rejoice at the sound of the organ. They spend their days in wealth, and in a moment go down to the grave. Therefore they say unto God, Depart from us; for we desire not the knowledge of thy ways. What is the Almighty, that we should serve him? and what profit should we have, if we pray unto him?

Lo, their good is not in their hand: the counsel of the wicked is far from me. How oft is the candle of the wicked put out!

and how oft cometh their destruction upon them! God distri-
buteth sorrows in his anger. . . .

Shall any teach God knowledge? seeing he judgeth those that
are high. One dieth in his full strength, being wholly at ease
and quiet. His breasts are full of milk, and his bones are moist-
ened with marrow. And another dieth in the bitterness of his
soul, and never eateth with pleasure. They shall lie down alike
in the dust, and the worms shall cover them. . . . How then
comfort ye me in vain, seeing in your answers there remaineth
falsehood?

Then Eliphaz the Temanite answered and said, Can a man be
profitable unto God, as he that is wise may be profitable unto
himself? Is it any pleasure to the Almighty, that thou art righteous? or is it gain to him, that thou makest thy ways perfect?
Will he reprove thee for fear of thee? will he enter with thee
into judgment? Is not thy wickedness great? and thine iniquities
infinite? For thou hast taken a pledge from thy brother for
nought, and stripped the naked of their clothing. Thou hast not
given water to the weary to drink, and thou hast withholden
bread from the hungry. . . . He shall deliver the island of the
innocent: and it is delivered by the pureness of thine hands.

Then Job answered and said, Even to day is my complaint bitter:
my stroke is heavier than my groaning. Oh that I knew where
I might find him! that I might come even to his seat! I would
order my cause before him, and fill my mouth with arguments.
I would know the words which he would answer me, and understand what he would say unto me. Will he plead against me
with his great power? No; but he would put strength in me.
There the righteous might dispute with him; so should I be
delivered for ever from my judge. Behold, I go forward, but he
is not there; and backward, but I cannot perceive him: on the

left hand, where he doth work, but I cannot behold him: he hideth himself on the right hand, that I cannot see him.

But he knoweth the way that I take: when he hath tried me, I shall come forth as gold. My foot hath held his steps, his way have I kept, and not declined. Neither have I gone back from the commandment of his lips; I have esteemed the words of his mouth more than my necessary food. But he is in one mind, and who can turn him? and what his soul desireth, even that he doeth. For he performeth the thing that is appointed for me: and many such things are with him. . . .

Why, seeing times are not hidden from the Almighty, do they that know him not see his days? Some remove the landmarks; they violently take away flocks, and feed thereof. They drive away the ass of the fatherless, they take the widow's ox for a pledge. They turn the needy out of the way: the poor of the earth hide themselves together. Behold, as wild asses in the desert, go they forth to their work; rising betimes for a prey: the wilderness yieldeth food for them and for their children. They reap every one his corn in the field: and they gather the vintage of the wicked. They cause the naked to lodge without clothing, that they have no covering in the cold. They are wet with the showers of the mountains, and embrace the rock for want of a shelter. They pluck the fatherless from the breast, and take a pledge of the poor. They cause him to go naked without clothing, and they take away the sheaf from the hungry; which make oil within their walls, and tread their winepresses, and suffer thirst. Men groan from out of the city, and the soul of the wounded crieth out: yet God layeth not folly to them. . . . And if it be not so now, who will make me a liar, and make my speech nothing worth?

Then answered Bildad the Shuhite, and said, Dominion and fear are with him, he maketh peace in his high places. Is there any number of his armies? and upon whom doth not his light arise? How then can man be justified with God? or how can he be clean that is born of a woman? Behold even to the moon, and it shineth not; yea, the stars are not pure in his sight. How much less man, that is a worm? and the son of man, which is a worm?

But Job answered and said, How hast thou helped him that is without power? how savest thou the arm that hath no strength? How hast thou counselled him that hath no wisdom? and how hast thou plentifully declared the thing as it is? . . .

Moreover Job continued his parable, and said, As God liveth, who hath taken away my judgment; and the Almighty, who hath vexed my soul; all the while my breath is in me, and the spirit of God is in my nostrils; my lips shall not speak wickedness, nor my tongue utter deceit. God forbid that I should justify you: till I die I will not remove mine integrity from me. My righteousness I hold fast, and will not let it go: my heart shall not reproach me so long as I live. Let mine enemy be as the wicked, and he that riseth up against me as the unrighteous. . . .

Surely there is a vein for the silver, and a place for gold where they refine it. Iron is taken out of the earth, and brass is molten out of the stone. He setteth an end to darkness, and searcheth out all perfection: the stones of darkness, and the shadow of death. . . . He cutteth out rivers among the rocks; and his eye seeth every precious thing. He bindeth the floods from overflowing; and the thing that is hid bringeth he forth to light.

But where shall wisdom be found? and where is the place of understanding? Man knoweth not the price thereof; neither is it found in the land of the living. The depth saith, It is not in me: and the sea saith, It is not with me. It cannot be gotten for gold, neither shall silver be weighed for the price thereof. . . .

Whence then cometh wisdom? and where is the place of understanding? Seeing it is hid from the eyes of all living, and kept close from the fowls of the air. Destruction and death say, We have heard the fame thereof with our ears. God understandeth the way thereof, and he knoweth the place thereof. For he looketh to the ends of the earth, and seeth under the whole heaven; to make the weight for the winds; and he weigheth the waters by measure. When he made a decree for the rain, and a way for the lightning of the thunder: then did he see it, and declare it; he prepared it, yea, and searched it out. And unto man he said, Behold, the fear of the Lord, that is wisdom; and to depart from evil is understanding.

Moreover Job continued his parable, and said, Oh that I were as in months past, as in the days when God preserved me; when his candle shined upon my head, and when by his light I walked through darkness; as I was in the days of my youth, when the secret of God was upon my tabernacle; when the Almighty was yet with me, when my children were about me; when I washed my steps with butter, and the rock poured me out rivers of oil; when I went out to the gate through the city, when I prepared my seat in the street! The young men saw me, and hid themselves: and the aged arose, and stood up. The princes refrained from talking, and laid their hand on their mouth. The nobles held their peace, and their tongue cleaved to the roof of their mouth. When the ear heard me, then it blessed me; and when the eye saw me, it gave witness to me: because I delivered the poor that cried, and the fatherless, and him that had none to help him. The blessing of him that was ready to perish came upon me: and I caused the widow's heart to sing for joy. . . .

And now my soul is poured out upon me; the days of affliction have taken hold upon me. My bones are pierced in me in the night season: and my sinews take no rest. By the great force of my disease is my garment changed: it bindeth me about as the collar of my coat. He hath cast me into the mire, and I am become like dust and ashes. I cry unto thee, and thou dost not hear me: I stand up, and thou regardest me not. Thou art become cruel to me: with thy strong hand thou opposest thyself against me. Thou liftest me up to the wind; thou causest me to ride upon it, and dissolvest my substance. For I know that thou wilt bring me to death, and to the house appointed for all living. Howbeit he will not stretch out his hand to the grave, though they cry in his destruction. Did not I weep for him that was in trouble? was not my soul grieved for the poor? When I looked for good, then evil came unto me: and when I waited for light, there came darkness. . . .

I made a covenant with mine eyes; why then should I think upon a maid? For what portion of God is there from above? and what inheritance of the Almighty from on high? Is not destruction to the wicked? and a strange punishment to the workers of iniquity? Doth not he see my ways, and count all my steps? If I have walked with vanity, or if my foot hath hasted to deceit; let me be weighed in an even balance, that God may know mine integrity. If my step hath turned out of the way, and mine heart walked after mine eyes, and if any blot hath cleaved to mine hands; then let me sow, and let another eat; yea, let my offspring be rooted out. If mine heart have been deceived by a woman, or if I have laid wait at my neighbour's door; then let my wife grind unto another, and let others bow down upon her. For this is an heinous crime; yea, it is an iniquity to be punished by the judge. For it is a fire that consumeth to destruction, and would root out all mine increase.

If I did despise the cause of my manservant or of my maidservant, when they contended with me; what then shall I do when God riseth up? and when he visiteth, what shall I answer him? Did not he that made me in the womb make him? and did not one fashion us in the womb?

If I have withheld the poor from their desire, or have caused the eyes of the widow to fail; or have eaten my morsel myself alone, and the fatherless hath not eaten thereof; (for from my youth he was brought up with me, as with a father, and I have guided her from my mother's womb;) if I have seen any perish for want of clothing, or any poor without covering; if his loins have not blessed me, and if he were not warmed with the fleece of my sheep; if I have lifted up my hand against the fatherless, when I saw my help in the gate: then let mine arm fall from my shoulder blade, and mine arm be broken from the bone. For destruction from God was a terror to me, and by reason of his highness I could not endure.

If I have made gold my hope, or have said to the fine gold, Thou art my confidence; if I rejoiced because my wealth was great, and because mine hand had gotten much; if I beheld the sun when it shined, or the moon walking in brightness; and my heart hath been secretly enticed, or my mouth hath kissed my hand:[1] this also were an iniquity to be punished by the judge: for I should have denied the God that is above.

If I rejoiced at the destruction of him that hated me, or lifted up myself when evil found him: neither have I suffered my mouth to sin by wishing a curse to his soul. . . . Oh that one would hear me! behold, my desire is, that the Almighty would answer me, and that mine adversary had written a book. Surely I would take it upon my shoulder, and bind it as a crown to me. I would declare unto him the number of my steps; as a prince would I go near unto him. . . . The words of Job are ended.

So these three men ceased to answer Job, because he was righteous in his own eyes. Then was kindled the wrath of Elihu the

---

[1] [An idolatrous ritual.]

son of Barachel the Buzite, of the kindred of Ram: against Job was his wrath kindled, because he justified himself rather than God. Also against his three friends was his wrath kindled, because they had found no answer, and yet had condemned Job. Now Elihu had waited till Job had spoken, because they were elder than he. When Elihu saw that there was no answer in the mouth of these three men, then his wrath was kindled.

And Elihu the son of Barachel the Buzite answered and said, I am young, and ye are very old; wherefore I was afraid, and durst not shew you mine opinion. I said, Days should speak, and multitude of years should teach wisdom. But there is a spirit in man: and the inspiration of the Almighty giveth them understanding. . . . Behold, I waited for your words; I gave ear to your reasons, whilst ye searched out what to say. Yea, I attended unto you, and, behold, there was none of you that convinced Job, or that answered his words. . . .

Wherefore, Job, I pray thee, hear my speeches, and hearken to all my words. Behold, now I have opened my mouth, my tongue hath spoken in my mouth. My words shall be of the uprightness of my heart: and my lips shall utter knowledge clearly. The spirit of God hath made me, and the breath of the Almighty hath given me life. If thou canst answer me, set thy words in order before me, stand up. Behold, I am according to thy wish in God's stead: I also am formed out of the clay. Behold, my terror shall not make thee afraid, neither shall my hand be heavy upon thee. Surely thou hast spoken in mine hearing, and I have heard the voice of thy words, saying, I am clean without transgression, I am innocent; neither is there iniquity in me. Behold, he findeth occasions against me, he counteth me for his enemy, he putteth my feet in the stocks, he marketh all my paths.

Behold, in this thou art not just: I will answer thee, that God is greater than man. Why dost thou strive against him? for he giveth not account of any of his matters. For God speaketh once, yea twice, yet man perceiveth it not. In a dream, in a vision of the night, when deep sleep falleth upon men, in slumberings upon the bed; then he openeth the ears of men, and sealeth their instruction, that he may withdraw man from his purpose, and hide pride from man. He keepeth back his soul from the pit, and his life from perishing by the sword.

He is chastened also with pain upon his bed, and the multitude of his bones with strong pain: so that his life abhorreth bread, and his soul dainty meat. His flesh is consumed away, that it cannot be seen; and his bones that were not seen stick out. Yea, his soul draweth near unto the grave, and his life to the destroyers. If there be a messenger with him, an interpreter, one among a thousand, to shew unto man his uprightness: then he is gracious unto him, and saith, Deliver him from going down to the pit: I have found a ransom. His flesh shall be fresher than a child's: he shall return to the days of his youth: he shall pray unto God, and he will be favourable unto him: and he shall see his face with joy: for he will render unto man his righteousness. He looketh upon men, and if any say, I have sinned, and perverted that which was right, and it profited me not; he will deliver his soul from going into the pit, and his life shall see the light.

Lo, all these things worketh God oftentimes with man, to bring back his soul from the pit, to be enlightened with the light of the living. Mark well, O Job, hearken unto me: hold thy peace, and I will speak. If thou hast any thing to say, answer me: speak, for I desire to justify thee. If not, hearken unto me: hold thy peace, and I shall teach thee wisdom.

Furthermore Elihu answered and said, . . . What man is like Job, who drinketh up scorning like water? Which goeth in company with the workers of iniquity, and walketh with wicked men. For he hath said, It profiteth a man nothing that he should delight himself with God. Therefore hearken unto me, ye men

of understanding: far be it from God, that he should do wickedness; and from the Almighty, that he should commit iniquity.
For the work of a man shall he render unto him, and cause
every man to find according to his ways. Yea, surely God will
not do wickedly, neither will the Almighty pervert judgment.
Who hath given him a charge over the earth? or who hath
disposed the whole world? If he set his heart upon man, if he
gather unto himself his spirit and his breath; all flesh shall perish
together, and man shall turn again unto dust.

If now thou hast understanding, hear this: hearken to the
voice of my words. Shall even he that hateth right govern? and
wilt thou condemn him that is most just? Is it fit to say to a
king, Thou art wicked? and to princes, Ye are ungodly? How
much less to him that accepteth not the persons of princes, nor
regardeth the rich more than the poor? . . .

Surely it is meet to be said unto God, I have borne chas-
tisement, I will not offend any more: that which I see not teach
thou me: if I have done iniquity, I will do no more. Should it
be according to thy mind? he will recompense it, whether thou
refuse, or whether thou choose; and not I: therefore speak what
thou knowest. Let men of understanding tell me, and let a wise
man hearken unto me. Job hath spoken without knowledge,
and his words were without wisdom. My desire is that Job may
be tried unto the end because of his answers for wicked men.
For he addeth rebellion unto his sin, he clappeth his hands
among us, and multiplieth his words against God.

Elihu spake moreover, and said, Thinkest thou this to be right,
that thou saidst, My righteousness is more than God's? For thou
saidst, What advantage will it be unto thee? and, What profit
shall I have, if I be cleansed from my sin? I will answer thee,
and thy companions with thee. Look unto the heavens, and see;
and behold the clouds which are higher than thou. If thou
sinnest, what doest thou against him? or if thy transgressions

be multiplied, what doest thou unto him? If thou be righteous, what givest thou him? or what receiveth he of thine hand? Thy wickedness may hurt a man as thou art; and thy righteousness may profit the son of man.

By reason of the multitude of oppressions they make the oppressed to cry: they cry out by reason of the arm of the mighty. But none saith, Where is God my maker, who giveth songs in the night; who teacheth us more than the beasts of the earth, and maketh us wiser than the fowls of heaven? There they cry, but none giveth answer, because of the pride of evil men. Surely God will not hear vanity, neither will the Almighty regard it. Although thou sayest thou shalt not see him, yet judgment is before him; therefore trust thou in him. But now, because it is not so, he hath visited in his anger; yet he knoweth it not in great extremity: therefore doth Job open his mouth in vain; he multiplieth words without knowledge.

Elihu also proceeded, and said, Suffer me a little, and I will shew thee that I have yet to speak on God's behalf. I will fetch my knowledge from afar, and will ascribe righteousness to my Maker. For truly my words shall not be false: he that is perfect in knowledge is with thee. Behold, God is mighty, and despiseth not any: he is mighty in strength and wisdom. He preserveth not the life of the wicked: but giveth right to the poor. . . . If they obey and serve him, they shall spend their days in prosperity, and their years in pleasures. But if they obey not, they shall perish by the sword, and they shall die without knowledge. But the hypocrites in heart heap up wrath: they cry not when he bindeth them. They die in youth, and their life is among the unclean. He delivereth the poor in his affliction, and openeth their ears in oppression.

Even so would he have removed thee out of the strait into a broad place, where there is no straitness; and that which should be set on thy table should be full of fatness. But thou hast fulfilled the judgment of the wicked: judgment and justice take hold on thee. Because there is wrath, beware lest he take thee away with his stroke: then a great ransom cannot deliver thee.

*   *   *

Hearken unto this, O Job: stand still, and consider the wondrous works of God. Dost thou know when God disposed them, and caused the light of his cloud to shine? Dost thou know the balancings of the clouds, the wondrous works of him which is perfect in knowledge? How thy garments are warm, when he quieteth the earth by the south wind? Hast thou with him spread out the sky, which is strong, and as a molten looking glass? Teach us what we shall say unto him; for we cannot order our speech by reason of darkness. Shall it be told him that I speak? if a man speak, surely he shall be swallowed up. And now men see not the bright light which is in the clouds: but the wind passeth, and cleanseth them. Fair weather cometh out of the north: with God is terrible majesty. Touching the Almighty, we cannot find him out: he is excellent in power, and in judgment, and in plenty of justice: he will not afflict. Men do therefore fear him: he respecteth not any that are wise of heart.

Then the Lord answered Job out of the whirlwind, and said, Who is this that darkeneth counsel by words without knowledge? Gird up now thy loins like a man; for I will demand of thee, and answer thou me.

   Where wast thou when I laid the foundations of the earth? declare, if thou hast understanding. Who hath laid the measures thereof, if thou knowest? or who hath stretched the line upon it? Whereupon are the foundations thereof fastened? or who laid the corner stone thereof; when the morning stars sang together, and all the sons of God shouted for joy? Or who shut up the sea with doors, when it brake forth, as if it had issued out of the womb? When I made the cloud the garment thereof, and thick darkness a swaddling-band for it, and brake it up for my decreed place, and set bars and doors, and said, Hitherto shalt thou come, but no further: and here shall thy proud waves be stayed?

Hast thou commanded the morning since thy days; and caused the dayspring to know his place; that it might take hold of the ends of the earth, that the wicked might be shaken out of it? It is turned as clay to the seal; and they stand as a garment. And from the wicked their light is withholden, and the high arm shall be broken. Hast thou entered into the springs of the sea? or hast thou walked in the search of the depth? Have the gates of death been opened unto thee? or hast thou seen the doors of the shadow of death? Hast thou perceived the breadth of the earth? declare if thou knowest it all. . . .

Who can number the clouds in wisdom? or who can stay the bottles of heaven, when the dust groweth into hardness, and the clods cleave fast together? Wilt thou hunt the prey for the lion? or fill the appetite of the young lions, when they couch in their dens, and abide in the covert to lie in wait? who provideth for the raven his food? when his young ones cry unto God, they wander for lack of meat.

Knowest thou the time when the wild goats of the rock bring forth? or canst thou mark when the hinds do calve? Canst thou number the months that they fulfil? or knowest thou the time when they bring forth? They bow themselves, they bring forth their young ones, they cast out their sorrows. Their young ones are in good liking, they grow up with corn; they go forth, and return not unto them.

Who hath sent out the wild ass free? or who hath loosed the bands of the wild ass? whose house I have made the wilderness, and the barren land his dwellings. He scorneth the multitude of the city, neither regardeth he the crying of the driver. The range of the mountains is his pasture, and he searcheth after every green thing.

Will the unicorn be willing to serve thee, or abide by thy crib? Canst thou bind the unicorn with his band in the furrow? or will he harrow the valleys after thee? Wilt thou trust him, because his strength is great? or wilt thou leave thy labour to him? Wilt thou believe him, that he will bring home thy seed, and gather it into thy barn? . . .

Moreover the Lord answered Job, and said, Shall he that contendeth with the Almighty instruct him? he that reproveth God, let him answer it.

Then Job answered the Lord, and said, Behold, I am vile; what shall I answer thee? I will lay mine hand upon my mouth. Once have I spoken; but I will not answer: yea, twice; but I will proceed no further.

Then answered the Lord unto Job out of the whirlwind, and said, Gird up thy loins now like a man: I will demand of thee, and declare thou unto me. Wilt thou also disannul my judgment? wilt thou condemn me, that thou mayest be righteous? Hast thou an arm like God? or canst thou thunder with a voice like him? Deck thyself now with majesty and excellency; and array thyself with glory and beauty. Cast abroad the rage of thy wrath: and behold every one that is proud, and abase him. Look on every one that is proud, and bring him low; and tread down the wicked in their place. Hide them in the dust together; and bind their faces in secret. Then will I also confess unto thee that thine own right hand can save thee.

Behold now, behemoth, which I made with thee; he eateth grass as an ox. Lo now, his strength is in his loins, and his force is in the navel of his belly. He moveth his tail like a cedar: the sinews of his stones are wrapped together. His bones are as strong pieces of brass; his bones are like bars of iron. He is the chief of the ways of God: he that made him can make his sword to approach unto him. . . .

Canst thou draw out leviathan with an hook? or his tongue with a cord which thou lettest down? Canst thou put an hook into his nose? or bore his jaw through with a thorn? . . . Lay thine hand upon him, remember the battle, do no more. Behold, the hope of him is in vain: shall not one be cast down even at the sight of him? None is so fierce that dare stir him up: who then is able to stand before me? Who hath prevented me, that I should repay him? whatsoever is under the whole heaven is mine. . . . Upon earth there is not his like, who is made without fear. He beholdeth all high things: he is a king over all the children of pride.

Then Job answered the Lord, and said, I know that thou canst do every thing, and that no thought can be withholden from thee. Who is he that hideth counsel without knowledge? therefore have I uttered that I understood not; things too wonderful for me, which I knew not. Hear, I beseech thee, and I will speak: I will demand of thee, and declare thou unto me. I have heard of thee by the hearing of the ear: but now mine eye seeth thee. Wherefore I abhor myself, and repent in dust and ashes.

And it was so, that after the Lord had spoken these words unto Job, the Lord said to Eliphaz the Temanite, My wrath is kindled against thee, and against thy two friends: for ye have not spoken of me the thing that is right, as my servant Job hath. Therefore take unto you now seven bullocks and seven rams, and go to my servant Job, and offer up for yourselves a burnt offering; and my servant Job shall pray for you: for him will I accept: lest I deal with you after your folly, in that ye have not spoken of me the thing which is right, like my servant Job. So Eliphaz the Temanite and Bildad the Shuhite and Zophar the Naamathite went, and did according as the Lord commanded them: the Lord also accepted Job.

And the Lord turned the captivity of Job, when he prayed for his friends: also the Lord gave Job twice as much as he had before. Then came there unto him all his brethren, and all his sisters, and all they that had been of his acquaintance before, and did eat bread with him in his house: and they bemoaned him, and comforted him over all the evil that the Lord had brought upon him: every man also gave him a piece of money, and every one an earring of gold. So the Lord blessed the latter end of Job more than his beginning: for he had fourteen thousand sheep, and six thousand camels, and a thousand yoke of oxen, and a thousand she-asses. He had also seven sons and three daughters. And he called the name of the first, Jemima; and the name of the second, Kezia; and the name of the third, Kerenhappuch. And in all the land were no women found so fair as the daughters of Job: and their father gave them inheritance among their brethren. After this lived Job an hundred and forty years, and saw his sons, and his sons' sons, even four generations. So Job died, being old and full of days.

JOHN STUART MILL, who claimed that his life was "uneventful," was born in 1806 in London, England. The son of a philosopher and reformer, Mill was faulted by his stern and domineering father for his "general slackness of mind," but he had learned Greek by the age of three, Latin at eight, logic at twelve, and political economy at thirteen. "The education which my father gave me," Mill noted, "was in itself much more fitted for training me to know than to do." As a young man, Mill went to work for his father at the British East India Company, where he remained for thirty-six years, writing works of philosophy and political economy meanwhile. When he was twenty, Mill experienced an emotional and intellectual crisis probably caused by overwork and his father's persistent meddling. He despaired of reason and read poetry for comfort. But Mill recovered: "I was no longer hopeless: I was not a stock or a stone." He met his future wife in 1830, but couldn't marry her until twenty years later, when her husband died. Their courtship was considered scandalous; Mill lost the esteem of many friends and his family. Mill's *Utilitarianism* was published in 1863. He served as a member of the House of Commons from 1865 to 1868 and died in Avignon, France, in 1873.

A selection from *Utilitarianism,* edited by Oskar Piest. Publisher: The Bobbs-Merrill Co., Inc., 1957. Pages 10–33 and 44–49.

Utilitarianism

What Utilitarianism Is

The creed which accepts as the foundation of morals "utility" or the "greatest happiness principle" holds that actions are right in proportion as they tend to promote happiness; wrong as they tend to produce the reverse of happiness. By happiness is intended pleasure and the absence of pain; by unhappiness, pain and the privation of pleasure. To give a clear view of the moral standard set up by the theory, much more requires to be said; in particular, what things it includes in the ideas of pain and pleasure, and to what extent this is left an open question. But these supplementary explanations do not affect the theory of life on which this theory of morality is grounded—namely, that pleasure and freedom from pain are the only things desirable as ends; and that all desirable things (which are as numerous in the utilitarian as in any other scheme) are desirable either for pleasure inherent in themselves or as means to the promotion of pleasure and the prevention of pain.

Now such a theory of life excites in many minds, and among them in some of the most estimable in feeling and purpose, inveterate dislike. To suppose that life has (as they express it) no higher end than pleasure—no better and nobler object of desire and pursuit—they designate as utterly mean and groveling, as a doctrine worthy only of swine, to whom the followers of Epicurus were, at a very early period, contemptuously likened; and modern holders of the doctrine are occasionally made the subject of equally polite comparisons by its German, French, and English assailants.

When thus attacked, the Epicureans have always answered that it is not they, but their accusers, who represent human nature in a degrading light, since the accusation supposes human beings to be capable of no pleasures except those of which swine are capable. If this supposition were true, the charge could not be gainsaid, but would then be no longer an imputation; for if the sources of pleasure were precisely the same to human beings and to swine, the rule of life which is good enough for the one would be good enough for the other. The comparison of the Epicurean life to that of beasts is felt as degrading, precisely because a beast's pleasures do not satisfy a human being's conceptions of happiness. Human beings have faculties more elevated than the animal appetites and, when once made conscious of them, do not regard anything as happiness which does not include their gratification. I do not, indeed, consider the Epicureans to have been by any means faultless in drawing out their scheme of consequences from the utilitarian principle. To do this in any sufficient manner, many Stoic, as well as Christian, elements require to be included. But there is no known Epicurean theory of life which does not assign to the pleasures of the intellect, of the feelings and imagination, and of the moral sentiments a much higher value as pleasures than to those of mere sensation. It must be admitted, however, that utilitarian writers in general have placed the superiority of mental over bodily pleasures chiefly in the greater permanency, safety, uncostliness, etc., of the former—that is, in their circumstantial advantages rather than in their intrinsic nature. And on all these points utilitarians have fully proved their case; but they might have taken the other and, as it may be called, higher ground with entire consistency. It is quite compatible with the principle of utility to recognize the fact that some kinds of pleasure are more desirable and more valuable than others. It would be absurd that, while in estimating all other things quality is considered as well as quantity, the estimation of pleasure should be supposed to depend on quantity alone.

If I am asked what I mean by difference of quality in pleasures, or what makes one pleasure more valuable than another, merely as a pleasure, except its being greater in amount, there is but one possible answer. Of two pleasures, if there be one to which all or almost all who have experience of both give a decided preference, irrespective of any feeling of moral obligation to prefer it, that is the more desirable pleasure. If one of the two is, by those who are competently acquainted with both, placed so far above the other that they prefer it, even though knowing it to be attended with a greater amount of discontent, and would not resign it for any quantity of the other pleasure which their nature is capable of, we are justified in ascribing to the preferred enjoyment a superiority in quality so far outweighing quantity as to render it, in comparison, of small account.

Now it is an unquestionable fact that those who are equally acquainted with and equally capable of appreciating and enjoying both do give a most marked preference to the manner of existence which employs their higher faculties. Few human creatures would consent to be changed into any of the lower animals for a promise of the fullest allowance of a beast's pleasures; no intelligent human being would consent to be a fool, no instructed person would be an ignoramus, no person of feeling and conscience would be selfish and base, even though they should be persuaded that the fool, the dunce, or the rascal is better satisfied with his lot than they are with theirs. They would not resign what they possess more than he for the most complete satisfaction of all the desires which they have in common with him. If they ever fancy they would, it is only in cases of unhappiness so extreme that to escape from it they would exchange their lot for almost any other, however undesirable in their own eyes. A being of higher faculties requires more to make him happy, is capable probably of more acute suffering, and certainly accessible to it at more points, than one of an inferior type; but in spite of these liabilities, he can never really wish to sink into what he feels to be a lower grade of existence. We may give what explanation we please of this unwillingness; we may attribute it to pride, a name which is given indiscriminately to some of the most and to some of the least estimable feelings of which mankind are capable; we may refer it to the love of liberty and personal independence, an appeal to which was with the Stoics one of the most effective means for the inculcation of it; to the love of power or to the love excitement, both of which do really enter into and contribute to it; but its most appropriate appellation is a sense of dignity, which all human beings possess in one form or other, and in some, though by no means in exact, proportion to their higher faculties, and which is so essential a part of the happiness of those in whom it is strong that nothing which conflicts with it could be otherwise than momentarily an object of desire to them. Whoever supposes that this preference takes place at a sacrifice of happiness—that the superior being, in anything like equal circumstances, is not happier than the inferior—confounds the two very different ideas of happiness and content. It is indisputable that the being whose capacities of enjoyment are low has the greatest chance of having them fully satisfied; and a highly endowed being will always feel that any happiness which he can look for, as the world is constituted, is imperfect. But he can learn to bear its imperfections, if they are at all bearable; and they will not make him envy the being who is indeed unconscious of the imperfections, but only because he feels not at all the good which those imperfections qualify. It is better to be a human being dissatisfied than a pig satisfied; better to be Socrates dissatisfied than a fool satisfied. And if the fool, or the pig, are of a different opinion, it is because they only know their own side of the question. The other party to the comparison knows both sides.

It may be objected that many who are capable of the higher pleasures occasionally, under the influence of temptation, postpone them to the lower. But this is quite compatible with a full appreciation of the intrinsic superiority of the higher. Men often, from infirmity of character, make their election for the nearer good, though they know it to be the less valuable; and this no less when the choice is between two bodily pleasures than when it is between bodily and mental. They pursue sensual indulgences to the injury of health, though perfectly aware that health is the greater good. It may be further objected that many who begin with youthful enthusiasm for everything noble, as they advance in years, sink into indolence and selfishness. But I do not believe that those who undergo this very common change voluntarily choose the lower description of pleasures in preference to the higher. I believe that, before they devote themselves exclusively to the one, they have already become incapable of the other. Capacity for the nobler feelings is in most natures a very tender plant, easily killed, not only by hostile influences, but by mere want of sustenance; and in the majority of young persons it speedily dies away if the occupations to which their position in life has devoted them, and the society into which it has thrown them, are not favorable to keeping that higher capacity in exercise. Men lose their high aspirations as they lose their intellectual tastes, because they have not time or opportunity for indulging them; and they addict themselves to inferior pleasures, not because they deliberately prefer them, but because they are either the only ones to which they have access or the only ones which they are any longer capable of enjoying. It may be questioned whether anyone who has remained equally susceptible to both classes of pleasures ever knowingly and calmly preferred the lower, though many, in all ages, have broken down in an ineffectual attempt to combine both.

From this verdict of the only competent judges, I apprehend there can be no appeal. On a question which is the best worth

having of two pleasures, or which of two modes of existence is
the most grateful to the feelings, apart from its moral attributes
and from its consequences, the judgment of those who are qualified by knowledge of both, or, if they differ, that of the majority
among them, must be admitted as final. And there needs be
the less hesitation to accept this judgment respecting the quality
of pleasures, since there is no other tribunal to be referred to
even on the question of quantity. What means are there of
determining which is the acutest of two pains, or the intensest
of two pleasurable sensations, except the general suffrage of those
who are familiar with both? Neither pains nor pleasures are
homogeneous, and pain is always heterogeneous with pleasure.
What is there to decide whether a particular pleasure is worth
purchasing at the cost of a particular pain, except the feelings
and judgment of the experienced? When, therefore, those feelings and judgment declare the pleasures derived from the higher
faculties to be preferable *in kind,* apart from the question of
intensity, to those of which the animal nature, disjoined from
the higher faculties, is susceptible, they are entitled on this
subject to the same regard.

I have dwelt on this point as being a necessary part of a
perfectly just conception of utility or happiness considered as
the directive rule of human conduct. But it is by no means an
indispensable condition to the acceptance of the utilitarian standard; for that standard is not the agent's own greatest happiness,
but the greatest amount of happiness altogether; and if it may
possibly be doubted whether a noble character is always the
happier for its nobleness, there can be no doubt that it makes
other people happier, and that the world in general is immensely
a gainer by it. Utilitarianism, therefore, could only attain its end
by the general cultivation of nobleness of character, even if each
individual were only benefited by the nobleness of others, and
his own, so far as happiness is concerned, were a sheer deduction
from the benefit. But the bare enunciation of such an absurdity
as this last renders refutation superfluous.

According to the greatest happiness principle, as above explained, the ultimate end, with reference to and for the sake of which all other things are desirable—whether we are considering our own good or that of other people—is an existence exempt as far as possible from pain, and as rich as possible in enjoyments, both in point of quantity and quality; the test of quality and the rule for measuring it against quantity being the preference felt by those who, in their opportunities of experience, to which must be added their habits of self-consciousness and self-observation, are best furnished with the means of comparison. This, being according to the utilitarian opinion the end of human action, is necessarily also the standard of morality, which may accordingly be defined "the rules and precepts for human conduct," by the observance of which an existence such as has been described might be, to the greatest extent possible, secured to all mankind; and not to them only, but, so far as the nature of things admits, to the whole sentient creation. . . .

Unquestionably it is possible to do without happiness; it is done involuntarily by nineteen-twentieths of mankind, even in those parts of our present world which are least deep in barbarism; and it often has to be done voluntarily by the hero or the martyr, for the sake of something which he prizes more than his individual happiness. But this something, what is it, unless the happiness of others or some of the requisites of happiness? It is noble to be capable of resigning entirely one's own portion of happiness, or chances of it; but, after all, this self-sacrifice must be for some end; it is not its own end; and if we are told that its end is not happiness but virtue, which is better than happiness, I ask, would the sacrifice be made if the hero or martyr did not believe that it would earn for others immunity from similar sacrifices? Would it be made if he thought that his renunciation of happiness for himself would produce no fruit for any of his fellow creatures, but to make their lot like his and place them also in the condition of persons who have renounced happiness? All honor to those who can abnegate for themselves the personal enjoyment of life when by such renunciation they contribute worthily to increase the amount of happiness in the world; but he who does it or professes to do it for any other purpose is no more deserving of admiration than the ascetic mounted on his pillar. He may be an inspiriting proof of what men *can* do, but assuredly not an example of what they *should*.

Though it is only in a very imperfect state of the world's arrangements that anyone can best serve the happiness of others by the absolute sacrifice of his own, yet, so long as the world is in that imperfect state, I fully acknowledge that the readiness to make such a sacrifice is the highest virtue which can be found in man. I will add that in this condition of the world, paradoxical as the assertion may be, the conscious ability to do without happiness gives the best prospect of realizing such happiness as is attainable. For nothing except that consciousness can raise a person above the chances of life by making him feel that, let fate and fortune do their worst, they have not power to subdue him; which, once felt, frees him from excess of anxiety concerning the evils of life and enables him, like many a Stoic in the worst times of the Roman Empire, to cultivate in tranquillity the sources of satisfaction accessible to him, without concerning himself about the uncertainty of their duration any more than about their inevitable end.

Meanwhile, let utilitarians never cease to claim the morality of self-devotion as a possession which belongs by as good a right to them as either to the Stoic or to the Transcendentalist. The utilitarian morality does recognize in human beings the power of sacrificing their own greatest good for the good of others. It only refuses to admit that the sacrifice is itself a good. A sacrifice which does not increase or tend to increase the sum total of happiness, it considers as wasted. The only self-renunciation which it applauds is devotion to the happiness, or to some of the means of happiness, of others, either of mankind collectively or of individuals within the limits imposed by the collective interests of mankind.

I must again repeat what the assailants of utilitarianism seldom have the justice to acknowledge, that the happiness which forms the utilitarian standard of what is right in conduct is not the agent's own happiness but that of all concerned. As between his own happiness and that of others, utilitarianism requires him to be as strictly impartial as a disinterested and benevolent spectator. In the golden rule of Jesus of Nazareth, we read the complete spirit of the ethics of utility. "To do as you would be done by," and "to love your neighbor as yourself," constitute the ideal perfection of utilitarian morality. As the means of making the nearest approach to this ideal, utility would enjoin, first, that laws and social arrangements should place the happiness or (as, speaking practically, it may be called) the interest of every individual as nearly as possible in harmony with the interest of the whole; and, secondly, that education and opinion, which have so vast a power over human character, should so use that power as to establish in the mind of every individual an indissoluble association between his own happiness and the good of the whole, especially between his own happiness and the practice of such modes of conduct, negative and positive, as regard for the universal happiness prescribes; so that not only he may be unable to conceive the possibility of happiness to himself, consistently with conduct opposed to the general good, but also that a direct impulse to promote the general good may be in every individual one of the habitual motives of action, and the sentiments connected therewith may fill a large and prominent place in every human being's sentient existence. If the impugners of the utilitarian morality represented it to their own minds in this its true character, I know not what recommendation possessed by any other morality they could possibly affirm to be wanting to it; what more beautiful or more exalted developments of human nature any other ethical system can be supposed to foster, or what springs of action, not accessible to the utilitarian, such systems rely on for giving effect to their mandates.

The objectors to utilitarianism cannot always be charged with representing it in a discreditable light. On the contrary, those among them who entertain anything like a just idea of its disinterested character sometimes find fault with its standard as being too high for humanity. They say it is exacting too much to require that people shall always act from the inducement of promoting the general interests of society. But this is to mistake the very meaning of a standard of morals and confound the rule of action with the motive of it. It is the business of ethics to tell us what are our duties, or by what test we may know them; but no system of ethics requires that the sole motive of all we do shall be a feeling of duty; on the contrary, ninety-nine hundredths of all our actions are done from other motives, and rightly so done if the rule of duty does not condemn them. It is the more unjust to utilitarianism that this particular misapprehension should be made a ground of objection to it, inasmuch as utilitarian moralists have gone beyond almost all others in affirming that the motive has nothing to do with the morality of the action, though much with the worth of the agent. He who saves a fellow creature from drowning does what is morally right, whether his motive be duty or the hope of being paid for his trouble; he who betrays the friend that trusts him is guilty of a crime, even if his object be to serve another friend to whom he is under greater obligations. . . .

It may not be superfluous to notice a few more of the common misapprehensions of utilitarian ethics, even those which are so obvious and gross that it might appear impossible for any person of candor and intelligence to fall into them; since persons, even of considerable mental endowment, often give themselves so little trouble to understand the bearings of any opinion against which they entertain a prejudice, and men are in general so little conscious of this voluntary ignorance as a defect that the vulgarest misunderstandings of ethical doctrines are continually met with in the deliberate writings of persons of the greatest pretensions both to high principle and to philosophy. We not uncommonly hear the doctrine of utility inveighed against as a *godless* doctrine. If it be necessary to say anything at all against so mere an assumption, we may say that the question depends upon what idea we have formed of the moral character of the Deity. If it be a true belief that God desires, above all things, the happiness of his creatures, and that this was his purpose in their creation, utility is not only not a godless doctrine, but more profoundly religious than any other. If it be meant that utilitarianism does not recognize the revealed will of God as the supreme law of morals, I answer that a utilitarian who believes in the perfect goodness and wisdom of God necessarily believes that whatever God has thought fit to reveal on the subject of morals must fulfill the requirements of utility in a supreme degree. But others besides utilitarians have been of opinion that the Christian revelation was intended, and is fitted, to inform the hearts and minds of mankind with a spirit which should enable them to find for themselves what is right, and incline them to do it when found, rather than to tell them, except in a very general way, what it is; and that we need a doctrine of ethics, carefully followed out, to *interpret* to us the will of God. Whether this opinion is correct or not, it is superfluous here to discuss; since whatever aid religion, either natural or revealed, can afford to ethical investigation is as open to the utilitarian moralist as to any other. He can use it as the testimony of God to the usefulness or hurtfulness of any given course of action by as good a right as others can use it for the indication of a transcendental law having no connection with usefulness or with happiness.

Again, utility is often summarily stigmatized as an immoral doctrine by giving it the name of "expediency," and taking advantage of the popular use of that term to contrast it with principle. But the expedient, in the sense in which it is opposed to the right, generally means that which is expedient for the particular interest of the agent himself; as when a minister sacrifices the interests of his country to keep himself in place. When it means anything better than this, it means that which is expedient for some immediate object, some temporary purpose, but which violates a rule whose observance is expedient in a much higher degree. The expedient, in this sense, instead of being the same thing with the useful, is a branch of the hurtful. Thus it would often be expedient, for the purpose of getting over some momentary embarrassment, or attaining some object immediately useful to ourselves or others, to tell a lie. But inasmuch as the cultivation in ourselves of a sensitive feeling on the subject of veracity is one of the most useful, and the enfeeblement of that feeling one of the most hurtful, things to which our conduct can be instrumental; and inasmuch as any, even unintentional, deviation from truth does that much toward weakening the trustworthiness of human assertion, which is not only the principal support of all present social well-being, but the insufficiency of which does more than any one thing that can be named to keep back civilization, virtue, everything on which human happiness on the largest scale depends—we feel that the violation, for a present advantage, of a rule of such transcendent expediency is not expedient, and that he who, for the sake of convenience to himself or to some other individual, does what depends on him to deprive mankind of the good, and inflict upon them the evil, involved in the greater or less reliance which they can place in each other's word, acts the part of one of their worst enemies. Yet that even this rule, sacred as it is, admits of possible exceptions is acknowledged by all moralists; the chief of which is when the withholding of some fact (as of information from a malefactor, or of bad news from a person dangerously ill) would save an individual (especially an individual other than oneself) from great and unmerited evil, and when the withholding can only be effected by denial. But in order that the exception may not extend itself beyond the need, and may have the least possible effect in weakening reliance on veracity, it ought to be recognized and, if possible, its limits defined; and, if the principle of utility is good for anything, it must be good for weighing these conflicting utilities against one another and marking out the region within which one or the other preponderates.

Again, defenders of utility often find themselves called upon to reply to such objections as this—that there is not time, previous to action, for calculating and weighing the effects of any line of conduct on the general happiness. This is exactly as if anyone were to say that it is impossible to guide our conduct by Christianity because there is not time, on every occasion on which anything has to be done, to read through the Old and New Testaments. The answer to the objection is that there has been ample time, namely, the whole past duration of the human species. During all that time mankind have been learning by experience the tendencies of actions; on which experience all the prudence as well as all the morality of life are dependent. People talk as if the commencement of this course of experience had hitherto been put off, and as if, at the moment when some man feels tempted to meddle with the property or life of another, he had to begin considering for the first time whether murder and theft are injurious to human happiness. Even then I do not think that he would find the question very puzzling; but, at all events, the matter is now done to his hand. It is truly a whimsical supposition that, if mankind were agreed in considering utility to be the test of morality, they would remain without any agreement as to what *is* useful, and would take no measures for having their notions on the subject taught to the young and enforced by law and opinion. There is no difficulty in proving any ethical standard whatever to work ill if we suppose universal idiocy to be conjoined with it; but on any hypothesis short of that, mankind must by this time have acquired positive beliefs as to the effects of some actions on their happiness; and the beliefs which have thus come down are the rules of morality for the multitude, and for the philosopher until he has succeeded in finding better. That philosophers might easily do this, even now, on many subjects; that the received code of ethics is by no means of divine right; and that mankind have still much to learn as to the effects of actions on the general happiness, I admit or rather earnestly maintain. The corollaries from the principle of utility, like the precepts of every practical art, admit of indefinite improvement, and, in a progressive state of the human mind, their improvement is perpetually going on. But to consider the rules of morality as improvable is one thing; to pass over the intermediate generalization entirely and endeavor to test each individual action directly by the first principle is another. It is a strange notion that the acknowledgment of a first principle is inconsistent with the admission of secondary ones. To inform a traveler respecting the place of his ultimate destination is not to forbid the use of landmarks and direction-posts on the way. The proposition that happiness is the end and aim of morality does not mean that no road ought to be laid down to that goal, or that persons going thither should not be advised to take one direction rather than another. Men really ought to leave off talking a kind of nonsense on this subject, which they would neither talk nor listen to on other matters of practical concernment. Nobody argues that the art of navigation is not founded on astronomy because sailors cannot wait to calculate the Nautical Almanac. Being rational creatures, they go to sea with it ready calculated; and all rational creatures go out upon the sea of life with their minds made up on the common questions of right and wrong, as well as on many of the far more difficult questions of wise and foolish. And this, as long as foresight is a human quality, it is to be presumed they will continue to do. Whatever we adopt as the fundamental principle of morality, we require subordinate principles to apply it by; the impossibility of doing without them, being common to all systems, can afford no argument against anyone in particular; but gravely to argue as if no such secondary principles could be had, and as if mankind had remained till now, and always must remain, without drawing any general conclusions from the experience of human life is as high a pitch, I think, as absurdity has ever reached in philosophical controversy.

The remainder of the stock arguments against utilitarianism mostly consist in laying to its charge the common infirmities of human nature, and the general difficulties which embarrass conscientious persons in shaping their course through life. We are told that a utilitarian will be apt to make his own particular case an exception to moral rules, and, when under temptation, will see a utility in the breach of a rule, greater than he will see in its observance. But is utility the only creed which is able to furnish us with excuses for evil-doing and means of cheating our own conscience? They are afforded in abundance by all doctrines which recognize as a fact in morals the existence of conflicting considerations, which all doctrines do that have been believed by sane persons. It is not the fault of any creed, but of the complicated nature of human affairs, that rules of conduct cannot be so framed as to require no exceptions, and that hardly any kind of action can safely be laid down as either always obligatory or always condemnable. There is no ethical creed which does not temper the rigidity of its laws by giving a certain latitude, under the moral responsibility of the agent, for accommodation to peculiarities of circumstances; and under every creed, at the opening thus made, self-deception and dishonest casuistry get in. There exists no moral system under which there do not arise unequivocal cases of conflicting obligation. These are the real difficulties, the knotty points both in the theory of ethics and in the conscientious guidance of personal conduct. They are overcome practically, with greater or with less success, according to the intellect and virtue of the individual; but it can hardly be pretended that anyone will be the less qualified for dealing with them, from possessing an ultimate standard to which conflicting rights and duties can be referred. If utility is the ultimate source of moral obligations, utility may be invoked to decide between them when their demands are incompatible. Though the application of the standard may be difficult, it is better than none at all; while in other systems, the moral laws all claiming independent authority, there is no common umpire entitled to interfere between them; their claims to precedence one over another rest on little better than sophistry, and, unless determined, as they generally are, by the unacknowledged influence of consideration of utility, afford a free scope for the action of personal desires and partialities. We must remember that only in these cases of conflict between secondary principles is it requisite that first principles should be appealed to. There is no case of moral obligation in which some secondary principle is not involved; and if only one, there can seldom be any real doubt which one it is, in the mind of any person by whom the principle itself is recognized.

PROOF OF THE PRINCIPLE

. . . Questions about ends are . . . questions [about] what things are desirable. The utilitarian doctrine is that happiness is desirable, and the only thing desirable, as an end; all other things being only desirable as means to that end. What ought to be required of this doctrine, what conditions is it requisite that the doctrine should fulfill—to make good its claim to be believed?

The only proof capable of being given that an object is visible is that people actually see it. The only proof that a sound is audible is that people hear it; and so of the other sources of our experience. In like manner, I apprehend, the sole evidence it is possible to produce that anything is desirable is that people do actually desire it. If the end which the utilitarian doctrine proposes to itself were not, in theory and in practice, acknowledged to be an end, nothing could ever convince any person that it was so. No reason can be given why the general happiness is desirable, except that each person, so far as he believes it to be attainable, desires his own happiness. This, however, being a fact, we have not only all the proof which the case admits of, but all which it is possible to require, that happiness is a good, that each person's happiness is a good to that person, and the general happiness, therefore, is a good to the aggregate of all persons. Happiness has made out its title as *one* of the ends of conduct and, consequently, one of the criteria of morality.

But it has not, by this alone, proved itself to be the sole criterion. To do that, it would seem, by the same rule, necessary to show not only that people desire happiness, but that they never desire anything else. Now it is palpable that they do desire things which, in common language, are decidedly distinguished from happiness. They desire, for example, virtue and the absence of vice no less really than pleasure and the absence of pain. The desire of virtue is not as universal, but it is as authentic a fact as the desire of happiness. And hence the opponents of the utilitarian standard deem they that have a right to infer that there are other ends of human action besides happiness, and that happiness is not the standard of approbation and disapprobation.

But does the utilitarian doctrine deny that people desire virtue, or maintain that virtue is not a thing to be desired? The very reverse. It maintains not only that virtue is to be desired, but that it is to be desired disinterestedly, for itself. Whatever may be the opinion of utilitarian moralists as to the original conditions by which virtue is made virtue, however they may believe (as they do) that actions and dispositions are only virtuous because they promote another end than virtue, yet this being granted, and it having been decided, from considerations of this description, what *is* virtuous, they not only place virtue at the very head of the things which are good as means to the ultimate end, but they also recognize as a psychological fact the possibility of its being, to the individual, a good in itself, without looking to any end beyond it; and hold that the mind is not in a right state, not in a state conformable to utility, not in the state most conducive to the general happiness, unless it does love virtue in this manner—as a thing desirable in itself, even although, in the individual instance, it should not produce those other desirable consequences which it tends to produce, and on account of which it is held to be virtue. This opinion is not, in the smallest degree, a departure from the happiness principle. The ingredients of happiness are very various, and each of them is desirable in itself, and not merely when considered as swelling an aggregate. The principle of utility does not mean that any given pleasure, as music, for instance, or any given exemption from pain, as for example health, is to be looked upon as means to a collective something termed happiness, and to be desired on that account. They are desired and desirable in and for themselves; besides being means, they are a part of the end. Virtue, according to the utilitarian doctrine, is not naturally and originally part of the end, but it is capable of becoming so; and in those who live it disinterestedly it has become so, and is desired and cherished, not as a means to happiness, but as a part of their happiness.

To illustrate this further, we may remember that virtue is not the only thing originally a means, and which if it were not a means to anything else would be and remain indifferent, but which by association with what it is a means to comes to be desired for itself, and that too with the utmost intensity. What, for example, shall we say of the love of money? There is nothing originally more desirable about money than about any heap of glittering pebbles. Its worth is solely that of the things which it will buy; the desires for other things than itself, which it is a means of gratifying. Yet the love of money is not only one of the strongest moving forces of human life, but money is, in many cases, desired in and for itself; the desire to possess it is often stronger than the desire to use it, and goes on increasing when all the desires which point to ends beyond it, to be compassed by it, are falling off. It may, then, be said truly that money is desired not for the sake of an end, but as part of the end. From being a means to happiness, it has come to be itself a principal ingredient of the individual's conception of happiness. The same may be said of the majority of the great objects of human life: power, for example, or fame, except that to each of these there is a certain amount of immediate pleasure annexed, which has at least the semblance of being naturally inherent in them—a thing which cannot be said of money. Still, however, the strongest natural attraction, both of power and of fame, is the immense aid they give to the attainment of our other wishes; and it is the strong association thus generated between them and all our objects of desire which gives to the direct desire of them the intensity it often assumes, so as in some characters to surpass in strength all other desires. In these cases the means have become a part of the end, and a more important part of it than any of the things which they are means to. What was once desired as an instrument for the attainment of happiness has come to be desired for its own sake. In being desired for its own sake it is, however, desired as *part* of happiness. The person is made, or thinks he would be made, happy by its mere possession; and is made unhappy by failure to obtain it. The desire of it is not a different thing from the desire of happiness any more than the love of music or the desire of health. They are included in happiness. They are some of the elements of which the desire of happiness is made up. Happiness is not an abstract idea but a concrete whole; and these are some of its parts. And the utilitarian standard sanctions and approves their being so. Life would be a poor thing, very ill provided with sources of happiness, if there were not this provision of nature by which things originally indifferent, but conducive to, or otherwise associated with, the satisfaction of our primitive desires, become in themselves sources of pleasure more valuable than the primitive pleasures, both in permanency, in the space of human existence that they are capable of covering, and even in intensity.

Virtue, according to the utilitarian conception, is a good of this description. There was no original desire of it, or motive to it, save its conduciveness to pleasure, and especially to protection from pain. But through the association thus formed it may be felt a good in itself, and desired as such with as great intensity as any other good; and with this difference between it and the love of money, of power, or of fame—that all of these may, and often do, render the individual noxious to the other members of the society to which he belongs, whereas there is nothing which makes him so much a blessing to them as the cultivation of the disinterested love of virtue. And consequently, the utilitarian standard, while it tolerates and approves those other acquired desires, up to the point beyond which they would be more injurious to the general happiness than promotive of it, enjoins and requires the cultivation of the love of virtue up to the greatest strength possible, as being above all things important to the general happiness.

It results from the preceding considerations that there is in reality nothing desired except happiness. Whatever is desired otherwise than as a means to some end beyond itself, and ultimately to happiness, is desired as itself a part of happiness, and is not desired for itself until it has become so. Those who desire virtue for its own sake desire it either because the consciousness of it is a pleasure, or because the consciousness of being without it is a pain, or for both reasons united; as in truth the pleasure and pain seldom exist separately, but almost always together—the same person feeling pleasure in the degree of virtue attained, and pain in not having attained more. If one of these gave him no pleasure, and the other no pain, he would not love or desire virtue, or would desire it only for the other benefits which it might produce to himself or to persons whom he cared for.

We have now, then, an answer to the question, of what sort of proof the principle of utility is susceptible. If the opinion which I have now stated is psychologically true—if human nature is so constituted as to desire nothing which is not either a part of happiness or a means of happiness—we can have no other proof, and we require no other, that these are the only things desirable. If so, happiness is the sole end of human action, and the promotion of it the test by which to judge of all human conduct; from whence it necessarily follows that it must be the criterion of morality, since a part is included in the whole.

And now to decide whether this is really so, whether mankind do desire nothing for itself but that which is a pleasure to them, or of which the absence is a pain, we have evidently arrived at a question of fact and experience, dependent, like all similar questions, upon evidence. It can only be determined by practiced self-consciousness and self-observation, assisted by observation of others. I believe that these sources of evidence, impartially consulted, will declare that desiring a thing and finding it pleasant, aversion to it and thinking of it as painful, are phenomena entirely inseparable or, rather, two parts of the same phenomenon—in strictness of language, two different modes of naming the same psychological fact; that to think of an object as desirable (unless for the sake of its consequences) and to think of it as pleasant are one and the same thing; and that to desire anything except in proportion as the idea of it is pleasant is a physical and metaphysical impossibility.

GEORGE BERNARD SHAW was born in Dublin, Ireland, in 1856. His family was genteel but had fallen on hard times. In 1875, Shaw's mother left Ireland for London. Shaw joined her there when he was twenty, worked for a telephone company, and "made a man of myself (at my mother's expense)" by writing five novels, none of which was published. (Shaw later satirized one in blank verse.) He became a member of the Fabian Society—an organization of intellectual, middle-class British socialists—a political pamphleteer and public speaker, an essayist, and a writer of music, theater, and literary criticism. Remarked Shaw, "Criticism is not only medicinally salutary: it has positive popular attractions in its cruelty, its gladiatorship. . . It may say things which many would like to say, but dare not. . ." In the 1880s, Shaw began to write plays, ostensibly to satisfy the demands of his own theater criticism. Shaw's prefaces to his plays were equally noted. His first published collection was *Plays, Pleasant and Unpleasant* (1898). Said Shaw of his "unpleasant" plays: ". . . their dramatic power is used to force the spectator to face unpleasant facts." Among his works are *Mrs. Warren's Profession* (1898), *Arms and the Man* (1898), *Man and Superman* (1903), *Pygmalion* (1916), and *Saint Joan* (1924). Shaw was awarded the Nobel Prize in 1925. When he died in 1950, he donated his estate to research into a forty-letter phonetic alphabet.

From *Caesar and Cleopatra: A History*. Publisher: Penguin Books, 1984.

Caesar and Cleopatra

PROLOGUE

In the doorway of the temple of Ra in Memphis. Deep gloom. An august personage with a hawk's head is mysteriously visible by his own light in the darkness within the temple. He surveys the modern audience with great contempt; and finally speaks the following words to them.

Peace! Be silent and hearken unto me, ye quaint little islanders. Give ear, ye men with white paper on your breasts and nothing written thereon (to signify the innocence of your minds). Hear me, ye women who adorn yourselves alluringly and conceal your thoughts from your men, leading them to believe that ye deem them wondrous strong and masterful whilst in truth ye hold them in your hearts as children without judgment. Look upon my hawk's head; and know that I am Ra, who was once in Egypt a mighty god. Ye cannot kneel nor prostrate yourselves; for ye are packed in rows without freedom to move, obstructing one another's vision; neither do any of ye regard it as seemly to do aught until ye see all the rest do so too; wherefore it commonly happens that in great emergencies ye do nothing, though each telleth his fellow that something must be done. I ask you not for worship, but for silence. Let not your men speak nor your women cough; for I am come to draw you back two thousand years over the graves of sixty generations. Ye poor posterity, think not that ye are the first. Other fools before ye have seen the sun rise and set, and the moon change her shape and her hour. As they were so ye are; and yet not so great; for the pyramids my people built stand to this day; whilst the

55

dustheaps on which ye slave, and which ye call empires, scatter in the wind even as ye pile your dead sons' bodies on them to make yet more dust.

Hearken to me then, oh ye compulsorily educated ones. Know that even as there is an old England and a new, and ye stand perplexed between the twain; so in the days when I was worshipped was there an old Rome and a new, and men standing perplexed between them. And the old Rome was poor and little, and greedy and fierce, and evil in many ways; but because its mind was little and its work was simple, it knew its own mind and did its own work; and the gods pitied it and helped it and strengthened it and shielded it; for the gods are patient with littleness. Then the old Rome, like the beggar on horseback, presumed on the favor of the gods, and said, "Lo! there is neither riches nor greatness in our littleness: the road to riches and greatness is through robbery of the poor and slaughter of the weak." So they robbed their own poor until they became great masters of that art, and knew by what laws it could be made to appear seemly and honest. And when they had squeezed their own poor dry, they robbed the poor of other lands, and added those lands to Rome until there came a new Rome, rich and huge. And I, Ra, laughed; for the minds of the Romans remained the same size whilst their dominion spread over the earth.

Now mark me, that ye may understand what ye are presently to see. Whilst the Romans still stood between the old Rome and the new, there arose among them a mighty soldier: Pompey the Great. And the way of the soldier is the way of death; but the way of the gods is the way of life; and so it comes that a god at the end of his way is wise and a soldier at the end of his way is a fool. So Pompey held by the old Rome, in which only soldiers could become great; but the gods turned to the new Rome, in which any man with wit enough could become what he would. And Pompey's friend Julius Caesar was on the side of the gods; for he saw that Rome had passed beyond the control of the little old Romans. This Caesar was a great talker and a politician: he bought men with words and with gold, even as ye are bought. And when they would not be satisfied with words and gold, and demanded also the glories of war, Caesar in his middle age turned his hand to that trade; and they that were against him when he sought their welfare, bowed down before him when he became a slayer and a conqueror; for such is the nature of you mortals. And as for Pompey, the gods grew tired of his triumphs and his airs of being himself a god; for he talked of law and duty and other matters that concerned not a mere human worm. And the gods smiled on Caesar; for he lived the life they had given him boldly, and was not forever rebuking us for our indecent ways of creation, and hiding our handiwork as a shameful thing. Ye know well what I mean; for this is one of your own sins.

And thus it fell out between the old Rome and the new, that Caesar said, "Unless I break the law of old Rome, I cannot take my share in ruling her; and the gift of ruling that the gods gave me will perish without fruit." But Pompey said, "The law is above all; and if thou break it thou shalt die." Then said Caesar, "I will break it: kill me who can." And he broke it. And Pompey went for him, as ye say, with a great army to slay him and uphold the old Rome. So Caesar fled across the Adriatic sea; for the high gods had a lesson to teach him, which lesson they shall also teach you in due time if ye continue to forget them and to worship that cad among gods, Mammon. Therefore before they raised Caesar to be master of the world, they were minded to throw him down into the dust, even beneath the feet of Pompey, and blacken his face before the nations. And Pompey they raised higher than ever, he and his laws and his high mind that aped the gods, so that his fall might be the more terrible. And Pompey followed Caesar, and overcame him with all the majesty of old Rome, and stood over him and over the whole world even as ye stand over it with your fleet that covers thirty miles of the sea. And when Caesar was brought down to utter nothingness, he made a last stand to die honorably, and did not despair; for he said, "Against me there is Pompey, and the old Rome, and the law and the legions: all all against me; but high above these are the gods; and Pompey is a fool." And the gods laughed and approved; and on the field of Pharsalia the impossible came to pass; the blood and iron ye pin your faith on fell before the spirit of man; for the spirit of man is the will of the gods; and Pompey's power crumbled in his hand, even as the power of imperial Spain crumbled when it was set against your fathers in the days when England was little, and knew her own mind, and had a mind to know instead of a circulation of newspapers. Wherefore look to it, lest some little people whom ye would enslave rise up and become in the hand of God the scourge of your boastings and your injustices and your lusts and stupidities.

And now, would ye know the end of Pompey, or will ye sleep while a god speaks? Heed my words well; for Pompey went where ye are gone, even to Egypt, where there was a Roman occupation even as there was but now a British one. And Caesar pursued Pompey to Egypt: a Roman fleeing, and a Roman pursuing: dog eating dog. And the Egyptians said, "Lo: these Romans which have lent money to our kings and levied a distraint upon us with their arms, call for ever upon us to be loyal to them by betraying our own country to them. But now behold two Romes! Pompey's Rome and Caesar's Rome! To which of the twain shall we pretend to be loyal?" So they turned in their perplexity to a soldier that had once served Pompey, and that knew the way of Rome and was full of her lusts. And they said to him, "Lo: in thy country dog eats dog; and both dogs are coming to eat us: what counsel hast thou to give us?" And this soldier, whose name was Lucius Septimius, and whom ye shall presently see before ye, replied, "Ye shall diligently consider which is the bigger dog of the two; and ye shall kill the other dog for his sake and thereby earn his favor." And the Egyptians said, "Thy counsel is expedient; but if we kill a man outside the law we set ourselves in the place of the gods; and this we dare not do. But thou, being a Roman, art accustomed to this kind of killing; for thou hast imperial instincts. Wilt thou there-

fore kill the lesser dog for us?" And he said, "I will; for I have
made my home in Egypt; and I desire consideration and influence among you." And they said, "We knew well thou wouldst
not do it for nothing: thou shalt have thy reward." Now when
Pompey came, he came alone in a little galley, putting his trust
in the law and the constitution. And it was plain to the people
of Egypt that Pompey was now but a very small dog. So when
he set his foot on the shore he was greeted by his old comrade
Lucius Septimius, who welcomed him with one hand and with
the other smote off his head, and kept it as it were a pickled
cabbage to make a present to Caesar. And mankind shuddered;
but the gods laughed; for Septimius was but a knife that Pompey
had sharpened; and when it turned against his own throat they
said that Pompey had better have made Septimius a ploughman
than so brave and readyhanded a slayer. Therefore again I bid
you beware, ye who would all be Pompeys if ye dared; for war
is a wolf that may come to your own door.

Are ye impatient with me? Do ye crave for a story of an
unchaste woman? Hath the name of Cleopatra tempted ye hither?
Ye foolish ones; Cleopatra is as yet but a child that is whipped
by her nurse. And what I am about to shew you for the good
of your souls is how Caesar, seeking Pompey in Egypt, found
Cleopatra; and how he received that present of a pickled cabbage
that was once the head of Pompey; and what things happened
between the old Caesar and the child queen before he left Egypt
and battled his way back to Rome to be slain there as Pompey
was slain, by men in whom the spirit of Pompey still lived. All
this ye shall see; and ye shall marvel, after your ignorant manner,
that men twenty centuries ago were already just such as you,
and spoke and lived as ye speak and live, no worse and no
better, no wiser and no sillier. And the two thousand years that
have past are to me, the god Ra, but a moment; nor is this day
any other than the day in which Caesar set foot in the land of
my people. And now I leave you; for ye are a dull folk, and
instruction is wasted on you; and I had not spoken so much
but that it is in the nature of a god to struggle for ever with

the dust and the darkness, and to drag from them, by the force of his longing for the divine, more life and more light. Settle ye therefore in your seats and keep silent; for ye are about to hear a man speak, and a great man he was, as ye count greatness. And fear not that I shall speak to you again: the rest of the story must ye learn from them that lived it. Farewell; and do not presume to applaud me. (*The temple vanishes in utter darkness.*)

*   *   *

AN ALTERNATIVE TO THE PROLOGUE

An October night on the Syrian border of Egypt towards the end of the XXXIII Dynasty, in the year 706 by Roman computation, afterwards reckoned by Christian computation as 48 B.C. *A great radiance of silver fire, the dawn of a moonlit night, is rising in the east. The stars and the cloudless sky are our own contemporaries, nineteen and a half centuries younger than we know them; but you would not guess that from their appearance. Below them are two notable drawbacks of civilization: a palace, and soldiers. The palace, an old, low, Syrian building of whitened mud, is not so ugly as Buckingham Palace; and the officers in the court-yard are more highly civilized than modern English officers: for example, they do not dig up the corpses of their dead enemies and mutilate them, as we dug up Cromwell and the Mahdi. They are in two groups: one intent on the gambling of their captain Belzanor, a warrior of fifty, who, with his spear on the ground beside his knee, is stooping to throw dice with a sly-looking young Persian recruit; the other gathered about a guardsman who has just finished telling a naughty story (still current in English barracks) at which they are laughing uproariously. They are about a dozen in number, all highly aristocratic young Egyptian guards-men, handsomely equipped with weapons and armor, very unEnglish in point of not being ashamed of and uncomfortable in their professional dress; on the contrary, rather ostentatiously and arrogantly warlike, as valuing themselves on their military caste.*

Belzanor is a typical veteran, tough and wilful; prompt, capable and crafty where brute force will serve; helpless and boyish when it will not: an active sergeant, an incompetent general, a deplorable dictator. Would, if influentially connected, be employed in the two last capacities by a modern European State on the strength of his success in the first. Is rather to be pitied just now in view of the fact that Julius Caesar is invading his country. Not knowing this, is intent on his game with the Persian, whom, as a foreigner, he considers quite capable of cheating him.

His subalterns are mostly handsome young fellows whose interest in the game and the story symbolize with tolerable completeness the main interests in life of which they are conscious. Their spears are leaning against the walls, or lying on the ground ready to their hands. The corner of the courtyard forms a triangle of which one side is the front of the palace, with a doorway, the other a wall with a gateway. The storytellers are on the palace side: the gamblers, on the gateway side. Close to the gateway, against the wall, is a stone block high enough to enable a Nubian sentinel, standing on it, to look over the wall. The yard is lighted by a torch stuck in the wall. As the laughter from the group round the storyteller dies away, the kneeling Persian, winning the throw, snatches up the stake from the ground.

BELZANOR: By Apis, Persian, thy gods are good to thee.

THE PERSIAN: Try yet again, O captain. Double or quits!

BELZANOR: No more. I am not in the vein.

THE SENTINEL (*poising his javelin as he peers over the wall*): Stand. Who goes there?

(*They all start, listening. A strange voice replies from without.*)

VOICE: The bearer of evil tidings.

BELZANOR (*calling to the sentry*): Pass him.

THE SENTINEL (*grounding his javelin*): Draw near, O bearer of evil tidings.

BELZANOR (*pocketing the dice and picking up his spear*): Let us receive this man with honor. He bears evil tidings.

(*The guardsmen seize their spears and gather about the gate, leaving a way through for the new comer.*)

PERSIAN (*rising from his knee*): Are evil tidings, then, so honorable?

BELZANOR: O barbarous Persian, hear my instruction. In Egypt the bearer of good tidings is sacrificed to the gods as a thank offering; but no god will accept the blood of the messenger of evil. When we have good tidings, we are careful to send them in the mouth of the cheapest slave we can find. Evil tidings are borne by young noblemen who desire to bring themselves into notice. (*They join the rest at the gate.*)

THE SENTINEL: Pass, O young captain; and bow the head in the House of the Queen.

VOICE: Go anoint thy javelin with fat of swine, O Blackamoor: for before morning the Romans will make thee eat it to the very butt.

(*The owner of the voice, a fairhaired dandy, dressed in a different fashion from that affected by the guardsmen, but no less extravagantly, comes through the gateway laughing. He is somewhat battlestained; and his left forearm, bandaged, comes through a torn sleeve. In his right hand he carries a Roman sword in its sheath. He swaggers down the courtyard, the Persian on his right, Belzanor on his left, and the guardsmen crowding down behind him.*)

BELZANOR: Who are thou that laughest in the House of Cleopatra the Queen, and in the teeth of Belzanor, the captain of her guard?

THE NEW COMER: I am Bel Affris, descended from the gods.

BELZANOR (*ceremoniously*): Hail, cousin!

ALL (*except the Persian*): Hail, cousin!

PERSIAN: All the Queen's guards are descended from the gods, O stranger, save myself. I am Persian, and descended from many kings.

BEL AFFRIS (*to the guardsmen*): Hail, cousins! (*To the Persian, condescendingly.*) Hail, mortal!

BELZANOR: You have been in battle, Bel Affris; and you are a soldier among soldiers. You will not let the Queen's women have the first of your tidings.

BEL AFFRIS: I have no tidings, except that we shall have our throats cut presently, women, soldiers, and all.

PERSIAN (*to Belzanor*): I told you so.

THE SENTINEL (*who has been listening*): Woe, alas!

BEL AFFRIS (*calling to him*): Peace, peace, poor Ethiop: destiny is with the gods who painted thee black. (*To Belzanor.*) What has this mortal (*indicating the Persian*) told you?

BELZANOR: He says that the Roman Julius Caesar, who has landed on our shores with a handful of followers, will make himself master of Egypt. He is afraid of the Roman soldiers. (*The guardsmen laugh with boisterous scorn.*) Peasants, brought up to scare crows and follow the plough! Sons of smiths and millers and tanners! And we nobles, consecrated to arms, descended from the gods!

PERSIAN: Belzanor: the gods are not always good to their poor relations.

BELZANOR (*hotly, to the Persian*): Man to man, are we worse than the slaves of Caesar?

BEL AFFRIS (*stepping between them*): Listen, cousin. Man to man, we Egyptians are as gods above the Romans.

THE GUARDSMEN (*exultantly*): Aha!

BEL AFFRIS: But this Caesar does not pit man against man: he throws a legion at you where you are weakest as he throws a stone from a catapult; and that legion is as a man with one head, a thousand arms, and no religion. I have fought against them; and I know.

BELZANOR (*derisively*): Were you frightened, cousin?

(*The guardsmen roar with laughter, their eyes sparkling at the wit of their captain.*)

BEL AFFRIS: No, cousin; but I was beaten. They were frightened (perhaps); but they scattered us like chaff.

(*The guardsmen, much damped, utter a growl of contemptuous disgust.*)

BELZANOR: Could you not die?

BEL AFFRIS: No: that was too easy to be worthy of a descendant of the gods. Besides, there was no time: all was over in a moment. The attack came just where we least expected it.

BELZANOR: That shews that the Romans are cowards.

BEL AFFRIS: They care nothing about cowardice, these Romans: they fight to win. The pride and honor of war are nothing to them.

PERSIAN: Tell us the tale of the battle. What befell?

THE GUARDSMEN (*gathering eagerly round Bel Affris*): Ay: the tale of the battle.

BEL AFFRIS: Know then, that I am a novice in the guard of the temple of Ra in Memphis, serving neither Cleopatra nor her brother Ptolemy, but only the high gods. We went a journey to inquire of Ptolemy why he had driven Cleopatra into Syria, and how we of Egypt should deal with the Roman Pompey, newly come to our shores after his defeat by Caesar at Pharsalia. What, think ye, did we learn? Even that Caesar is coming also in hot pursuit of his foe, and that Ptolemy has slain Pompey, whose severed head he holds in readiness to present to the conqueror. (*Sensation among the guardsmen.*) Nay, more: we found that Caesar is already come; for we had not made half a day's journey on our way back when we came upon a city rabble flying from his legions, whose landing they had gone out to withstand.

BELZANOR: And ye, the temple guard! did ye not withstand these legions?

BEL AFFRIS: What man could, that we did. But there came the sound of a trumpet whose voice was as the cursing of a black mountain. Then saw we a moving wall of shields coming towards us. You know how the heart burns when you charge a fortified wall; but how if the fortified wall were to charge you?

THE PERSIAN (*exulting in having told them so*): Did I not say it?

BEL AFFRIS: When the wall came nigh, it changed into a line of men—common fellows enough, with helmets, leather tunics, and breastplates. Every man of them flung his javelin: the one that came my way drove through my shield as through a papyrus—lo there! (*he points to the bandage on his left arm*) and would have gone through my neck had I not stooped. They were charging at the double then, and were upon us with short swords almost as soon as their javelins. When a man is close to you with such a sword, you can do nothing with our weapons: they are all too long.

THE PERSIAN: What did you do?

BEL AFFRIS: Doubled my fist and smote my Roman on the sharpness of his jaw. He was but mortal after all: he lay down in a stupor; and I took his sword and laid it on. (*Drawing the sword.*) Lo! a Roman sword with Roman blood on it!

THE GUARDSMEN (*approvingly*): Good! (*They take the sword and hand it round, examining it curiously.*)

THE PERSIAN: And your men?

BEL AFFRIS: Fled. Scattered like sheep.

BELZANOR (*furiously*): The cowardly slaves! Leaving the descendants of the gods to be butchered!

BEL AFFRIS (*with acid coolness*): The descendants of the gods did not stay to be butchered, cousin. The battle was not to the strong; but the race was to the swift. The Romans who have no chariots, sent a cloud of horsemen in pursuit, and slew multitudes. Then our high priest's captain rallied a dozen descendants of the gods and exhorted us to die fighting. I said to myself: surely it is safer to stand than to lose my breath and be stabbed in the back; so I joined our captain and stood. Then the Romans treated us with respect; for no man attacks a lion when the field is full of sheep, except for the pride and honor of war, of which these Romans know nothing. So we escaped with our lives; and I am come to warn you that you must open your gates to Caesar; for his advance guard is scarce an hour behind me; and not an Egyptian warrior is left standing between you and his legions.

THE SENTINEL: Woe, alas! (*He throws down his javelin and flies into the palace.*)

BELZANOR: Nail him to the door, quick! (*The guardsmen rush for him with their spears; but he is too quick for them.*) Now this news will run through the palace like fire through stubble.

BEL AFFRIS: What shall we do to save the women from the Romans?

BELZANOR: Why not kill them?

PERSIAN: Because we should have to pay blood money for some of them. Better let the Romans kill them: it is cheaper.

BELZANOR (*awestruck at his brain power*): O subtle one! O serpent!

BEL AFFRIS: But your Queen?

BELZANOR: True: we must carry off Cleopatra.

BEL AFFRIS: Will ye not await her command?

BELZANOR: Command! a girl of sixteen! Not we. At Memphis ye deem her a Queen: here we know better. I will take her on the crupper of my horse. When we soldiers have carried her out of Caesar's reach, then the priests and the nurses and the rest of them can pretend she is a queen again, and put their commands into her mouth.

PERSIAN: Listen to me, Belzanor.

BELZANOR: Speak, O subtle beyond thy years.

THE PERSIAN: Cleopatra's brother Ptolemy is at war with her. Let us sell her to him.

THE GUARDSMEN: O subtle one! O serpent!

BELZANOR: We dare not. We are descended from the gods; but Cleopatra is descended from the river Nile; and the lands of our fathers will grow no grain if the Nile rises not to water them. Without our father's gifts we should live the lives of dogs.

PERSIAN: It is true: the Queen's guard cannot live on its pay. But hear me further, O ye kinsmen of Osiris.

THE GUARDSMEN: Speak, O subtle one. Hear the serpent begotten!

PERSIAN: Have I heretofore spoken truly to you of Caesar, when you thought I mocked you?

GUARDSMEN: Truly, truly.

BELZANOR (*reluctantly admitting it*): So Bel Affris says.

PERSIAN: Hear more of him, then. This Caesar is a great lover of women: he makes them his friends and counsellors.

BELZANOR: Faugh! This rule of women will be the ruin of Egypt.

THE PERSIAN: Let it rather be the ruin of Rome! Caesar grows old now: he is past fifty and full of labors and battles. He is too old for the young women; and the old women are too wise to worship him.

BEL AFFRIS: Take heed, Persian. Caesar is by this time almost within earshot.

PERSIAN: Cleopatra is not yet a woman: neither is she wise. But she already troubles men's wisdom.

BELZANOR: Ay: that is because she is descended from the river Nile and a black kitten of the sacred White Cat. What then?

PERSIAN: Why, sell her secretly to Ptolemy, and then offer ourselves to Caesar as volunteers to fight for the overthrow of her brother and the rescue of our Queen, the Great Granddaughter of the Nile.

THE GUARDSMEN: O serpent!

PERSIAN: He will listen to us if we come with her picture in our mouths. He will conquer and kill her brother, and reign in Egypt with Cleopatra for his Queen. And we shall be her guard.

GUARDSMEN: O subtlest of all the serpents! O admiration! O wisdom!

BEL AFFRIS: He will also have arrived before you have done talking, O word spinner.

BELZANOR: That is true. (*An affrighted uproar in the palace interrupts him.*) Quick: the flight has begun: guard the door. (*They rush to the door and form a cordon before it with their spears. A mob of women-servants and nurses surges out. Those in front recoil from the spears, screaming to those behind to keep*

back. Belzanor's voice dominates the disturbance as he shouts.)
Back there. In again, unprofitable cattle.

THE GUARDSMEN: Back, unprofitable cattle.

BELZANOR: Send us out Ftatateeta, the Queen's chief nurse.

THE WOMEN (*calling into the palace*): Ftatateeta, Ftatateeta.
Come, come. Speak to Belzanor.

A WOMAN: Oh, keep back. You are thrusting me on the spear-
heads.

(*A huge grim woman, her face covered with a network of tiny
wrinkles, and her eyes old, large, and wise; sinewy handed, very
tall, very strong; with the mouth of a bloodhound and the jaws of
a bulldog, appears on the threshold. She is dressed like a person
of consequence in the palace, and confronts the guardsmen insolently.*)

FTATATEETA: Make way for the Queen's chief nurse.

BELZANOR (*with solemn arrogance*): Ftatateeta: I am Belzanor,
the captain of the Queen's guard, descended from the gods.

FTATATEETA (*retorting his arrogance with interest*): Belzanor: I
am Ftatateeta, the Queen's chief nurse; and your divine ances-
tors were proud to be painted on the wall in the pyramids
of the kings whom my fathers served.

(*The women laugh triumphantly.*)

BELZANOR (*with grim humor*): Ftatateeta: daughter of a long-
tongued, swivel-eyed chameleon, the Romans are at hand.
(*A cry of terror from the women: they would fly but for the
spears.*) Not even the descendants of the gods can resist them;
for they have each man seven arms, each carrying seven spears.
The blood in their veins is boiling quicksilver; and their wives
become mothers in three hours, and are slain and eaten the
next day.

(*A shudder of horror from the women. Ftatateeta, despising them
and scorning the soldiers, pushes her way through the crowd and
confronts the spear points undismayed.*)

FTATATEETA: Then fly and save yourselves, O cowardly sons of the cheap clay gods that are sold to fish porters; and leave us to shift for ourselves.

BELZANOR: Not until you have first done our bidding, O terror of manhood. Bring out Cleopatra the Queen to us; and then go whither you will.

FTATATEETA (*with a derisive laugh*): Now I know why the gods have taken her out of our hands. (*The guardsmen start and look at one another.*) Know, thou foolish soldier, that the Queen has been missing since an hour past sundown.

BELZANOR (*furiously*): Hag: you have hidden her to sell to Caesar or her brother. (*He grasps her by the left wrist, and drags her, helped by a few of the guards, to the middle of the courtyard, where, as they fling her on her knees, he draws a murderous looking knife.*) Where is she? Where is she? or—(*he threatens to cut her throat*).

FTATATEETA (*savagely*): Touch me, dog; and the Nile will not rise on your fields for seven times seven years of famine.

BELZANOR (*frightened, but desperate*): I will sacrifice: I will pay. Or stay. (*To the Persian.*) You, O subtle one: your father's lands lie far from the Nile. Slay her.

PERSIAN (*threatening her with his knife*): Persia has but one god; yet he loves the blood of old women. Where is Cleopatra?

FTATATEETA: Persian: as Osiris lives, I do not know. I chid her for bringing evil days upon us by talking to the sacred cats of the priests, and carrying them in her arms. I told her she would be left alone here when the Romans came as a punishment for her disobedience. And now she is gone—run away—hidden. I speak the truth. I call Osiris to witness—

THE WOMEN (*protesting officiously*): She speaks the truth, Belzanor.

BELZANOR: You have frightened the child: she is hiding. Search—quick—into the palace—search every corner.

(*The guards, led by Belzanor, shoulder their way into the palace through the flying crowd of women, who escape through the courtyard gate.*)

FTATATEETA (*screaming*): Sacrilege! Men in the Queen's chambers! Sa— (*her voice dies away as the Persian puts his knife to her throat*).

BEL AFFRIS (*laying a hand on Ftatateeta's left shoulder*): Forbear her yet a moment, Persian. (*To Ftatateeta, very significantly.*) Mother: your gods are asleep or away hunting; and the sword is at your throat. Bring us to where the Queen is hid, and you shall live.

FTATATEETA (*contemptuously*): Who shall stay the sword in the hand of a fool, if the high gods put it there? Listen to me, ye young men without understanding. Cleopatra fears me; but she fears the Romans more. There is but one power greater in her eyes than the wrath of the Queen's nurse and the cruelty of Caesar; and that is the power of the Sphinx that sits in the desert watching the way to the sea. What she would have it know, she tells into the ears of the sacred cats; and on her birthday she sacrifices to it and decks it with poppies. Go ye therefore into the desert and seek Cleopatra in the shadow of the Sphinx; and on your heads see to it that no harm comes to her.

BEL AFFRIS (*to the Persian*): May we believe this, O subtle one?

PERSIAN: Which way come the Romans?

BEL AFFRIS: Over the desert, from the sea, by this very Sphinx.

PERSIAN (*to Ftatateeta*): O mother of guile! O aspic's tongue! You have made up this tale so that we two may go into the desert and perish on the spears of the Romans. (*Lifting his knife.*) Taste death.

FTATATEETA: Not from thee, baby. (*She snatches his ankle from under him and flies stooping along the palace wall, vanishing in the darkness within its precinct. Bel Affris roars with laughter as the Persian tumbles. The guardsmen rush out of the palace with Belzanor and a mob of fugitives, mostly carrying bundles.*)

PERSIAN: Have you found Cleopatra?

BELZANOR: She is gone. We have searched every corner.

THE SENTINEL (*appearing at the door of the palace*): Woe! Alas! Fly, fly!

BELZANOR: What is the matter now?

THE SENTINEL: The sacred white cat has been stolen.

ALL: Woe! woe! (*General panic. They all fly with cries of consternation. The torch is thrown down and extinguished in the rush. The noise of the fugitives dies away. Darkness and dead silence.*)

ACT I

The same darkness into which the temple of Ra and the Syrian palace vanished. The same silence. Suspense. Then the blackness and stillness break softly into silver mist and strange airs as the windswept harp of Memnon plays at the dawning of the moon. It rises full over the desert; and a vast horizon comes into relief, broken by a huge shape which soon reveals itself in the spreading radiance as a Sphinx pedestalled on the sands. The light still clears, until the upraised eyes of the image are distinguished looking straight forward and upward in infinite fearless vigil, and a mass of color between its great paws defines itself as a heap of red poppies on which a girl lies motionless, her silken vest heaving gently and regularly with the breathing of a dreamless sleeper, and her braided hair glittering in a shaft of moonlight like a bird's wing.

Suddenly there comes from afar a vaguely fearful sound (it might be the bellow of a Minotaur softened by great distance) and Memnon's music stops. Silence: then a few faint high-ringing trumpet notes. Then silence again. Then a man comes from the south with stealing steps, ravished by the mystery of the night, all wonder, and halts, lost in contemplation, opposite the left flank of the Sphinx, whose bosom, with its burden, is hidden from him by its massive shoulder.

THE MAN: Hail, Sphinx: salutation from Julius Caesar! I have wandered in many lands, seeking the lost regions from which my birth into this world exiled me, and the company of creatures such as I myself. I have found flocks and pastures, men and cities, but no other Caesar, no air native to me, no man kindred to me, none who can do my day's deed, and think my night's thought. In the little world yonder, Sphinx, my place is as high as yours in this great desert; only I wander, and you sit still; I conquer, and you endure; I work and wonder, you watch and wait; I look up and am dazzled, look down and am darkened, look round and am puzzled, whilst your eyes never turn from looking out—out of the world—to the lost region—the home from which we have strayed. Sphinx, you and I, strangers to the race of men, are no strangers to one another: have I not been conscious of you and of this place since I was born? Rome is a madman's dream: this is my Reality. These starry lamps of yours I have seen from afar in Gaul, in Britain, in Spain, in Thessaly, signalling great secrets to some eternal sentinel below, whose post I never could find. And here at last is their sentinel—an image of the constant and immortal part of my life, silent, full of thoughts, alone in the silver desert. Sphinx, Sphinx: I have climbed mountains at night to hear in the distance the stealthy footfall of the winds that chase your sands in forbidden play—our invisible children, O Sphinx, laughing in whispers. My way hither was the way of destiny; for I am he of whose genius you are the symbol: part brute, part woman, and part god—nothing of man in me at all. Have I read your riddle, Sphinx?

THE GIRL (*who has wakened, and peeped cautiously from her nest to see who is speaking*): Old gentleman.

CAESAR (*starting violently, and clutching his sword*): Immortal gods!

THE GIRL: Old gentleman: dont run away.

CAESAR (*stupefied*): "Old gentleman: dont run away"!!! This! to Julius Caesar!

THE GIRL (*urgently*): Old gentleman.

CAESAR: Sphinx: you presume on your centuries. I am younger than you, though your voice is but a girl's voice as yet.

THE GIRL: Climb up here, quickly; or the Romans will come and eat you.

CAESAR (*running forward past the Sphinx's shoulder, and seeing her*): A child at its breast! a divine child!

THE GIRL: Come up quickly. You must get up at its side and creep round.

CAESAR (*amazed*): Who are you?

THE GIRL: Cleopatra, Queen of Egypt.

CAESAR: Queen of the Gypsies, you mean.

CLEOPATRA: You must not be disrespectful to me, or the Sphinx will let the Romans eat you. Come up. It is quite cosy here.

CAESAR (*to himself*): What a dream! What a magnificent dream! Only let me not wake, and I will conquer ten continents to pay for dreaming it out to the end. (*He climbs to the Sphinx's flank, and presently reappears to her on the pedestal, stepping round to its right shoulder.*)

CLEOPATRA: Take care. Thats right. Now sit down: you may have its other paw. (*She seats herself comfortably on its left paw.*) It is very powerful and will protect us; but (*shivering, and with plaintive loneliness*) it would not take any notice of me or keep me company. I am glad you have come: I was very lonely. Did you happen to see a white cat anywhere?

CAESAR (*sitting slowly down on the right paw in extreme wonderment*): Have you lost one?

CLEOPATRA: Yes: the sacred white cat: is it not dreadful? I brought him here to sacrifice him to the Sphinx; but when we got a little way from the city a black cat called him, and he jumped out of my arms and ran away to it. Do you think that the black cat can have been my great-great-great-grandmother?

CAESAR (*staring at her*): Your great-great-great-grandmother! Well, why not? Nothing would surprise me on this night of nights.

CLEOPATRA: I think it must have been. My great-grandmother's great-grandmother was a black kitten of the sacred white cat; and the river Nile made her his seventh wife. That is why my hair is so wavy. And I always want to be let do as I like, no matter whether it is the will of the gods or not: that is because my blood is made with Nile water.

CAESAR: What are you doing here at this time of night? Do you live here?

CLEOPATRA: Of course not: I am the Queen; and I shall live in the palace at Alexandria when I have killed my brother, who drove me out of it. When I am old enough I shall do just what I like. I shall be able to poison the slaves and see them wriggle, and pretend to Ftatateeta that she is going to be put into the fiery furnace.

CAESAR: Hm! Meanwhile why are you not at home and in bed?

CLEOPATRA: Because the Romans are coming to eat us all. You are not at home and in bed either.

CAESAR (*with conviction*): Yes I am. I live in a tent; and I am now in that tent, fast asleep and dreaming. Do you suppose that I believe you are real, you impossible little dream witch?

CLEOPATRA (*giggling and leaning trustfully towards him*): You are a funny old gentleman. I like you.

CAESAR: Ah, that spoils the dream. Why dont you dream that I am young?

CLEOPATRA: I wish you were; only I think I should be more afraid of you. I like men, especially young men with round strong arms; but I am afraid of them. You are old and rather thin and stringy; but you have a nice voice; and I like to have somebody to talk to, though I think you are a little mad. It is the moon that makes you talk to yourself in that silly way.

CAESAR: What! you heard that, did you? I was saying my prayers to the great Sphinx.

CLEOPATRA: But this isnt the great Sphinx.

CAESAR (*much disappointed, looking up at the statue*): What!

CLEOPATRA: This is only a dear little kitten of a Sphinx. Why, the great Sphinx is so big that it has a temple between its paws. This is my pet Sphinx. Tell me: do you think the Romans have any sorcerers who could take us away from the Sphinx by magic?

CAESAR: Why? Are you afraid of the Romans?

CLEOPATRA (*very seriously*): Oh, they would eat us if they caught us. They are barbarians. Their chief is called Julius Caesar. His father was a tiger and his mother a burning mountain; and his nose is like an elephant's trunk. (CAESAR *involuntarily rubs his nose.*) They all have long noses, and ivory tusks, and little tails, and seven arms with a hundred arrows in each; and they live on human flesh.

CAESAR: Would you like me to shew you a real Roman?

CLEOPATRA (*terrified*): No. You are frightening me.

CAESAR: No matter: this is only a dream—

CLEOPATRA (*excitedly*): It is not a dream: it is not a dream. See, see. (*She plucks a pin from her hair and jabs it repeatedly into his arm.*)

CAESAR: Ffff—Stop. (*Wrathfully.*) How dare you?

CLEOPATRA (*abashed*): You said you were dreaming. (*Whimpering.*) I only wanted to shew you—

CAESAR (*gently*): Come, come: dont cry. A queen mustnt cry. (*He rubs his arm, wondering at the reality of the smart.*) Am I awake? (*He strikes his hand against the Sphinx to test its solidity. It feels so real that he begins to be alarmed, and says perplexedly:*) Yes, I— (*quite panicstricken*) no: impossible: madness, madness! (*Desperately.*) Back to camp—to camp. (*He rises to spring down from the pedestal.*)

CLEOPATRA (*flinging her arms in terror round him*): No: you shant leave me. No, no, no: dont go. I'm afraid—afraid of the Romans.

CAESAR (*as the conviction that he is really awake forces itself on him*): Cleopatra: can you see my face well?

CLEOPATRA: Yes. It is so white in the moonlight.

CAESAR: Are you sure it is the moonlight that makes me look whiter than an Egyptian? (*Grimly.*) Do you notice that I have a rather long nose?

CLEOPATRA (*recoiling, paralysed by a terrible suspicion*): Oh!

CAESAR: It is a Roman nose, Cleopatra.

CLEOPATRA: Ah! (*With a piercing scream she springs up; darts round the left shoulder of the Sphinx; scrambles down to the sand; and falls on her knees in frantic supplication, shrieking.*) Bite him in two, Sphinx: bite him in two. I meant to sacrifice the white cat—I did indeed—I (*Caesar, who has slipped down from the pedestal, touches her on the shoulder.*)—Ah! (*She buries her head in her arms.*)

CAESAR: Cleopatra: shall I teach you a way to prevent Caesar from eating you?

CLEOPATRA (*clinging to him piteously*): Oh do, do, do. I will steal Ftatateeta's jewels and give them to you. I will make the river Nile water your lands twice a year.

CAESAR: Peace, peace, my child. Your gods are afraid of the Romans: you see the Sphinx dare not bite me, nor prevent me carrying you off to Julius Caesar.

CLEOPATRA (*in pleading murmurings*): You wont, you wont. You said you wouldnt.

CAESAR: Caesar never eats women.

CLEOPATRA (*springing up full of hope*): What!

CAESAR (*impressively*): But he eats girls (*she relapses*) and cats. Now you are a silly little girl; and you are descended from the black kitten. You are both a girl and a cat.

CLEOPATRA (*trembling*): And will he eat me?

CAESAR: Yes; unless you make him believe that you are a woman.

CLEOPATRA: Oh, you must get a sorcerer to make a woman of me. Are you a sorcerer?

CAESAR: Perhaps. But it will take a long time; and this very night you must stand face to face with Caesar in the palace of your fathers.

CLEOPATRA: No, no. I darent.

CAESAR: Whatever dread may be in your soul—however terrible Caesar may be to you—you must confront him as a brave woman and a great queen; and you must feel no fear. If your hand shakes: if your voice quavers; then—night and death!

(*She moans.*) But if he thinks you worthy to rule, he will set you on the throne by his side and make you the real ruler of Egypt.

CLEOPATRA (*despairingly*): No: he will find me out: he will find me out.

CAESAR (*rather mournfully*): He is easily deceived by women. Their eyes dazzle him; and he sees them not as they are, but as he wishes them to appear to him.

CLEOPATRA (*hopefully*): Then we will cheat him. I will put on Ftatateeta's head-dress; and he will think me quite an old woman.

CAESAR: If you do that he will eat you at one mouthful.

CLEOPATRA: But I will give him a cake with my magic opal and seven hairs of the white cat baked in it; and—

CAESAR (*abruptly*): Pah! you are a little fool. He will eat your cake and you too. (*He turns contemptuously from her.*)

CLEOPATRA (*running after him and clinging to him*): Oh please, please! I will do whatever you tell me. I will be good. I will be your slave. (*Again the terrible bellowing note sounds across the desert, now closer at hand. It is the bucina, the Roman war trumpet.*)

CAESAR: Hark!

CLEOPATRA (*trembling*): What was that?

CAESAR: Caesar's voice.

CLEOPATRA (*pulling at his hand*): Let us run away. Come. Oh, come.

CAESAR: You are safe with me until you stand on your throne to receive Caesar. Now lead me thither.

CLEOPATRA (*only too glad to get away*): I will, I will. (*Again the bucina.*) Oh come, come, come: the gods are angry. Do you feel the earth shaking?

CAESAR: It is the tread of Caesar's legions.

CLEOPATRA (*drawing him away*): This way, quickly. And let us look for the white cat as we go. It is he that has turned you into a Roman.

CAESAR: Incorrigible, oh, incorrigible! Away! (*He follows her, the bucina sounding louder as they steal across the desert. The moonlight wanes: the horizon again shews black against the sky, broken only by the fantastic silhouette of the Sphinx. The sky itself vanishes in darkness, from which there is no relief until the gleam of a distant torch falls on great Egyptian pillars supporting the roof of a majestic corridor. At the further end of this corridor a Nubian slave appears carrying the torch. Caesar, still led by Cleopatra, follows him. They come down the corridor, Caesar peering keenly about at the strange architecture, and at the pillar shadows between which, as the passing torch makes them hurry noiselessly backwards, figures of men with wings and hawk's heads, and vast black marble cats, seem to flit in and out of ambush. Further along, the wall turns a corner and makes a spacious transept in which Caesar sees, on his right, a throne, and behind the throne a door. On each side of the throne is a slender pillar with a lamp on it.*)

CAESAR: What place is this?

CLEOPATRA: This is where I sit on the throne when I am allowed to wear my crown and robes. (*The slave holds his torch to shew the throne.*)

CAESAR: Order the slave to light the lamps.

CLEOPATRA (*shyly*): Do you think I may?

CAESAR: Of course. You are the Queen. (*She hesitates.*) Go on.

CLEOPATRA (*timidly, to the slave*): Light all the lamps.

FTATATEETA (*suddenly coming from behind the throne*): Stop. (*The slave stops. She turns sternly to Cleopatra, who quails like a naughty child.*) Who is this you have with you; and how dare you order the lamps to be lighted without my permission? (*Cleopatra is dumb with apprehension.*)

CAESAR: Who is she?

CLEOPATRA: Ftatateeta.

FTATATEETA (*arrogantly*): Chief nurse to—

CAESAR (*cutting her short*): I speak to the Queen. Be silent. (*To Cleopatra.*) Is this how your servants know their places? Send her away; and do you (*to the slave*) do as the Queen has bidden. (*The slave lights the lamps. Meanwhile Cleopatra stands hesitating, afraid of Ftatateeta.*) You are the Queen: send her away.

CLEOPATRA (*cajoling*): Ftatateeta, dear: you must go away—just for a little.

CAESAR: You are not commanding her to go away: you are begging her. You are no Queen. You will be eaten. Farewell. (*He turns to go.*)

CLEOPATRA (*clutching him*): No, no, no. Dont leave me.

CAESAR: A Roman does not stay with queens who are afraid of their slaves.

CLEOPATRA: I am not afraid. Indeed I am not afraid.

FTATATEETA: We shall see who is afraid here. (*Menacingly.*) Cleopatra—

CAESAR: On your knees, woman: am I also a child that you dare trifle with me? (*He points to the floor at Cleopatra's feet. Ftatateeta, half cowed, half savage, hesitates. Caesar calls to the Nubian.*) Slave. (*The Nubian comes to him.*) Can you cut off a head? (*The Nubian nods and grins ecstatically, showing all his teeth. Caesar takes his sword by the scabbard, ready to offer the hilt to the Nubian, and turns again to Ftatateeta, repeating his gesture.*) Have you remembered yourself, mistress?

(*Ftatateeta, crushed, kneels before Cleopatra, who can hardly believe her eyes.*)

FTATATEETA (*hoarsely*): O Queen, forget not thy servant in the days of thy greatness.

CLEOPATRA (*blazing with excitement*): Go. Begone. Go away. (*Ftatateeta rises with stooped head, and moves backwards towards the door. Cleopatra watches her submission eagerly, almost clapping her hands, which are trembling. Suddenly she cries:*) Give me something to beat her with. (*She snatches a snake-skin from the throne and dashes after Ftatateeta, whirling it like a scourge in the air. Caesar makes a bound and manages to catch her and hold her while Ftatateeta escapes.*)

CAESAR: You scratch, kitten, do you?

CLEOPATRA (*breaking from him*): I will beat somebody. I will beat him. (*She attacks the slave.*) There, there, there! (*The slave flies for his life up the corridor and vanishes. She throws the snake-skin away and jumps on the step of the throne with her arms waving, crying.*) I am a real Queen at last—a real, real Queen! Cleopatra the Queen! (*Caesar shakes his head dubiously, the advantage of the change seeming open to question from the point of view of the general welfare of Egypt. She turns and looks at him exultantly. Then she jumps down from the steps, runs to him, and flings her arms round him rapturously, crying:*) Oh, I love you for making me a Queen.

CAESAR: But queens love only kings.

CLEOPATRA: I will make all the men I love kings. I will make you a king. I will have many young kings, with round, strong arms; and when I am tired of them I will whip them to death; but you shall always be my king: my nice, kind, wise, good old king.

CAESAR: Oh, my wrinkles, my wrinkles! And my child's heart! You will be the most dangerous of all Caesar's conquests.

CLEOPATRA (*appalled*): Caesar! I forgot Caesar. (*Anxiously.*) You will tell him that I am a Queen, will you not?—a real Queen. Listen! (*stealthily coaxing him*): let us run away and hide until Caesar is gone.

CAESAR: If you fear Caesar, you are no true queen; and though you were to hide beneath a pyramid, he would go straight to it and lift it with one hand. And then—! (*He chops his teeth together.*)

CLEOPATRA (*trembling*): Oh!

CAESAR: Be afraid if you dare. (*The note of the bucina resounds again in the distance. She moans with fear. Caesar exults in it, exclaiming:*) Aha! Caesar approaches the throne of Cleopatra. Come: take your place. (*He takes her hand and leads her to the throne. She is too downcast to speak.*) Ho, there, Teetatota. How do you call your slaves?

CLEOPATRA (*spiritlessly, as she sinks on the throne and cowers there, shaking*): Clap your hands.

(*He claps his hands. Ftatateeta returns.*)

CAESAR: Bring the Queen's robes, and her crown, and her women; and prepare her.

CLEOPATRA (*eagerly—recovering herself a little*): Yes, the crown, Ftatateeta: I shall wear the crown.

FTATATEETA: For whom must the Queen put on her state?

CAESAR: For a citizen of Rome. A king of kings, Totateeta.

CLEOPATRA (*stamping at her*): How dare you ask questions? Go and do as you are told. (*Ftatateeta goes out with a grim smile. Cleopatra goes on eagerly, to Caesar.*) Caesar will know that I am a Queen when he sees my crown and robes, will he not?

CAESAR: No. How shall he know that you are not a slave dressed up in the Queen's ornaments?

CLEOPATRA: You must tell him.

CAESAR: He will not ask me. He will know Cleopatra by her pride, her courage, her majesty, and her beauty. (*She looks very doubtful.*) Are you trembling?

CLEOPATRA (*shivering with dread*): No, I—I— (*in a very sickly voice*) No.

(*Ftatateeta and three women come in with the regalia.*)

FTATATEETA: Of all the Queen's women, these three alone are left. The rest are fled. (*They begin to deck Cleopatra, who submits, pale and motionless.*)

CAESAR: Good, good. Three are enough. Poor Caesar generally has to dress himself.

FTATATEETA (*contemptuously*): The queen of Egypt is not a Roman barbarian. (*To Cleopatra.*) Be brave, my nursling. Hold up your head before this stranger.

CAESAR (*admiring Cleopatra, and placing the crown on her head*): Is it sweet or bitter to be a Queen, Cleopatra?

CLEOPATRA: Bitter.

CAESAR: Cast out fear; and you will conquer Caesar. Tota: are the Romans at hand?

FTATATEETA: They are at hand; and the guard has fled.

THE WOMEN (*wailing subduedly*): Woe to us!

(*The Nubian comes running down the hall.*)

NUBIAN: The Romans are in the courtyard. (*He bolts through the door. With a shriek, the women fly after him. Ftatateeta's jaw expresses savage resolution: she does not budge. Cleopatra can hardly restrain herself from following them. Caesar grips her wrist, and looks steadfastly at her. She stands like a martyr.*)

CAESAR: The Queen must face Caesar alone. Answer "So be it."

CLEOPATRA (*white*): So be it.

CAESAR (*releasing her*): Good.

(*A tramp and tumult of armed men is heard. Cleopatra's terror increases. The bucina sounds close at hand, followed by a formidable clangor of trumpets. This is too much for Cleopatra: she utters a cry and darts towards the door. Ftatateeta stops her ruthlessly.*)

FTATATEETA: You are my nursling. You have said "So be it"; and if you die for it, you must make the Queen's word good. (*She hands Cleopatra to Caesar, who takes her back, almost beside herself with apprehension, to the throne.*)

CAESAR: Now, if you quail—! (*He seats himself on the throne.*)

(*She stands on the step, all but unconscious, waiting for death. The Roman soldiers troop in tumultuously through the corridor, headed by their ensign with his eagle, and their bucinator, a burly fellow with his instrument coiled round his body, its brazen bell shaped like the head of a howling wolf. When they reach the transept, they stare in amazement at the throne; dress into ordered rank opposite; draw their swords and lift them in the air with a shout of* Hail, Caesar. *Cleopatra turns and stares wildly at Caesar; grasps the situation; and, with a great sob of relief, falls into his arms.*)

ACT II

Alexandria. A hall on the first floor of the Palace, ending in a loggia approached by two steps. Through the arches of the loggia the Mediterranean can be seen, bright in the morning sun. The clean lofty walls, painted with a procession of the Egyptian theocracy, presented in profile as flat ornament, and the absence of mirrors, sham perspectives, stuffy upholstery and textiles, make the place handsome, wholesome, simple and cool, or, as a rich English manufacturer would express it, poor, bare, ridiculous and unhomely. For Tottenham Court Road civilization is to this Egyptian civilization as glass bead and tattoo civilization is to Tottenham Court Road.

The young king Ptolemy Dionysus (aged ten) is at the top of the steps, on his way in through the loggia, led by his guardian Pothinus, who has him by the hand. The court is assembled to receive him. It is made up of men and women (some of the women being officials) of various complexions and races, mostly Egyptian; some of them, comparatively fair, from lower Egypt, some, much darker, from upper Egypt; with a few Greeks and Jews. Prominent in a group on Ptolemy's right hand is Theodotus, Ptolemy's tutor. Another group, on Ptolemy's left, is headed by Achillas, the general of Ptolemy's troops. Theodotus is a little old man, whose features are as cramped and wizened as his limbs, except his tall straight forehead, which occupies more space than all the rest of his face. He maintains an air of magpie keenness and profundity, listening to what the others say with the sarcastic vigilance of a philosopher listening to the exercises of his disciples. Achillas is a tall handsome man of thirty-five, with a fine black beard curled like the coat of a poodle. Apparently not a clever man, but distinguished and dignified, Pothinus is a vigorous man of fifty, a eunuch, passionate, energetic and quick witted, but of common mind and character; impatient and unable to control his temper. He has fine tawny hair, like fur. Ptolemy, the King, looks much older than an English boy of ten; but he has the childish air, the habit of being in leading strings, the mixture of impotence and petulance, the appearance of being excessively washed, combed and dressed by other hands, which is exhibited by court-bred princes of all ages.

All receive the King with reverences. He comes down the steps to a chair of state which stands a little to his right, the only seat in the hall. Taking his place before it, he looks nervously for instructions to Pothinus, who places himself at his left hand.

POTHINUS: The King of Egypt has a word to speak.

THEODOTUS (*in a squeak which he makes impressive by sheer self-opinionativeness*): Peace for the King's word!

PTOLEMY (*without any vocal inflexions: he is evidently repeating a lesson*): Take notice of this all of you. I am the first-born son of Auletes the Flute Blower who was your King. My sister Berenice drove him from his throne and reigned in his stead but—but—(*he hesitates*)—

POTHINUS (*stealthily prompting*): —but the gods would not suffer—

PTOLEMY: Yes—the gods would not suffer—not suffer— (*He stops; then, crestfallen:*) I forgot what the gods would not suffer.

THEODOTUS: Let Pothinus, the King's guardian, speak for the King.

POTHINUS (*suppressing his impatience with difficulty*): The King wished to say that the gods would not suffer the impiety of his sister to go unpunished.

PTOLEMY (*hastily*): Yes: I remember the rest of it. (*He resumes his monotone.*) Therefore the gods sent a stranger one Mark Antony a Roman captain of horsemen across the sands of the desert and he set my father again upon the throne. And my father took Berenice my sister and struck her head off. And now that my father is dead yet another of his daughters my sister Cleopatra would snatch the kingdom from me and reign in my place. But the gods would not suffer—(*Pothinus coughs admonitorily.*)—the gods—the gods would not suffer—

POTHINUS (*prompting*): —will not maintain—

PTOLEMY: Oh yes—will not maintain such iniquity they will give her head to the axe even as her sister's. But with the help of the witch Ftatateeta she hath cast a spell on the Roman Julius Caesar to make him uphold her false pretence to rule in Egypt. Take notice then that I will not suffer—that I will not suffer—(*pettishly, to Pothinus:*) What is it that I will not suffer?

POTHINUS (*suddenly exploding with all the force and emphasis of political passion*): The King will not suffer a foreigner to take from him the throne of our Egypt. (*A shout of applause.*) Tell the King, Achillas, how many soldiers and horsemen follow the Roman?

THEODOTUS: Let the King's general speak!

ACHILLAS: But two Roman legions, O King. Three thousand soldiers and scarce a thousand horsemen.

(*The court breaks into derisive laughter; and a great chattering begins, amid which Rufio, a Roman officer, appears in the loggia. He is a burly, black-bearded man of middle age, very blunt, prompt and rough, with small clear eyes, and plump nose and cheeks, which, however, like the rest of his flesh, are in ironhard condition.*)

RUFIO (*from the steps*): Peace, ho! (*The laughter and chatter cease abruptly.*) Caesar approaches.

THEODOTUS (*with much presence of mind*): The King permits the Roman commander to enter!

(*Caesar, plainly dressed, but wearing an oak wreath to conceal his baldness, enters from the loggia, attended by Britannus, his secretary, a Briton, about forty, tall, solemn, and already slightly bald, with a heavy, drooping, hazel-colored moustache trained so as to lose its ends in a pair of trim whiskers. He is carefully dressed in blue, with portfolio, inkhorn, and reed pen at his girdle. His serious air and sense of the importance of the business in hand is in marked contrast to the kindly interest of Caesar, who looks at the scene, which is new to him, with the frank curiosity of a child, and then turns to the King's chair: Britannus and Rufio posting themselves near the steps at the other side.*)

CAESAR (*looking at Pothinus and Ptolemy*): Which is the King? the man or the boy?

POTHINUS: I am Pothinus, the guardian of my lord the King.

CAESAR (*patting Ptolemy kindly on the shoulder*): So you are the King. Dull work at your age, eh? (*To Pothinus.*) Your servant, Pothinus. (*He turns away unconcernedly and comes slowly along the middle of the hall, looking from side to side at the courtiers until he reaches Achillas.*) And this gentleman?

THEODOTUS: Achillas, the King's general.

CAESAR (*to Achillas, very friendly*): A general, eh? I am a general myself. But I began too old, too old. Health and many victories, Achillas!

ACHILLAS: As the gods will, Caesar.

CAESAR (*turning to Theodotus*): And you, sir, are—?

THEODOTUS: Theodotus, the King's tutor.

CAESAR: You teach men how to be kings, Theodotus. That is very clever of you. (*Looking at the gods on the walls as he turns away from Theodotus and goes up again to Pothinus.*) And this place?

POTHINUS: The council chamber of the chancellors of the King's treasury, Caesar.

CAESAR: Ah! that reminds me. I want some money.

POTHINUS: The King's treasury is poor, Caesar.

CAESAR: Yes: I notice that there is but one chair in it.

RUFIO (*shouting gruffly*): Bring a chair there, some of you, for Caesar.

PTOLEMY (*rising shyly to offer his chair*): Caesar—

CAESAR (*kindly*): No, no, my boy: that is your chair of state. Sit down.

(*He makes Ptolemy sit down again. Meanwhile Rufio, looking about him, sees in the nearest corner an image of the god Ra, represented as a seated man with the head of a hawk. Before the image is a bronze tripod, about as large as a three-legged stool, with a stick of incense burning on it. Rufio, with Roman resourcefulness and indifference to foreign superstitions, promptly seizes the tripod; shakes off the incense; blows away the ash; and dumps it down behind Caesar, nearly in the middle of the hall.*)

RUFIO: Sit on that, Caesar.

(*A shiver runs through the court, followed by a hissing whisper of* Sacrilege!)

CAESAR (*seating himself*): Now, Pothinus, to business. I am badly in want of money.

BRITANNUS (*disapproving of these informal expressions*): My master would say that there is a lawful debt due to Rome by Egypt, contracted by the King's deceased father to the Triumvirate; and that it is Caesar's duty to his country to require immediate payment.

CAESAR (*blandly*): Ah, I forgot. I have not made my companions known here. Pothinus: this is Britannus, my secretary. He is an islander from the western end of the world, a day's voyage from Gaul. (*Britannus bows stiffly.*) This gentleman is Rufio, my comrade in arms. (*Rufio nods.*) Pothinus: I want 1,600 talents.

(*The courtiers, appalled, murmur loudly, and Theodotus and Achillas appeal mutely to one another against so monstrous a demand.*)

POTHINUS (*aghast*): Forty million sesterces! Impossible. There is not so much money in the King's treasury.

CAESAR (*encouragingly*): Only sixteen hundred talents, Pothinus. Why count it in sesterces? A sestertius is only worth a loaf of bread.

POTHINUS: And a talent is worth a racehorse. I say it is impossible. We have been at strife here, because the King's sister Cleopatra falsely claims his throne. The King's taxes have not been collected for a whole year.

CAESAR: Yes they have, Pothinus. My officers have been collecting them all morning. (*Renewed whisper and sensation, not without some stifled laughter, among the courtiers.*)

RUFIO (*bluntly*): You must pay, Pothinus. Why waste words? You are getting off cheaply enough.

POTHINUS (*bitterly*): Is it possible that Caesar, the conqueror of the world, has time to occupy himself with such a trifle as our taxes?

CAESAR: My friend: taxes are the chief business of a conqueror of the world.

POTHINUS: Then take warning, Caesar. This day, the treasures of the temple and the gold of the King's treasury shall be sent to the mint to be melted down for our ransom in the sight of the people. They shall see us sitting under bare walls and drinking from wooden cups. And their wrath be on your head, Caesar, if you force us to this sacrilege!

CAESAR: Do not fear, Pothinus: the people know how well wine tastes in wooden cups. In return for your bounty, I will settle this dispute about the throne for you, if you will. What say you?

POTHINUS: If I say no, will that hinder you?

RUFIO (*defiantly*): No.

CAESAR: You say the matter has been at issue for a year, Pothinus. May I have ten minutes at it?

POTHINUS: You will do your pleasure, doubtless.

CAESAR: Good! But first, let us have Cleopatra here.

THEODOTUS: She is not in Alexandria: she is fled into Syria.

CAESAR: I think not. (*To Rufio.*) Call Totateeta.

RUFIO (*calling*): Ho there, Teetatota.

(*Ftatateeta enters the loggia, and stands arrogantly at the top of the steps.*)

FTATATEETA: Who pronounces the name of Ftatateeta, the Queen's chief nurse?

CAESAR: Nobody can pronounce it, Tota, except yourself. Where is your mistress?

(*Cleopatra, who is hiding behind Ftatateeta, peeps out at them, laughing. Caesar rises.*)

CAESAR: Will the Queen favor us with her presence for a moment?

CLEOPATRA (*pushing Ftatateeta aside and standing haughtily on the brink of the steps*): Am I to behave like a Queen?

CAESAR: Yes.

(*Cleopatra immediately comes down to the chair of state; seizes Ptolemy; drags him out of his seat; then takes his place in the chair. Ftatateeta seats herself on the step of the loggia, and sits there, watching the scene with sibylline intensity.*)

PTOLEMY (*mortified, and struggling with his tears*): Caesar: this is how she treats me always. If I am king why is she allowed to take everything from me?

CLEOPATRA: You are not to be King, you little cry-baby. You are to be eaten by the Romans.

CAESAR (*touched by Ptolemy's distress*): Come here, my boy, and stand by me.

(*Ptolemy goes over to Caesar, who, resuming his seat on the tripod, takes the boy's hand to encourage him. Cleopatra, furiously jealous, rises and glares at them.*)

CLEOPATRA (*with flaming cheeks*): Take your throne: I dont want it. (*She flings away from the chair, and approaches Ptolemy, who shrinks from her.*) Go this instant and sit down in your place.

CAESAR: Go, Ptolemy. Always take a throne when it is offered to you.

RUFIO: I hope you will have the good sense to follow your own advice when we return to Rome, Caesar.

(*Ptolemy slowly goes back to the throne, giving Cleopatra a wide berth, in evident fear of her hands. She takes his place beside Caesar.*)

CAESAR: Pothinus—

CLEOPATRA (*interrupting him*): Are you not going to speak to me?

CAESAR: Be quiet. Open your mouth again before I give you leave, and you shall be eaten.

CLEOPATRA: I am not afraid. A queen must not be afraid. Eat my husband there, if you like: he is afraid.

CAESAR (*starting*): Your husband! What do you mean?

CLEOPATRA (*pointing to Ptolemy*): That little thing.

(*The two Romans and the Briton stare at one another in amazement.*)

THEODOTUS: Caesar: you are a stranger here, and not conversant with our laws. The kings and queens of Egypt may not marry except with their own royal blood. Ptolemy and Cleopatra are born king and consort just as they are born brother and sister.

BRITANNUS (*shocked*): Caesar: this is not proper.

THEODOTUS (*outraged*): How!

CAESAR (*recovering his self-possession*): Pardon him, Theodotus: he is a barbarian, and thinks that the customs of his tribe and island are the laws of nature.

BRITANNUS: On the contrary, Caesar, it is these Egyptians who are barbarians; and you do wrong to encourage them. I say it is a scandal.

CAESAR: Scandal or not, my friend, it opens the gate of peace. (*He addresses Pothinus seriously.*) Pothinus: hear what I propose.

RUFIO: Hear Caesar there.

CAESAR: Ptolemy and Cleopatra shall reign jointly in Egypt.

ACHILLAS: What of the King's younger brother and Cleopatra's younger sister?

RUFIO (*explaining*): There is another little Ptolemy, Caesar: so they tell me.

CAESAR: Well, the little Ptolemy can marry the other sister; and we will make them both a present of Cyprus.

POTHINUS (*impatiently*): Cyprus is of no use to anybody.

CAESAR: No matter: you shall have it for the sake of peace.

BRITANNUS (*unconsciously anticipating a later statesman*): Peace with honor, Pothinus.

POTHINUS (*mutinously*): Caesar: be honest. The money you demand is the price of our freedom. Take it; and leave us to settle our own affairs.

THE BOLDER COURTIERS (*encouraged by Pothinus' tone and Caesar's quietness*): Yes, yes. Egypt for the Egyptians!

(*The conference now becomes an altercation, the Egyptians becoming more and more heated. Caesar remains unruffled; but Rufio grows fiercer and doggeder, and Britannus haughtily indignant.*)

RUFIO (*contemptuously*): Egypt for the Egyptians! Do you forget that there is a Roman army of occupation here, left by Aulus Gabinius when he set up your toy king for you?

ACHILLAS (*suddenly asserting himself*): And now under my command. *I* am the Roman general here, Caesar.

CAESAR (*tickled by the humor of the situation*): And also the Egyptian general, eh?

POTHINUS (*triumphantly*): That is so, Caesar.

CAESAR (*to Achillas*): So you can make war on the Egyptians in the name of Rome, and on the Romans—on me, if necessary—in the name of Egypt?

ACHILLAS: That is so, Caesar.

CAESAR: And which side are you on at present, if I may presume to ask, general?

ACHILLAS: On the side of the right and of the gods.

CAESAR: Hm! How many men have you?

ACHILLAS: That will appear when I take the field.

RUFIO (*truculently*): Are your men Romans? If not, it matters not how many there are, provided you are no stronger than 500 to ten.

POTHINUS: It is useless to try to bluff us, Rufio. Caesar has been defeated before and may be defeated again. A few weeks ago Caesar was flying for his life before Pompey: a few months hence he may be flying for his life before Cato and Juba of Numidia, the African King.

ACHILLAS (*following up Pothinus' speech menacingly*): What can you do with 4,000 men?

THEODOTUS (*following up Achillas' speech with a raucous squeak*): And without money? Away with you.

ALL THE COURTIERS (*shouting fiercely and crowding towards Caesar*): Away with you. Egypt for the Egyptians! Begone.

(*Rufio bites his beard, too angry to speak. Caesar sits as comfortably as if he were at breakfast, and the cat were clamoring for a piece of Finnan-haddie.*)

CLEOPATRA: Why do you let them talk to you like that, Caesar? Are you afraid?

CAESAR: Why, my dear, what they say is quite true.

CLEOPATRA: But if you go away, I shall not be Queen.

CAESAR: I shall not go away until you are Queen.

POTHINUS: Achillas: if you are not a fool, you will take that girl whilst she is under your hand.

RUFIO (*daring them*): Why not take Caesar as well, Achillas?

POTHINUS (*retorting the defiance with interest*): Well said, Rufio. Why not?

RUFIO: Try, Achillas. (*Calling.*) Guard there.

(*The loggia immediately fills with Caesar's soldiers, who stand, sword in hand, at the top of the steps, waiting the word to charge from their centurion, who carries a cudgel. For a moment the Egyptians face them proudly: then they retire sullenly to their former places.*)

BRITANNUS: You are Caesar's prisoners, all of you.

CAESAR (*benevolently*): Oh no, no, no. By no means. Caesar's guests, gentlemen.

CLEOPATRA: Wont you cut their heads off?

CAESAR: What! Cut off your brother's head?

CLEOPATRA: Why not? He would cut off mine, if he got the chance. Wouldnt you, Ptolemy?

PTOLEMY (*pale and obstinate*): I would. I will, too, when I grow up.

(*Cleopatra is rent by a struggle between her newly-acquired dignity as a queen, and a strong impulse to put out her tongue at him. She takes no part in the scene which follows, but watches it with curiosity and wonder, fidgeting with the restlessness of a child, and sitting down on Caesar's tripod when he rises.*)

POTHINUS: Caesar: if you attempt to detain us—

RUFIO: He will succeed, Egyptian: make up your mind to that. We hold the palace, the beach, and the eastern harbor. The road to Rome is open; and you shall travel it if Caesar chooses.

CAESAR (*courteously*): I could do no less, Pothinus, to secure the retreat of my own soldiers. I am accountable for every life among them. But you are free to go. So are all here, and in the palace.

RUFIO (*aghast at this clemency*): What! Renegades and all?

CAESAR (*softening the expression*): Roman army of occupation and all, Rufio.

POTHINUS (*bewildered*): But—but—but—

CAESAR: Well, my friend?

POTHINUS: You are turning us out of our own palace into the streets; and you tell us with a grand air that we are free to go! It is for you to go.

CAESAR: Your friends are in the street, Pothinus. You will be safer there.

POTHINUS: This is a trick. I am the King's guardian: I refuse to stir. I stand on my right here. Where is your right?

CAESAR: It is in Rufio's scabbard, Pothinus. I may not be able to keep it there if you wait too long.

(*Sensation.*)

POTHINUS (*bitterly*): And this is Roman justice!

THEODOTUS: But not Roman gratitude, I hope.

CAESAR: Gratitude! Am I in your debt for any service, gentlemen?

THEODOTUS: Is Caesar's life of so little account to him that he forgets that we have saved it?

CAESAR: My life! Is that all?

THEODOTUS: Your life. Your laurels. Your future.

POTHINUS: It is true. I can call a witness to prove that but for us, the Roman army of occupation, led by the greatest soldier in the world, would now have Caesar at its mercy. (*Calling through the loggia.*) Ho, there, Lucius Septimius (*Caesar starts, deeply moved*): if my voice can reach you, come forth and testify before Caesar.

CAESAR (*shrinking*): No, no.

THEODOTUS: Yes, I say. Let the military tribune bear witness.

(*Lucius Septimius, a clean shaven, trim athlete of about 40, with symmetrical features, resolute mouth, and handsome, thin Roman nose, in the dress of a Roman officer, comes in through the loggia and confronts Caesar, who hides his face with his robe for a moment; then, mastering himself, drops it, and confronts the tribune with dignity.*)

POTHINUS: Bear witness, Lucius Septimius. Caesar came hither in pursuit of his foe. Did we shelter his foe?

LUCIUS: As Pompey's foot touched the Egyptian shore, his head fell by the stroke of my sword.

THEODOTUS (*with viperish relish*): Under the eyes of his wife and child! Remember that, Caesar! They saw it from the ship he had just left. We have given you a full and sweet measure of vengeance.

CAESAR (*with horror*): Vengeance!

POTHINUS: Our first gift to you, as your galley came into the roadstead, was the head of your rival for the empire of the world. Bear witness, Lucius Septimius: is it not so?

LUCIUS: It is so. With this hand, that slew Pompey, I placed his head at the feet of Caesar.

CAESAR: Murderer! So would you have slain Caesar, had Pompey been victorious at Pharsalia.

LUCIUS: Woe to the vanquished, Caesar! When I served Pompey, I slew as good men as he, only because he conquered them. His turn came at last.

THEODOTUS (*flatteringly*): The deed was not yours, Caesar, but ours—nay, mine; for it was done by my counsel. Thanks to us, you keep your reputation for clemency, and have your vengeance too.

CAESAR: Vengeance! Vengeance!! Oh, if I could stoop to vengeance, what would I not extract from you as the price of this murdered man's blood? (*They shrink back, appalled and disconcerted.*) Was he not my son-in-law, my ancient friend, for 20 years the master of great Rome, for 30 years the compeller of victory? Did not I, as a Roman, share his glory? Was the Fate that forced us to fight for the mastery of the world, of our making? Am I Julius Caesar, or am I a wolf, that you fling to me the grey head of the old soldier, the laurelled conqueror, the mighty Roman, treacherously struck down by this callous ruffian, and then claim my gratitude for it! (*To Lucius Septimius.*) Begone: you fill me with horror.

LUCIUS (*cold and undaunted*): Pshaw! You have seen severed heads before, Caesar, and severed right hands too, I think; some thousands of them, in Gaul, after you vanquished Vercingetorix. Did you spare him, with all your clemency? Was that vengeance?

CAESAR: No, by the gods! would that it had been! Vengeance at least is human. No, I say: those severed right hands, and the brave Vercingetorix basely strangled in a vault beneath the Capitol were (*with shuddering satire*) a wise severity, a necessary protection to the commonwealth, a duty of statesmanship—follies and fictions ten times bloodier than honest vengeance! What a fool was I then! To think that men's lives should be at the mercy of such fools! (*Humbly*.) Lucius Septimius, pardon me: why should the slayer of Vercingetorix rebuke the slayer of Pompey? You are free to go with the rest. Or stay if you will: I will find a place for you in my service.

LUCIUS: The odds are against you, Caesar. I go. (*He turns to go out through the loggia.*)

RUFIO (*full of wrath at seeing his prey escaping*): That means that he is a Republican.

LUCIUS (*turning defiantly on the loggia steps*): And what are you?

RUFIO: A Caesarian, like all Caesar's soldiers.

CAESAR (*courteously*): Lucius: believe me, Caesar is no Caesarian. Were Rome a true republic, then were Caesar the first of Republicans. But you have made your choice. Farewell.

LUCIUS: Farewell. Come, Achillas, whilst there is yet time.

(*Caesar, seeing that Rufio's temper threatens to get the worse of him, puts his hand on his shoulder and brings him down the hall out of harm's way, Britannus accompanying them and posting himself on Caesar's right hand. This movement brings the three in a little group to the place occupied by Achillas, who moves haughtily away and joins Theodotus on the other side. Lucius Septimius goes out through the soldiers in the loggia. Pothinus, Theodotus and Achillas follow him with the courtiers, very mistrustful of the soldiers, who close up in their rear and go out after them, keeping them moving without much ceremony. The King is left in his chair, piteous, obstinate, with twitching face and fingers. During these movements Rufio maintains an energetic grumbling, as follows—*)*

RUFIO (*as Lucius departs*): Do you suppose he would let us go if he had our heads in his hands?

CAESAR: I have no right to suppose that his ways are any baser than mine.

RUFIO: Psha!

CAESAR: Rufio: if I take Lucius Septimius for my model, and become exactly like him, ceasing to be Caesar, will you serve me still?

BRITANNUS: Caesar: this is not good sense. Your duty to Rome demands that her enemies should be prevented from doing further mischief. (*Caesar, whose delight in the moral eye-to-business of his British secretary is inexhaustible, smiles indulgently.*)

RUFIO: It is no use talking to him, Britannus: you may save your breath to cool your porridge. But mark this, Caesar. Clemency is very well for you; but what is it for your soldiers, who have to fight tomorrow the men you spared yesterday? You may give what orders you please; but I tell you that your next victory will be a massacre, thanks to your clemency. I, for one, will take no prisoners. I will kill my enemies in the field; and then you can preach as much clemency as you please: I shall never have to fight them again. And now, with your leave, I will see these gentry off the premises. (*He turns to go.*)

CAESAR (*turning also and seeing Ptolemy*): What! have they left the boy alone! Oh shame, shame!

RUFIO (*taking Ptolemy's hand and making him rise*): Come, your majesty!

PTOLEMY (*to Caesar, drawing away his hand from Rufio*): Is he turning me out of my palace?

RUFIO (*grimly*): You are welcome to stay if you wish.

CAESAR (*kindly*): Go, my boy. I will not harm you; but you will be safer away, among your friends. Here you are in the lion's mouth.

PTOLEMY (*turning to go*): It is not the lion I fear, but (*looking at Rufio*) the jackal. (*He goes out through the loggia.*)

CAESAR (*laughing approvingly*): Brave boy!

CLEOPATRA (*jealous of Caesar's approbation, calling after Ptolemy*): Little silly. You think that very clever.

CAESAR: Britannus: attend the King. Give him in charge to that Pothinus fellow. (*Britannus goes out after Ptolemy.*)

RUFIO (*pointing to Cleopatra*): And this piece of goods? What is to be done with her? However, I suppose I may leave that to you. (*He goes out through the loggia.*)

CLEOPATRA (*flushing suddenly and turning on Caesar*): Did you mean me to go with the rest?

CAESAR (*a little preoccupied, goes with a sigh to Ptolemy's chair, whilst she waits for his answer with red cheeks and clenched fists*): You are free to do just as you please, Cleopatra.

CLEOPATRA: Then you do not care whether I stay or not?

CAESAR (*smiling*): Of course I had rather you stayed.

CLEOPATRA: Much, much rather?

CAESAR (*nodding*): Much, much rather.

CLEOPATRA: Then I consent to stay, because I am asked. But I do not want to, mind.

CAESAR: That is quite understood. (*Calling.*) Totateeta.

(*Ftatateeta, still seated, turns her eyes on him with a sinister expression, but does not move.*)

CLEOPATRA (*with a splutter of laughter*): Her name is not Totateeta: it is Ftatateeta. (*Calling.*) Ftatateeta. (*Ftatateeta instantly rises and comes to Cleopatra.*)

CAESAR (*stumbling over the name*): Tfatafeeta will forgive the erring tongue of a Roman. Tota: the Queen will hold her state here in Alexandria. Engage women to attend upon her; and do all that is needful.

FTATATEETA: Am I then the mistress of the Queen's household?

CLEOPATRA (*sharply*): No: *I* am the mistress of the Queen's household. Go and do as you are told, or I will have you thrown into the Nile this very afternoon, to poison the poor crocodiles.

CAESAR (*shocked*): Oh no, no.

CLEOPATRA: Oh yes, yes. You are very sentimental, Caesar; but you are clever; and if you do as I tell you, you will soon learn to govern.

(*Caesar, quite dumbfounded by this impertinence, turns in his chair and stares at her. Ftatateeta, smiling grimly, and shewing a splendid set of teeth, goes, leaving them alone together.*)

CAESAR: Cleopatra: I really think I must eat you, after all.

CLEOPATRA (*kneeling beside him and looking at him with eager interest, half real, half affected to shew how intelligent she is*): You must not talk to me now as if I were a child.

CAESAR: You have been growing up since the sphinx introduced us the other night; and you think you know more than I do already.

CLEOPATRA (*taken down, and anxious to justify herself*): No: that would be very silly of me: of course I know that. But— (*suddenly*) are you angry with me?

CAESAR: No.

CLEOPATRA (*only half believing him*): Then why are you so thoughtful?

CAESAR (*rising*): I have work to do, Cleopatra.

CLEOPATRA (*drawing back*): Work! (*Offended.*) You are tired of talking to me; and that is your excuse to get away from me.

CAESAR (*sitting down again to appease her*): Well, well: another minute. But then—work!

CLEOPATRA: Work! what nonsense! You must remember that you are a king now: I have made you one. Kings dont work.

CAESAR: Oh! Who told you that, little kitten? Eh?

CLEOPATRA: My father was King of Egypt; and he never worked. But he was a great king, and cut off my sister's head because she rebelled against him and took the throne from him.

CAESAR: Well; and how did he get his throne back again?

CLEOPATRA (*eagerly, her eyes lighting up*): I will tell you. A beautiful young man, with strong round arms, came over the desert with many horsemen, and slew my sister's husband and gave my father back his throne. (*Wistfully.*) I was only twelve then. Oh, I wish he would come again, now that I am queen. I would make him my husband.

CAESAR: It might be managed, perhaps; for it was I who sent that beautiful young man to help your father.

CLEOPATRA (*enraptured*): You know him!

CAESAR (*nodding*): I do.

CLEOPATRA: Has he come with you? (*Caesar shakes his head: she is cruelly disappointed.*) Oh, I wish he had, I wish he had. If only I were a little older; so that he might not think me a mere kitten, as you do! But perhaps that is because you are old. He is many many years younger than you, is he not?

CAESAR (*as if swallowing a pill*): He is somewhat younger.

CLEOPATRA: Would he be my husband, do you think, if I asked him?

CAESAR: Very likely.

CLEOPATRA: But I should not like to ask him. Could you not persuade him to ask me—without knowing that I wanted him to?

CAESAR (*touched by her innocence of the beautiful young man's character*): My poor child!

CLEOPATRA: Why do you say that as if you were sorry for me? Does he love anyone else?

CAESAR: I am afraid so.

CLEOPATRA (*tearfully*): Then I shall not be his first love.

CAESAR: Not quite the first. He is greatly admired by women.

CLEOPATRA: I wish I could be the first. But if he loves me, I will make him kill all the rest. Tell me: is he still beautiful? Do his strong round arms shine in the sun like marble?

CAESAR: He is in excellent condition—considering how much he eats and drinks.

CLEOPATRA: Oh, you must not say common, earthly things about him; for I love him. He is a god.

CAESAR: He is a great captain of horsemen, and swifter of foot than any other Roman.

CLEOPATRA: What is his real name?

CAESAR (*puzzled*): His real name?

CLEOPATRA: Yes, I always call him Horus, because Horus is the most beautiful of our gods. But I want to know his real name.

CAESAR: His name is Mark Antony.

CLEOPATRA (*musically*): Mark Antony, Mark Antony, Mark Antony! What a beautiful name! (*She throws her arms round Caesar's neck.*) Oh, how I love you for sending him to help my father! Did you love my father very much?

CAESAR: No, my child; but your father, as you say, never worked. I always work. So when he lost his crown he had to promise me 16,000 talents to get it back for him.

CLEOPATRA: Did he ever pay you?

CAESAR: Not in full.

CLEOPATRA: He was quite right: it was too dear. The whole world is not worth 16,000 talents.

CAESAR: That is perhaps true, Cleopatra. Those Egyptians who work paid as much of it as he could drag from them. The rest is still due. But as I most likely shall not get it, I must go back to my work. So you must run away for a little and send my secretary to me.

CLEOPATRA (*coaxing*): No: I want to stay and hear you talk about Mark Antony.

CAESAR: But if I do not get to work, Pothinus and the rest of them will cut us off from the harbor; and then the way from Rome will be blocked.

CLEOPATRA: No matter: I dont want you to go back to Rome.

CAESAR: But you want Mark Antony to come from it.

CLEOPATRA (*springing up*): Oh yes, yes, yes: I forgot. Go quickly and work, Caesar; and keep the way over the sea open for my Mark Antony. (*She runs out through the loggia, kissing her hand to Mark Antony across the sea.*)

CAESAR (*going briskly up the middle of the hall to the loggia steps*): Ho, Brittanus. (*He is startled by the entry of a wounded Roman soldier, who confronts him from the upper step.*) What now?

SOLDIER (*pointing to his bandaged head*): This, Caesar; and two of my comrades killed in the market place.

CAESAR (*quiet, but attending*): Ay. Why?

SOLDIER: There is an army come to Alexandria, calling itself the Roman army.

CAESAR: The Roman army of occupation. Ay?

SOLDIER: Commanded by one Achillas.

CAESAR: Well?

SOLDIER: The citizens rose against us when the army entered the gates. I was with two others in the market place when the news came. They set upon us. I cut my way out; and here I am.

CAESAR: Good. I am glad to see you alive. (*Rufio enters the loggia hastily, passing behind the soldier to look out through one of the arches at the quay beneath.*) Rufio: we are besieged.

RUFIO: What! Already?

CAESAR: Now or tomorrow: what does it matter? We shall be besieged.

(*Britannus runs in.*)

BRITANNUS: Caesar—

CAESAR (*anticipating him*): Yes: I know. (*Rufio and Britannus come down the hall from the loggia at opposite sides, past Caesar, who waits for a moment near the step to say to the soldier:*) Comrade: give the word to turn out on the beach and stand by the boats. Get your wound attended to. Go. (*The soldier hurries out. Caesar comes down the hall between Rufio and Britannus.*) Rufio: we have some ships in the west harbor. Burn them.

RUFIO (*staring*): Burn them! !

CAESAR: Take every boat we have in the east harbor, and seize the Pharos—that island with the lighthouse. Leave half our men behind to hold the beach and the quay outside this palace: that is the way home.

RUFIO (*disapproving strongly*): Are we to give up the city?

CAESAR: We have not got it, Rufio. This palace we have; and—what is that building next door?

RUFIO: The theatre.

CAESAR: We will have that too: it commands the strand. For the rest, Egypt for the Egyptians!

RUFIO: Well, you know best, I suppose. Is that all?

CAESAR: That is all. Are those ships burnt yet?

RUFIO: Be easy: I shall waste no more time. (*He runs out.*)

BRITANNUS: Caesar: Pothinus demands speech of you. In my opinion he needs a lesson. His manner is most insolent.

CAESAR: Where is he?

BRITANNUS: He waits without.

CAESAR: Ho there! admit Pothinus.

(*Pothinus appears in the loggia, and comes down the hall very haughtily to Caesar's left hand.*)

CAESAR: Well, Pothinus?

POTHINUS: I have brought you our ultimatum, Caesar.

CAESAR: Ultimatum! The door was open: you should have gone out through it before you declared war. You are my prisoner now. (*He goes to the chair and loosens his toga.*)

POTHINUS (*scornfully*): I your prisoner! Do you know that you are in Alexandria, and that King Ptolemy, with an army outnumbering your little troop a hundred to one, is in possession of Alexandria?

CAESAR (*unconcernedly taking off his toga and throwing it on the chair*): Well, my friend, get out if you can. And tell your friends not to kill any more Romans in the market place. Otherwise my soldiers, who do not share my celebrated clemency, will probably kill you. Britannus: pass the word to the guard; and fetch my armor. (*Britannus runs out. Rufio returns.*) Well?

RUFIO (*pointing from the loggia to a cloud of smoke drifting over the harbor*): See there! (*Pothinus runs eagerly up the steps to look out.*)

CAESAR: What, ablaze already! Impossible!

RUFIO: Yes, five good ships, and a barge laden with oil grappled to each. But it is not my doing: the Egyptians have saved me the trouble. They have captured the west harbor.

CAESAR (*anxiously*): And the east harbor? The lighthouse, Rufio?

RUFIO (*with a sudden splutter of raging ill usage, coming down to Caesar and scolding him*): Can I embark a legion in five minutes? The first cohort is already on the beach. We can do no more. If you want faster work, come and do it yourself.

CAESAR (*soothing him*): Good, good. Patience, Rufio, patience.

RUFIO: Patience! Who is impatient here, you or I? Would I be here, if I could not oversee them from that balcony?

CAESAR: Forgive me, Rufio; and (*anxiously*) hurry them as much as—

(*He is interrupted by an outcry as of an old man in the extremity of misfortune. It draws near rapidly; and Theodotus rushes in, tearing his hair, and squeaking the most lamentable exclamations. Rufio steps back to stare at him, amazed at his frantic condition. Pothinus turns to listen.*)

THEODOTUS (*on the steps, with uplifted arms*): Horror unspeakable! Woe, alas! Help!

RUFIO: What now?

CAESAR (*frowning*): Who is slain?

THEODOTUS: Slain! Oh, worse than the death of ten thousand men! Loss irreparable to mankind!

RUFIO: What has happened, man?

THEODOTUS (*rushing down the hall between them*): The fire has spread from your ships. The first of the seven wonders of the world perishes. The library of Alexandria is in flames.

RUFIO: Psha! (*Quite relieved, he goes up to the loggia and watches the preparations of the troops on the beach.*)

CAESAR: Is that all?

THEODOTUS (*unable to believe his senses*): All! Caesar: will you go down to posterity as a barbarous soldier too ignorant to know the value of books?

CAESAR: Theodotus: I am an author myself; and I tell you it is better that the Egyptians should live their lives than dream them away with the help of books.

THEODOTUS (*kneeling, with genuine literary emotion: the passion of the pedant*): Caesar: once in ten generations of men, the world gains an immortal book.

CAESAR (*inflexible*): If it did not flatter mankind, the common executioner would burn it.

THEODOTUS: Without history, death will lay you beside your meanest soldier.

CAESAR: Death will do that in any case. I ask no better grave.

THEODOTUS: What is burning there is the memory of mankind.

CAESAR: A shameful memory. Let it burn.

THEODOTUS (*wildly*): Will you destory the past?

CAESAR: Ay, and build the future with its ruins. (*Theodotus, in despair, strikes himself on the temples with his fists.*) But harken, Theodotus, teacher of kings: you who valued Pompey's head no more than a shepherd values an onion, and who now kneel to me, with tears in your old eyes, to plead for a few sheepskins scrawled with errors. I cannot spare you a man or a bucket of water just now; but you shall pass freely out of the palace. Now, away with you to Achillas; and borrow his legions to put out the fire. (*He hurries him to the steps.*)

POTHINUS (*significantly*): You understand, Theodotus: I remain a prisoner.

THEODOTUS: A prisoner!

CAESAR: Will you stay to talk whilst the memory of mankind is burning? (*Calling through the loggia.*) Ho there! Pass Theodotus out. (*To Theodotus.*) Away with you.

THEODOTUS (*to Pothinus*): I must go to save the library. (*He hurries out.*)

CAESAR: Follow him to the gate, Pothinus. Bid him urge your people to kill no more of my soldiers, for your sake.

POTHINUS: My life will cost you dear if you take it, Caesar. (*He goes out after Theodotus.*)

(*Rufio, absorbed in watching the embarkation, does not notice the departure of the two Egyptians.*)

RUFIO (*shouting from the loggia to the beach*): All ready, there?

A CENTURION (*from below*): All ready. We wait for Caesar.

CAESAR: Tell them Caesar is coming—the rogues! (*Calling.*) Britannicus. (*This magniloquent version of his secretary's name is one of Caesar's jokes. In later years it would have meant, quite seriously and officially, Conqueror of Britain.*)

RUFIO (*calling down*): Push off, all except the longboat. Stand by it to embark, Caesar's guard there. (*He leaves the balcony and comes down into the hall.*) Where are those Egyptians? Is this more clemency? Have you let them go?

CAESAR (*chuckling*): I have let Theodotus go to save the library. We must respect literature, Rufio.

RUFIO (*raging*): Folly on folly's head! I believe if you could bring back all the dead of Spain, Gaul, and Thessaly to life, you would do it that we might have the trouble of fighting them over again.

CAESAR: Might not the gods destroy the world if their only thought were to be at peace next year? (*Rufio, out of all patience, turns away in anger. Caesar suddenly grips his sleeve, and adds slyly in his ear:*) Besides, my friend: every Egyptian we imprison means imprisoning two Roman soldiers to guard him. Eh?

RUFIO: Agh! I might have known there was some fox's trick behind your fine talking. (*He gets away from Caesar with an ill-humored shrug, and goes to the balcony for another look at the preparations; finally goes out.*)

CAESAR: Is Britannus asleep? I sent him for my armor an hour ago. (*Calling.*) Britannicus, thou British islander. Britannicus!

(*Cleopatra runs in through the loggia with Caesar's helmet and sword, snatched from Britannus, who follows her with a cuirass and greaves. They come down to Caesar, she to his left hand, Britannus to his right.*)

CLEOPATRA: I am going to dress you, Caesar. Sit down. (*He

obeys.) These Roman helmets are so becoming! (*She takes off his wreath.*) Oh! (*She bursts out laughing at him.*)

CAESAR: What are you laughing at?

CLEOPATRA: Youre bald (*beginning with a big B, and ending with a splutter*).

CAESAR (*almost annoyed*): Cleopatra! (*He rises, for the convenience of* BRITANNUS, *who puts the cuirass on him.*)

CLEOPATRA: So that is why you wear the wreath—to hide it.

BRITANNUS: Peace, Egyptian: they are the bays of the conqueror. (*He buckles the cuirass.*)

CLEOPATRA: Peace, thou: islander! (*To Caesar.*) You should rub your head with strong spirits of sugar, Caesar. That will make it grow.

CAESAR (*with a wry face*): Cleopatra: do you like to be reminded that you are very young?

CLEOPATRA (*pouting*): No.

CAESAR (*sitting down again, and setting out his leg for Britannus, who kneels to put on his greaves*): Neither do I like to be reminded that I am—middle aged. Let me give you ten of my superfluous years. That will make you 26, and leave me only—no matter. Is it a bargain?

CLEOPATRA: Agreed. 26, mind. (*She puts the helmet on him.*) Oh! How nice! You look only about 50 in it!

BRITANNUS (*looking up severely at Cleopatra*): You must not speak in this manner to Caesar.

CLEOPATRA: Is it true that when Caesar caught you on that island, you were painted all over blue?

BRITANNUS: Blue is the color worn by all Britons of good standing. In war we stain our bodies blue; so that though our enemies may strip us of our clothes and our lives, they cannot strip us of our respectability. (*He rises.*)

CLEOPATRA (*with Caesar's sword*): Let me hang this on. Now you look splendid. Have they made any statues of you in Rome?

CAESAR: Yes, many statues.

CLEOPATRA: You must send for one and give it to me.

RUFIO(*coming back into the loggia, more impatient than ever*): Now Caesar: have you done talking? The moment your foot is aboard there will be no holding our men back: the boats will race one another for the lighthouse.

CAESAR (*drawing his sword and trying the edge*): Is this well set today, Britannicus? At Pharsalia it was as blunt as a barrel-hoop.

BRITANNUS: It will split one of the Egyptian's hairs today, Caesar. I have set it myself.

CLEOPATRA(*suddenly throwing her arms in terror round Caesar*): Oh, you are not really going into battle to be killed?

CAESAR: No, Cleopatra. No man goes to battle to be killed.

CLEOPATRA: But they do get killed. My sister's husband was killed in battle. You must not go. Let him go (*pointing to Rufio. They all laugh at her*). Oh please, please dont go. What will happen to me if you never come back?

CAESAR (*gravely*): Are you afraid?

CLEOPATRA (*shrinking*): No.

CAESAR (*with quiet authority*): Go to the balcony; and you shall see us take the Pharos. You must learn to look on battles. Go. (*She goes, downcast, and looks out from the balcony.*) That is well. Now, Rufio. March.

CLEOPATRA (*suddenly clapping her hands*): Oh, you will not be able to go!

CAESAR: Why? What now?

CLEOPATRA: They are drying up the harbor with buckets—a multitude of soldiers—over there (*pointing out across the sea to her left*)—they are dipping up the water.

RUFIO (*hastening to look*): It is true. The Egyptian army! Crawling over the edge of the west harbor like locusts. (*With sudden anger he strides down to Caesar.*) This is your accursed clemency, Caesar. Theodotus has brought them.

CAESAR (*delighted at his own cleverness*): I meant him to, Rufio. They have come to put out the fire. The library will keep them busy whilst we seize the lighthouse. Eh? (*He rushes out buoyantly through the loggia, followed by Britannus.*)

RUFIO (*disgustedly*): More foxing! Agh! (*He rushes off. A shout from the soldiers announces the appearance of Caesar below.*)

CENTURION (*below*): All aboard. Give way there. (*Another shout.*)

CLEOPATRA (*waving her scarf through the loggia arch*): Goodbye, goodbye, dear Caesar. Come back safe. Goodbye!

ACT III

The edge of the quay in front of the palace, looking out west over the east harbor of Alexandria to Pharos island, just to the end of which, and connected with it by a narrow mole, is the famous lighthouse, a gigantic square tower of white marble diminishing in size storey by storey to the top, on which stands a cresset beacon. The island is joined to the main land by the Heptastadium, a great mole or causeway five miles long bounding the harbor on the south.

In the middle of the quay a Roman sentinel stands on guard, pilum in hand, looking out to the lighthouse with strained attention, his left hand shading his eyes. The pilum is a stout wooden shaft 4½ feet long, with an iron spit about three feet long fixed in it. The sentinel is so absorbed that he does not notice the approach from the north end of the quay of four Egyptian market porters carrying rolls of carpet, preceded by Ftatateeta and Apollodorus the Sicilian. Apollodorus is a dashing young man of about 24, handsome and debonair, dressed with deliberate aestheticism in the most delicate purples and dove greys, with ornaments of bronze, oxydized silver, and stones of jade and agate. His sword, designed as carefully as a medieval cross, has a blued blade shewing through an openwork scabbard of purple leather and filigree. The porters, conducted by Ftatateeta, pass along the quay behind the sentinel to the steps of the palace, where they put down their bales and squat on the ground. Apollodorus does not pass along with them: he halts, amused by the preoccupation of the sentinel.

APOLLODORUS (*calling to the sentinel*): Who goes there, eh?

SENTINEL (*starting violently and turning with his pilum at the charge, revealing himself as a small, wiry, sandy-haired, conscientious young man with an elderly face*): Whats this? Stand. Who are you?

APOLLODORUS: I am Apollodorus the Sicilian. Why, man, what are you dreaming of? Since I came through the lines beyond the theatre there, I have brought my caravan past three sentinels, all so busy staring at the lighthouse that not one of them challenged me. Is this Roman discipline?

SENTINEL: We are not here to watch the land but the sea. Caesar has just landed on the Pharos. (*Looking at Ftatateeta.*) What have you here? Who is this piece of Egyptian crockery?

FTATATEETA: Apollodorus: rebuke this Roman dog; and bid him bridle his tongue in the presence of Ftatateeta, the mistress of the Queen's household.

APOLLODORUS: My friend: this is a great lady, who stands high with Caesar.

SENTINEL (*not at all impressed, pointing to the carpets*): And what is all this truck?

APOLLODORUS: Carpets for the furnishing of the Queen's apartments in the palace. I have picked them from the best carpets in the world; and the Queen shall choose the best of my choosing.

SENTINEL: So you are the carpet merchant?

APOLLODORUS (*hurt*): My friend: I am a patrician.

SENTINEL: A patrician! A patrician keeping a shop instead of following arms!

APOLLODORUS: I do not keep a shop. Mine is a temple of the arts. I am a worshipper of beauty. My calling is to choose beautiful things for beautiful queens. My motto is Art for Art's sake.

SENTINEL: That is not the password.

APOLLODORUS: It is a universal password.

SENTINEL: I know nothing about universal passwords. Either give me the password for the day or get back to your shop.

(*Ftatateeta, roused by his hostile tone, steals towards the edge of the quay with the step of a panther, and gets behind him.*)

APOLLODORUS: How if I do neither?

SENTINEL: Then I will drive this pilum through you.

APOLLODORUS: At your service, my friend. (*He draws his sword, and springs to his guard with unruffled grace.*)

FTATATEETA (*suddenly seizing the sentinel's arms from behind*): Thrust your knife into the dog's throat, Apollodorus. (*The chivalrous Apollodorus laughingly shakes his head; breaks ground away from the sentinel towards the palace; and lowers his point.*)

SENTINEL (*struggling vainly*): Curse on you! Let me go. Help ho!

FTATATEETA (*lifting him from the ground*): Stab the little Roman reptile. Spit him on your sword.

(*A couple of Roman soldiers, with a centurion, come running along the edge of the quay from the north end. They rescue their comrade, and throw off Ftatateeta, who is sent reeling away on the left hand of the sentinel.*)

CENTURION (*an unattractive man of fifty, short in his speech and manners, with a vinewood cudgel in his hand*): How now? What is all this?

FTATATEETA (*to Apollodorus*): Why did you not stab him? There was time!

APOLLODORUS: Centurion: I am here by order of the Queen to—

CENTURION (*interrupting him*): The Queen! Yes, yes: (*to the sentinel*) pass him in. Pass all these bazaar people in to the Queen, with their goods. But mind you pass no one out that you have not passed in—not even the Queen herself.

SENTINEL: This old woman is dangerous: she is as strong as three men. She wanted the merchant to stab me.

APOLLODORUS: Centurion: I am not a merchant. I am a patrician and a votary of art.

CENTURION: Is the woman your wife?

APOLLODORUS (*horrified*): No, no! (*Correcting himself politely.*) Not that the lady is not a striking figure in her own way. But (*emphatically*) she is not my wife.

FTATATEETA (*to the centurion*): Roman: I am Ftatateeta, the mistress of the Queen's household.

CENTURION: Keep your hands off our men, mistress; or I will have you pitched into the harbor, though you were as strong as ten men. (*To his men.*) To your posts: march! (*He returns with his men the way they came.*)

FTATATEETA (*looking malignantly after him*): We shall see whom Isis loves best: her servant Ftatateeta or a dog of a Roman.

SENTINEL (*to Apollodorus, with a wave of his pilum towards the palace*): Pass in there; and keep your distance. (*Turning to Ftatateeta.*) Come within a yard of me, you old crocodile; and I will give you this (*the pilum*) in your jaws.

CLEOPATRA (*calling from the palace*): Ftatateeta, Ftatateeta.

FTATATEETA (*looking up, scandalized*): Go from the window, go from the window. There are men here.

CLEOPATRA: I am coming down.

FTATATEETA (*distracted*): No, no. What are you dreaming of? O ye gods, ye gods! Apollodorus: bid your men pick up your bales; and in with me quickly.

APOLLODORUS: Obey the mistress of the Queen's household.

FTATATEETA (*impatiently, as the porters stoop to lift the bales*): Quick, quick: she will be out upon us. (*Cleopatra comes from the palace and runs across the quay to Ftatateeta.*) Oh that ever I was born!

CLEOPATRA (*eagerly*): Ftatateeta: I have thought of something. I want a boat—at once.

FTATATEETA: A boat! No, no: you cannot. Apollodorus: speak to the Queen.

APOLLODORUS (*gallantly*): Beautiful queen: I am Apollodorus the Sicilian, your servant, from the bazaar. I have brought you the three most beautiful Persian carpets in the world to choose from.

CLEOPATRA: I have no time for carpets today. Get me a boat.

FTATATEETA: What whim is this? You cannot go on the water except in the royal barge.

APOLLODORUS: Royalty, Ftatateeta, lies not in the barge but in the Queen. (*To Cleopatra.*) The touch of your majesty's foot on the gunwale of the meanest boat in the harbor will make it royal. (*He turns to the harbor and calls seaward.*) Ho there, boatman! Pull in to the steps.

CLEOPATRA: Apollodorus: you are my perfect knight; and I will always buy my carpets through you. (*Apollodorus bows joyously. An oar appears above the quay; and the boatman, a bullet-headed, vivacious, grinning fellow, burnt almost black by the sun, comes up a flight of steps from the water on the sentinel's right, oar in hand, and waits at the top.*) Can you row, Apollodorus?

APOLLODORUS: My oars shall be your majesty's wings. Whither shall I row my Queen?

CLEOPATRA: To the lighthouse. Come. (*She makes for the steps.*)

SENTINEL (*opposing her with his pilum at the charge*): Stand. You cannot pass.

CLEOPATRA (*flushing angrily*): How dare you? Do you know that I am the Queen?

SENTINEL: I have my orders. You cannot pass.

CLEOPATRA: I will make Caesar have you killed if you do not obey me.

SENTINEL: He will do worse to me if I disobey my officer. Stand back.

CLEOPATRA: Ftatateeta: strangle him.

SENTINEL (*alarmed—looking apprehensively at Ftatateeta, and brandishing his pilum*): Keep off, there.

CLEOPATRA (*running to Apollodorus*): Apollodorus: make your slaves help us.

APOLLODORUS: I shall not need their help, lady. (*He draws his sword.*) Now, soldier: choose which weapon you will defend yourself with. Shall it be sword against pilum, or sword against sword?

SENTINEL: Roman against Sicilian, curse you. Take that. (*He hurls his pilum at Apollodorus, who drops expertly on one knee. The pilum passes whizzing over his head and falls harmless.*

Apollodorus, with a cry of triumph, springs up and attacks the sentinel, who draws his sword and defends himself, crying:) Ho there, guard. Help!

(*Cleopatra, half frightened, half delighted, takes refuge near the palace, where the porters are squatting among the bales. The boatman, alarmed, hurries down the steps out of harm's way, but stops, with his head just visible above the edge of the quay, to watch the fight. The sentinel is handicapped by his fear of an attack in the rear from Ftatateeta. His swordsmanship, which is of a rough and ready sort, is heavily taxed, as he has occasionally to strike at her to keep her off between a blow and a guard with Apollodorus. The centurion returns with several soldiers. Apollodorus springs back towards Cleopatra as this reinforcement confronts him.*)

CENTURION (*coming to the sentinel's right hand*): What is this? What now?

SENTINEL (*panting*): I could do well enough by myself if it werent for the old woman. Keep her off me: that is all the help I need.

CENTURION: Make your report, soldier. What has happened?

FTATATEETA: Centurion: he would have slain the Queen.

SENTINEL (*bluntly*): I would, sooner than let her pass. She wanted to take boat, and go—so she said—to the lighthouse. I stopped her, as I was ordered to; and she set this fellow on me. (*He goes to pick up his pilum and returns to his place with it.*)

CENTURION (*turning to Cleopatra*): Cleopatra: I am loth to offend you; but without Caesar's express order we dare not let you pass beyond the Roman lines.

APOLLODORUS: Well, Centurion; and has not the lighthouse been within the Roman lines since Caesar landed there?

CLEOPATRA: Yes, yes. Answer that, if you can.

CENTURION (*to Apollodorus*): As for you, Apollodorus, you may thank the gods that you are not nailed to the palace door with a pilum for your meddling.

APOLLODORUS (*urbanely*): My military friend, I was not born to be slain by so ugly a weapon. When I fall, it will be (*holding up his sword*) by this white queen of arms, the only weapon fit for an artist. And now that you are convinced that we do not want to go beyond the lines, let me finish killing your sentinel and depart with the Queen.

CENTURION (*as the sentinel makes an angry demonstration*): Peace there, Cleopatra: I must abide by my orders, and not by the subtleties of this Sicilian. You must withdraw into the palace and examine your carpets there.

CLEOPATRA (*pouting*): I will not: I am the Queen. Caesar does not speak to me as you do. Have Caesar's centurions changed manners with his scullions?

CENTURION (*sulkily*): I do my duty. That is enough for me.

APOLLODORUS: Majesty: when a stupid man is doing something he is ashamed of, he always declares that it is his duty.

CENTURION (*angry*): Apollodorus—

APOLLODORUS (*interrupting him with defiant elegance*): I will make amends for that insult with my sword at fitting time and place. Who says artist, says duellist. (*To Cleopatra.*) Hear my counsel, star of the east. Until word comes to these soldiers from Caesar himself, you are a prisoner. Let me go to him with a message from you, and a present; and before the sun has stooped half way to the arms of the sea, I will bring you back Caesar's order of release.

CENTURION (*sneering at him*): And you will sell the Queen the present, no doubt.

APOLLODORUS: Centurion: the Queen shall have from me, without payment, as the unforced tribute of Sicilian taste to Egyptian beauty, the richest of these carpets for her present to Caesar.

CLEOPATRA (*exultantly, to the centurion*): Now you see what an ignorant common creature you are!

CENTURION (*curtly*): Well, a fool and his wares are soon parted. (*He turns to his men.*) Two more men to this post here; and

see that no one leaves the palace but this man and his mer-
chandize. If he draws his sword again inside the lines, kill
him. To your posts. March.

(*He goes out, leaving two auxiliary sentinels with the other.*)

APOLLODORUS (*with polite goodfellowship*): My friends: will you
not enter the palace and bury our quarrel in a bowl of wine?
(*He takes out his purse, jingling the coins in it.*) The Queen
has presents for you all.

SENTINEL (*very sulky*): You heard our orders. Get about your
business.

FIRST AUXILIARY: Yes: you ought to know better. Off with
you.

SECOND AUXILIARY (*looking longingly at the purse—this sentinel
is a hooknosed man, unlike his comrade, who is squab faced*): Do
not tantalize a poor man.

APOLLODORUS (*to Cleopatra*): Pearl of Queens: the centurion is
at hand; and the Roman soldier is incorruptible when his
officer is looking. I must carry your word to Caesar.

CLEOPATRA (*who has been meditating among the carpets*): Are
these carpets very heavy?

APOLLODORUS: It matters not how heavy. There are plenty of
porters.

CLEOPATRA: How do they put the carpets into boats? Do they
throw them down?

APOLLODORUS: Not into small boats, majesty. It would sink
them.

CLEOPATRA: Not into that man's boat, for instance? (*Pointing
to the boatman.*)

APOLLODORUS: No. Too small.

CLEOPATRA: But you can take a carpet to Caesar in it if I send
one?

APOLLODORUS: Assuredly.

CLEOPATRA: And you will have it carried gently down the steps
and take great care of it?

APOLLODORUS: Depend on me.

CLEOPATRA: Great, great care?

APOLLODORUS: More than of my own body.

CLEOPATRA: You will promise me not to let the porters drop it or throw it about?

APOLLODORUS: Place the most delicate glass goblet in the palace in the heart of the roll, Queen; and if it be broken, my head shall pay for it.

CLEOPATRA: Good. Come, Ftatateeta. (*Ftatateeta comes to her. Apollodorus offers to squire them into the palace.*) No, Apollodorus, you must not come. I will choose a carpet for myself. You must wait here. (*She runs into the palace.*)

APOLLODORUS (*to the porters*): Follow this lady (*indicating Ftatateeta*) and obey her.

(*The porters rise and take up their bales.*)

FTATATEETA (*addressing the porters as if they were vermin*): This way. And take your shoes off before you put your feet on those stairs.

(*She goes in, followed by the porters with the carpets. Meanwhile Apollodorus goes to the edge of the quay and looks out over the harbor. The sentinels keep their eyes on him malignantly.*)

APOLLODORUS (*addressing the sentinel*): My friend—

SENTINEL (*rudely*): Silence there.

FIRST AUXILIARY: Shut your muzzle, you.

SECOND AUXILIARY (*in a half whisper, glancing apprehensively towards the north end of the quay*): Cant you wait a bit?

APOLLODORUS: Patience, worthy three-headed donkey. (*They mutter ferociously; but he is not at all intimidated.*) Listen: were you set here to watch me, or to watch the Egyptians?

SENTINEL: We know our duty.

APOLLODORUS: Then why dont you do it? There is something going on over there (*pointing southwestward to the mole*).

SENTINEL (*sulkily*): I do not need to be told what to do by the like of you.

APOLLODORUS: Blockhead. (*He begins shouting.*) Ho there, Centurion. Hoiho!

SENTINEL: Curse your meddling. (*Shouting.*) Hoiho! Alarm! Alarm!

FIRST AND SECOND AUXILIARIES: Alarm! alarm! Hoiho!

(*The centurion comes running in with his guard.*)

CENTURION: What now? Has the old woman attacked you again? (*Seeing Apollodorus.*) Are y o u here still?

APOLLODORUS (*pointing as before*): See there. The Egyptians are moving. They are going to recapture the Pharos. They will attack by sea and land: by land along the great mole; by sea from the west harbor. Stir yourselves, my military friends: the hunt is up. (*A clangor of trumpets from several points along the quay.*) Aha! I told you so.

CENTURION (*quickly*): The two extra men pass the alarm to the south posts. One man keep guard here. The rest with me — quick.

(*The two auxiliary sentinels run off to the south. The centurion and his guard run off northward; and immediately afterwards the bucina sounds. The four porters come from the palace carrying a carpet, followed by Ftatateeta.*)

SENTINEL (*handling his pilum apprehensively*): You again! (*The porters stop.*)

FTATATEETA: Peace, Roman fellow: you are now single-handed. Apollodorus: this carpet is Cleopatra's present to Caesar. It has rolled up in it ten precious goblets of the thinnest Iberian crystal, and a hundred eggs of the sacred blue pigeon. On your honor, let not one of them be broken.

APOLLODORUS: On my head be it! (*To the porters.*) Into the boat with them carefully.

(*The porters carry the carpet to the steps.*)

FIRST PORTER (*looking down at the boat*): Beware what you do, sir. Those eggs of which the lady speaks must weigh more than a pound apiece. This boat is too small for such a load.

BOATMAN (*excitedly rushing up the steps*): Oh thou injurious porter! Oh thou unnatural son of a she-camel! (*To Apollodorus.*) My boat, sir, hath often carried five men. Shall it not carry your lordship and a bale of pigeon's eggs? (*To the porter.*) Thou mangey dromedary, the gods shall punish thee for this envious wickedness.

FIRST PORTER (*stolidly*): I cannot quit this bale now to beat thee; but another day I will lie in wait for thee.

APOLLODORUS (*going between them*): Peace there. If the boat were but a single plank, I would get to Caesar on it.

FTATATEETA (*anxiously*): In the name of the gods, Apollodorus, run no risks with that bale.

APOLLODORUS: Fear not, thou venerable grotesque: I guess its great worth. (*To the porters.*) Down with it, I say; and gently; or ye shall eat nothing but stick for ten days.

(*The boatman goes down the steps, followed by the porters with the bale: Ftatateeta and Apollodorus watching from the edge.*)

APOLLODORUS: Gently, my sons, my children—(*with sudden alarm*) gently, ye dogs. Lay it level in the stern—so—tis well.

FTATATEETA (*screaming down at one of the porters*): Do not step on it, do not step on it. Oh thou brute beast!

FIRST PORTER (*ascending*): Be not excited, mistress: all is well.

FTATATEETA (*panting*): All well! Oh, thou hast given my heart a turn! (*She clutches her side, gasping.*)

(*The four porters have now come up and are waiting at the stairhead to be paid.*)

APOLLODORUS: Here, ye hungry ones. (*He gives money to the first porter, who holds it in his hand to shew to the others. They crowd greedily to see how much it is, quite prepared, after the Eastern fashion, to protest to heaven against their patron's stinginess. But his liberality overpowers them.*)

FIRST PORTER: O bounteous prince!

SECOND PORTER: O lord of the bazaar!

THIRD PORTER: O favored of the gods!

FOURTH PORTER: O father to all the porters of the market!

SENTINEL (*enviously, threatening them fiercely with his pilum*): Hence, dogs: off. Out of this. (*They fly before him northward along the quay.*)

APOLLODORUS: Farewell, Ftatateeta. I shall be at the lighthouse before the Egyptians. (*He descends the steps.*)

FTATATEETA: The gods speed thee and protect my nursling!

(*The sentry returns from chasing the porters and looks down at the boat, standing near the stairhead lest Ftatateeta should attempt to escape.*)

APOLLODORUS (*from beneath, as the boat moves off*): Farewell, valiant pilum pitcher.

SENTINEL: Farewell, shopkeeper.

APOLLODORUS: Ha, ha! Pull, thou brave boatman, pull. Soho-o-o-o-o! (*He begins to sing in barcarolle measure to the rhythm of the oars.*)

> My heart, my heart, spread out thy wings:
> Shake off thy heavy load of love—

Give me the oars, O son of a snail.

SENTINEL (*threatening Ftatateeta*): Now mistress: back to your henhouse. In with you.

FTATATEETA (*falling on her knees and stretching her hands over the waters*): Gods of the seas, bear her safely to the shore!

SENTINEL: Bear who safely? What do you mean?

FTATATEETA (*looking darkly at him*): Gods of Egypt and of Vengeance, let this Roman fool be beaten like a dog by his captain for suffering her to be taken over the waters.

SENTINEL: Accursed one: is she then in the boat? (*He calls over the sea:*) Hoiho, there, boatman! Hoiho!

APOLLODORUS (*singing in the distance*):

> My heart, my heart, be whole and free:
> Love is thine only enemy.

(*Meanwhile Rufio, the morning's fighting done, sits munching dates on a faggot of brushwood outside the door of the lighthouse, which towers gigantic to the clouds on his left. His helmet, full of dates, is between his knees; and a leathern bottle of wine is by his side. Behind him the great stone pedestal of the lighthouse is shut in from the open sea by a low stone parapet, with a couple of steps in the middle to the broad coping. A huge chain with a hook hangs down from the lighthouse crane above his head. Faggots like the one he sits on lie beneath it ready to be drawn up to feed the beacon.*

Caesar is standing on the step at the parapet looking out anxiously, evidently ill at ease. Britannus comes out of the lighthouse door.)

RUFIO: Well, my British islander. Have you been up to the top?

BRITANNUS: I have. I reckon it at 200 feet high.

RUFIO: Anybody up there?

BRITANNUS: One elderly Tyrian to work the crane; and his son, a well conducted youth of 14.

RUFIO (*looking at the chain*): What! An old man and a boy work that! Twenty men, you mean.

BRITANNUS: Two only, I assure you. They have counter-weights, and a machine with boiling water in it which I do not understand: it is not of British design. They use it to haul up barrels of oil and faggots to burn in the brazier on the roof.

RUFIO: But—

BRITANNUS: Excuse me: I came down because there are messengers coming along the mole to us from the island. I must see what their business is. (*He hurries out past the lighthouse.*)

CAESAR (*coming away from the parapet, shivering and out of sorts*): Rufio: this has been a mad expedition. We shall be beaten. I wish I knew how our men are getting on with that barricade across the great mole.

RUFIO (*angrily*): Must I leave my food and go starving to bring you a report?

CAESAR (*soothing him nervously*): No, Rufio, no. Eat, my son, eat. (*He takes another turn, Rufio chewing dates meanwhile.*) The Egyptians cannot be such fools as not to storm the barricade and swoop down on us here before it is finished. It is the first time I have ever run an avoidable risk. I should not have come to Egypt.

RUFIO: An hour ago you were all for victory.

CAESAR (*apologetically*): Yes: I was a fool—rash, Rufio—boyish.

RUFIO: Boyish! Not a bit of it. Here (*offering him a handful of dates*).

CAESAR: What are these for?

RUFIO: To eat. Thats whats the matter with you. When a man comes to your age, he runs down before his midday meal. Eat and drink; and then have another look at our chances.

CAESAR (*taking the dates*): My age! (*He shakes his head and bites a date.*) Yes, Rufio: I am an old man—worn out now —true, quite true. (*He gives way to melancholy contemplation, and eats another date.*) Achillas is still in his prime: Ptolemy is a boy. (*He eats another date, and plucks up a little.*) Well, every dog has his day; and I have had mine: I cannot complain. (*With sudden cheerfulness.*) These dates are not bad, Rufio. (*Britannus returns, greatly excited, with a leathern bag. Caesar is himself again in a moment.*) What now?

BRITANNUS (*triumphantly*): Our brave Rhodian mariners have captured a treasure. There! (*He throws the bag down at Caesar's feet.*) Our enemies are delivered into our hands.

CAESAR: In that bag?

BRITANNUS: Wait till you hear, Caesar. This bag contains all the letters which have passed between Pompey's party and the army of occupation here.

CAESAR: Well?

BRITANNUS (*impatient of Caesar's slowness to grasp the situation*): Well, we shall now know who your foes are. The name of every man who has plotted against you since you crossed the Rubicon may be in these papers, for all we know.

CAESAR: Put them in the fire.

BRITANNUS: Put them—(*he gasps*)!!!!

CAESAR: In the fire. Would you have me waste the next three years of my life of proscribing and condemning men who will be my friends when I have proved that my friendship is worth more than Pompey's was—than Cato's is. O incorrigible British islander: am I a bull dog, to seek quarrels merely to shew how stubborn my jaws are?

BRITANNUS: But your honor—the honor of Rome—

CAESAR: I do not make human sacrifices to my honor, as your Druids do. Since you will not burn these, at least I can drown them. (*He picks up the bag and throws it over the parapet into the sea.*)

BRITANNUS: Caesar: this is mere eccentricity. Are traitors to be allowed to go free for the sake of a paradox?

RUFIO (*rising*): Caesar: when the islander has finished preaching, call me again. I am going to have a look at the boiling water machine. (*He goes into the lighthouse.*)

BRITANNUS (*with genuine feeling*): O Caesar, my great master, if I could but persuade you to regard life seriously, as men do in my country!

CAESAR: Do they truly do so, Britannus?

BRITANNUS: Have you not been there? Have you not seen them? What Briton speaks as you do in your moments of levity? What Briton neglects to attend the services at the sacred grove? What Briton wears clothes of many colors as you do, instead of plain blue, as all solid, well esteemed men should? These are moral questions with us.

CAESAR: Well, well, my friend: some day I shall settle down and have a blue toga, perhaps. Meanwhile, I must get on as best I can in my flippant Roman way. (*Apollodorus comes past the lighthouse.*) What now?

BRITANNUS (*turning quickly, and challenging the stranger with official haughtiness*): What is this? Who are you? How did you come here?

APOLLODORUS: Calm yourself, my friend: I am not going to eat you. I have come by boat, from Alexandria, with precious gifts for Caesar.

CAESAR: From Alexandria!

BRITANNUS (*severely*): This is Caesar, sir.

RUFIO (*appearing at the lighthouse door*): Whats the matter now?

APOLLODORUS: Hail, great Caesar! I am Apollodorus the Sicilian, an artist.

BRITANNUS: An artist! Why have they admitted this vagabond?

CAESAR: Peace, man. Apollodorus is a famous patrician amateur.

BRITANNUS (*disconcerted*): I crave the gentleman's pardon. (*To Caesar.*) I understood him to say that he was a professional. (*Somewhat out of countenance, he allows Apollodorus to approach Caesar, changing places with him. Rufio, after looking Apollodorus up and down with marked disparagement, goes to the other side of the platform.*)

CAESAR: You are welcome, Apollodorus. What is your business?

APOLLODORUS: First, to deliver to you a present from the Queen of Queens.

CAESAR: Who is that?

APOLLODORUS: Cleopatra of Egypt.

CAESAR (*taking him into his confidence in his most winning manner*): Apollodorus: this is no time for playing with presents. Pray you, go back to the Queen, and tell her that if all goes well I shall return to the palace this evening.

APOLLODORUS: Caesar: I cannot return. As I approached the lighthouse, some fool threw a great leathern bag into the sea. It broke the nose of my boat; and I had hardly time to get myself and my charge to the shore before the poor little cockleshell sank.

CAESAR: I am sorry, Apollodorus. The fool shall be rebuked. Well, well: what have you brought me? The Queen will be hurt if I do not look at it.

RUFIO: Have we time to waste on this trumpery? The Queen is only a child.

CAESAR: Just so: that is why we must not disappoint her. What is the present, Apollodorus?

APOLLODORUS: Caesar: it is a Persian carpet—a beauty! And in it are—so I am told—pigeons' eggs and crystal goblets and fragile precious things. I dare not for my head have it carried up that narrow ladder from the causeway.

RUFIO: Swing it up by the crane, then. We will send the eggs to the cook; drink our wine from the goblets; and the carpet will make a bed for Caesar.

APOLLODORUS: The crane! Caesar: I have sworn to tender this bale of carpet as I tender my own life.

CAESAR (*cheerfully*): Then let them swing you up at the same time; and if the chain breaks, you and the pigeons' eggs will perish together. (*He goes to the chain and looks up along it, examining it curiously.*)

APOLLODORUS (*to Britannus*): Is Caesar serious?

BRITANNUS: His manner is frivolous because he is an Italian; but he means what he says.

APOLLODORUS: Serious or not, he spake well. Give me a squad of soldiers to work the crane.

BRITANNUS: Leave the crane to me. Go and await the descent of the chain.

APOLLODORUS: Good. You will presently see me there (*turning to them all and pointing with an eloquent gesture to the sky above the parapet*) rising like the sun with my treasure.

(*He goes back the way he came. Britannus goes into the lighthouse.*)

RUFIO (*ill-humoredly*): Are you really going to wait here for this foolery, Caesar?

CAESAR (*backing away from the crane as it gives signs of working*): Why not?

RUFIO: The Egyptians will let you know why not if they have the sense to make a rush from the shore end of the mole before our barricade is finished. And here we are waiting like children to see a carpet full of pigeons' eggs.

(*The chain rattles, and is drawn up high enough to clear the parapet. It then swings round out of sight behind the lighthouse.*)

CAESAR: Fear not, my son Rufio. When the first Egyptian takes his first step along the mole, the alarm will sound; and we two will reach the barricade from our end before the Egyptians reach it from their end—we two, Rufio: I, the old man, and you, his biggest boy. And the old man will be there first. So peace; and give me some more dates.

APOLLODORUS (*from the causeway below*): Soho, haul away. So-ho-o-o-o! (*The chain is drawn up and comes round again from behind the lighthouse. Apollodorus is swinging in the air with his bale of carpet at the end of it. He breaks into song as he soars above the parapet.*)

> Aloft, aloft, behold the blue
> That never shone in woman's eyes

Easy there: stop her. (*He ceases to rise.*) Further round! (*The chain comes forward above the platform.*)

RUFIO (*calling up*): Lower away there. (*The chain and its load begin to descend.*)

APOLLODORUS (*calling up*): Gently—slowly—mind the eggs.

RUFIO (*calling up*): Easy there—slowly—slowly.

(*Apollodorus and the bale are deposited safely on the flags in the middle of the platform. Rufio and Caesar help Apollodorus to cast off the chain from the bale.*)

RUFIO: Haul up.

(*The chain rises clear of their heads with a rattle. Britannus comes from the lighthouse and helps them to uncord the carpet.*)

APOLLODORUS (*when the cords are loose*): Stand off, my friends: let Caesar see. (*He throws the carpet open.*)

RUFIO: Nothing but a heap of shawls. Where are the pigeons' eggs?

APOLLODORUS: Approach, Caesar; and search for them among the shawls.

RUFIO (*drawing his sword*): Ha, treachery! Keep back, Caesar: I saw the shawl move: there is something alive there.

BRITANNUS (*drawing his sword*): It is a serpent.

APOLLODORUS: Dares Caesar thrust his hand into the sack where the serpent moves?

RUFIO (*turning on him*): Treacherous dog—

CAESAR: Peace. Put up your swords. Apollodorus: your serpent seems to breathe very regularly. (*He thrusts his hand under the shawls and draws out a bare arm.*) This is a pretty little snake.

RUFIO (*drawing out the other arm*): Let us have the rest of you.

(*They pull Cleopatra up by the wrists into a sitting position. Britannus, scandalized, sheathes his sword with a drive of protest.*)

CLEOPATRA (*gasping*): Oh, I'm smothered. Oh, Caesar, a man stood on me in the boat; and a great sack of something fell upon me out of the sky; and then the boat sank; and then I was swung up into the air and bumped down.

CAESAR(*petting her as she rises and takes refuge on his breast*): Well, never mind: here you are safe and sound at last.

RUFIO: Ay, and now that she i s here, what are we to do with her?

BRITANNUS: She cannot stay here, Caesar, without the companionship of some matron.

CLEOPATRA(*jealously, to Caesar, who is obviously perplexed*): Arnt you glad to see me?

CAESAR: Yes, yes; I am very glad. But Rufio is very angry; and Britannus is shocked.

CLEOPATRA (*contemptuously*): You can have their heads cut off, can you not?

CAESAR: They would not be so useful with their heads cut off as they are now, my sea bird.

RUFIO (*to Cleopatra*): We shall have to go away presently and cut some of your Egyptians' heads off. How will you like being left here with the chance of being captured by that little brother of yours if we are beaten?

CLEOPATRA: But you mustnt leave me alone. Caesar: you will not leave me alone, will you?

RUFIO: What! not when the trumpet sounds and all our lives depend on Caesar's being at the barricade before the Egyptians reach it? Eh?

CLEOPATRA: Let them lose their lives: they are only soldiers.

CAESAR (*gravely*): Cleopatra: when that trumpet sounds, we must take every man his life in his hand, and throw it in the face of Death. And of my soldiers who have trusted me there is not one whose hand I shall not hold more sacred than your head. (*Cleopatra is overwhelmed. Her eyes fill with tears.*) Apollodorus: you must take her back to the palace.

APOLLODORUS: Am I a dolphin, Caesar, to cross the seas with young ladies on my back? My boat is sunk: all yours are either at the barricade or have returned to the city. I will hail one if I can: that is all I can do. (*He goes back to the causeway.*)

CLEOPATRA (*struggling with her tears*): It does not matter. I will not go back. Nobody cares for me.

CAESAR: Cleopatra—

CLEOPATRA: You want me to be killed.

CAESAR (*still more gravely*): My poor child: your life matters little here to anyone but yourself. (*She gives way altogether at this, casting herself down on the faggots weeping. Suddenly a great tumult is heard in the distance, bucinas and trumpets sounding through a storm of shouting. Britannus rushes to the* parapet and looks along the mole. Caesar and Rufio turn to one* *another with quick intelligence.*)

CAESAR: Come, Rufio.

CLEOPATRA (*scrambling to her knees and clinging to him*): No no. Do not leave me, Caesar. (*He snatches his skirt from her clutch.*) Oh!

BRITANNUS (*from the parapet*): Caesar: we are cut off. The Egyptians have landed from the west harbor between us and the barricade! ! !

RUFIO (*running to see*): Curses! It is true. We are caught like rats in a trap.

CAESAR (*ruthfully*): Rufio, Rufio: my men at the barricade are between the sea party and the shore party. I have murdered them.

RUFIO (*coming back from the parapet to Caesar's right hand*): Ay: that comes of fooling with this girl here.

APOLLODORUS (*coming up quickly from the causeway*): Look over the parapet, Caesar.

CAESAR: We have looked, my friend. We must defend ourselves here.

APOLLODORUS: I have thrown the ladder into the sea. They cannot get in without it.

RUFIO: Ay; and we cannot get out. Have you thought of that?

APOLLODORUS: Not get out! Why not? You have ships in the east harbor.

BRITANNUS (*hopefully, at the parapet*): The Rhodian galleys are standing in towards us already. (*Caesar quickly joins Britannus at the parapet.*)

RUFIO (*to Apollodorus, impatiently*): And by what road are we to walk to the galleys, pray?

APOLLODORUS (*with gay, defiant rhetoric*): By the road that leads everywhere—the diamond path of the sun and moon. Have you never seen the child's shadow play of The Broken Bridge? "Ducks and geese with ease get over"—eh? (*He throws away his cloak and cap, and binds his sword on his back.*)

RUFIO: What are you talking about?

APOLLODORUS: I will shew you. (*Calling to Britannus.*) How far off is the nearest galley?

BRITANNUS: Fifty fathom.

CAESAR: No, no: they are further off than they seem in this clear air to your British eyes. Nearly quarter of a mile, Apollodorus.

APOLLODORUS: Good. Defend yourselves here until I send you a boat from that galley.

RUFIO: Have you wings, perhaps?

APOLLODORUS: Water wings, soldier. Behold!

(*He runs up the steps between Caesar and Britannus to the coping of the parapet; springs into the air; and plunges head foremost into the sea.*)

CAESAR (*like a schoolboy—wildly excited*): Bravo, bravo! (*Throwing off his cloak.*) By Jupiter, I will do that too.

RUFIO (*seizing him*): You are mad. You shall not.

CAESAR: Why not? Can I not swim as well as he?

RUFIO (*frantic*): Can an old fool dive and swim like a young one? He is twenty-five and you are fifty.

CAESAR (*breaking loose from Rufio*): Old!!!

BRITANNUS (*shocked*): Rufio: you forget yourself.

CAESAR: I will race you to the galley for a week's pay, father Rufio.

CLEOPATRA: But me! me!! me!!! what is to become of me?

CAESAR: I will carry you on my back to the galley like a dolphin. Rufio: when you see me rise to the surface, throw her in: I will answer for her. And then in with you after her, both of you.

CLEOPATRA: No, no, NO. I shall be drowned.

BRITANNUS: Caesar: I am a man and a Briton, not a fish. I must have a boat. I cannot swim.

CLEOPATRA: Neither can I.

BRITANNUS (*anxiously*): One last word, Caesar. Do not let yourself be seen in the fashionable part of Alexandria until you have changed your clothes.

CAESAR (*calling over the sea*): Ho, Apollodorus: (*He points skyward and quotes the barcarolle:*)

The white upon the blue above—

APOLLODORUS (*swimming in the distance*):

Is purple on the green below—

CAESAR (*exultantly*): Aha! (*He plunges into the sea.*)

CLEOPATRA (*running excitedly to the steps*): Oh, let me see. He will be drowned (*Rufio seizes her*)—Ah—ah—ah—ah! (*He pitches her screaming into the sea. Rufio and Britannus roar with laughter.*)

RUFIO (*looking down after her*): He has got her. (*To Britannus.*) Hold the fort, Briton. Caesar will not forget you. (*He springs off.*)

BRITANNUS (*running to the steps to watch them as they swim*): All safe, Rufio?

RUFIO (*swimming*): All safe.

CAESAR (*swimming further off*): Take refuge up there by the beacon; and pile the fuel on the trap door, Britannus.

BRITANNUS (*calling in reply*): I will first do so, and then commend myself to my country's gods. (*A sound of cheering from the sea. Britannus gives full vent to his excitement.*) The boat has reached him: Hip, hip, hip, hurrah!

ACT IV

Cleopatra's sousing in the east harbor of Alexandria was in October 48 B.C. In March 47 she is passing the afternoon in her boudoir in the palace, among a bevy of her ladies, listening to a slave girl who is playing the harp in the middle of the room. The harpist's master, an old musician, with a lined face, prominent brows, white beard, moustache and eyebrows twisted and horned at the ends, and a consciously keen and pretentious expression, is squatting on the floor close to her on her right, watching her performance. Ftatateeta is in attendance near the door, in front of a group of female slaves. Except the harp player all are seated: Cleopatra in a chair opposite the door on the other side of the room; the rest on the ground. Cleopatra's ladies are all young, the most conspicuous being Charmian and Iras, her favorites. Charmian is a hatchet faced, terra cotta colored little goblin, swift in her movements, and neatly finished at the hands and feet. Iras is a plump, goodnatured creature, rather fatuous, with a profusion of red hair, and a tendency to giggle on the slightest provocation.

CLEOPATRA: Can I—

FTATATEETA (*insolently, to the player*): Peace, thou! The Queen speaks. (*The player stops.*)

CLEOPATRA (*to the old musician*): I want to learn to play the harp with my own hands. Caesar loves music. Can you teach me?

MUSICIAN: Assuredly I and no one else can teach the queen. Have I not discovered the lost method of the ancient Egyptians, who could make a pyramid tremble by touching a bass string? All the other teachers are quacks: I have exposed them repeatedly.

CLEOPATRA: Good: you shall teach me. How long will it take?

MUSICIAN: Not very long: only four years. Your Majesty must first become proficient in the philosophy of Pythagoras.

CLEOPATRA:: Has she (*indicating the slave*) become proficient in the philosophy of Pythagoras?

MUSICIAN: Oh, she is but a slave. She learns as a dog learns.

CLEOPATRA: Well, then, I will learn as a dog learns; for she plays better than you. You shall give me a lesson every day for a fortnight. (*The musician hastily scrambles to his feet and bows profoundly.*) After that, whenever I strike a false note you shall be flogged; and if I strike so many that there is not time to flog you, you shall be thrown into the Nile to feed the crocodiles. Give the girl a piece of gold; and send them away.

MUSICIAN (*much taken aback*): But true art will not be thus forced.

FTATATEETA (*pushing him out*): What is this? Answering the Queen, forsooth. Out with you.

(*He is pushed out by Ftatateeta, the girl following with her harp, amid the laughter of the ladies and slaves.*)

CLEOPATRA: Now, can any of you amuse me? Have you any stories or any news?

IRAS: Ftatateeta—

CLEOPATRA: Oh, Ftatateeta, Ftatateeta, always Ftatateeta. Some new tale to set me against her.

IRAS: No: this time Ftatateeta has been virtuous. (*All the ladies laugh—not the slaves.*) Pothinus has been trying to bribe her to let him speak with you.

CLEOPATRA (*wrathfully*): Ha! you all sell audiences with me, as if I saw whom you please, and not whom I please. I should like to know how much of her gold piece that harp girl will have to give up before she leaves the palace.

IRAS: We can easily find out that for you.

(*The ladies laugh.*)

CLEOPATRA (*frowning*): You laugh; but take care, take care. I will find out some day how to make myself served as Caesar is served.

CHARMIAN: Old hooknose! (*They laugh again.*)

CLEOPATRA (*revolted*): Silence. Charmian: do not you be a silly little Egyptian fool. Do you know why I allow you all to chatter impertinently just as you please, instead of treating you as Ftatateeta would treat you if she were Queen?

CHARMIAN: Because you try to imitate Caesar in everything; and he lets everybody say what they please to him.

CLEOPATRA: No; but because I asked him one day why he did so; and he said "Let your women talk; and you will learn something from them." What have I to learn from them? I said. "What they a r e," said he; and oh! you should have seen his eye as he said it. You would have curled up, you shallow things. (*They laugh. She turns fiercely on Iras.*) At whom are you laughing—at me or at Caesar?

IRAS: At Caesar.

CLEOPATRA: If you were not a fool, you would laugh at me; and if you were not a coward you would not be afraid to tell me so. (*Ftatateeta returns.*) Ftatateeta: they tell me that Pothinus has offered you a bribe to admit him to my presence.

FTATATEETA (*protesting*): Now by my father's gods—

CLEOPATRA (*cutting her short despotically*): Have I not told you not to deny things? You would spend the day calling your father's gods to witness to your virtues if I let you. Go take the bribe; and bring in Pothinus. (*Ftatateeta is about to reply.*) Dont answer me. Go.

(*Ftatateeta goes out; and Cleopatra rises and begins to prowl to and fro between her chair and the door, meditating. All rise and stand.*)

IRAS (*as she reluctantly rises*): Heigho! I wish Caesar were back in Rome.

CLEOPATRA (*threateningly*): It will be a bad day for you all when he goes. Oh, if I were not ashamed to let him see that I am as cruel at heart as my father, I would make you repent that speech! Why do you wish him away?

CHARMIAN: He makes you so terribly prosy and serious and learned and philosophical. It is worse than being religious, at our ages. (*The ladies laugh.*)

CLEOPATRA: Cease that endless cackling, will you. Hold your tongues.

CHARMIAN (*with mock resignation*): Well, well: we must try to live up to Caesar.

(*They laugh again. Cleopatra rages silently as she continues to prowl to and fro. Ftatateeta comes back with Pothinus, who halts on the threshold.*)

FTATATEETA (*at the door*): Pothinus craves the ear of the—

CLEOPATRA: There, there: that will do: let him come in. (*She resumes her seat. All sit down except Pothinus, who advances to the middle of the room. Ftatateeta takes her former place.*) Well, Pothinus: what is the latest news from your rebel friends?

POTHINUS (*haughtily*): I am no friend of rebellion. And a prisoner does not receive news.

CLEOPATRA: You are no more a prisoner than I am—than Caesar is. These six months we have been besieged in this palace by my subjects. You are allowed to walk on the beach among the soldiers. Can I go further myself, or can Caesar?

POTHINUS: You are but a child, Cleopatra, and do not understand these matters.

(*The ladies laugh. Cleopatra looks inscrutably at him.*)

CHARMIAN: I see you do not know the latest news, Pothinus.

POTHINUS: What is that?

CHARMIAN: That Cleopatra is no longer a child. Shall I tell you how to grow much older, and much, m u c h wiser in one day?

POTHINUS: I should prefer to grow wiser without growing older.

CHARMIAN: Well, go up to the top of the lighthouse; and get somebody to take you by the hair and throw you into the sea. (*The ladies laugh.*)

CLEOPATRA: She is right, Pothinus: you will come to the shore with much conceit washed out of you. (*The ladies laugh. Cleopatra rises impatiently.*) Begone, all of you. I will speak with Pothinus alone. Drive them out, Ftatateeta. (*They run out laughing. Ftatateeta shuts the door on them.*) What are you waiting for?

FTATATEETA: It is not meet that the Queen remain alone with—

CLEOPATRA (*interrupting her*): Ftatateeta: must I sacrifice you to your father's gods to teach you that *I* am Queen of Egypt, and not you?

FTATATEETA (*indignantly*): You are like the rest of them. You want to be what these Romans call a New Woman. (*She goes out, banging the door.*)

CLEOPATRA (*sitting down again*): Now, Pothinus: why did you bribe Ftatateeta to bring you hither?

POTHINUS (*studying her gravely*): Cleopatra: what they tell me is true. You are changed.

CLEOPATRA: Do you speak with Caesar every day for six months: and you will be changed.

POTHINUS: It is the common talk that you are infatuated with this old man?

CLEOPATRA: Infatuated? What does that mean? Made foolish, is it not? Oh no: I wish I were.

POTHINUS: You wish you were made foolish! How so?

CLEOPATRA: When I was foolish, I did what I liked, except when Ftatateeta beat me; and even then I cheated her and did it by stealth. Now that Caesar has made me wise, it is no use my liking or disliking: I do what must be done, and have no time to attend to myself. That is not happiness; but it is greatness. If Caesar were gone, I think I could govern the Egyptians; for what Caesar is to me, I am to the fools around me.

POTHINUS (*looking hard at her*): Cleopatra: this may be the vanity of youth.

CLEOPATRA: No, no: it is not that I am so clever, but that the others are so stupid.

POTHINUS (*musingly*): Truly, that is the great secret.

CLEOPATRA: Well, now tell me what you came to say?

POTHINUS (*embarrassed*): I! Nothing.

CLEOPATRA: Nothing!

POTHINUS: At least—to beg for my liberty: that is all.

CLEOPATRA: For that you would have knelt to Caesar. No, Pothinus: you came with some plan that depended on Cleopatra being a little nursery kitten. Now that Cleopatra is a Queen, the plan is upset.

POTHINUS (*bowing his head submissively*): It is so.

CLEOPATRA (*exultant*): Aha!

POTHINUS (*raising his eyes keenly to hers*): Is Cleopatra then indeed a Queen, and no longer Caesar's prisoner and slave?

CLEOPATRA: Pothinus: we are all Caesar's slaves—all we in this land of Egypt—whether we will or no. And she who is wise enough to know this will reign when Caesar departs.

POTHINUS: You harp on Caesar's departure.

CLEOPATRA: What if I do?

POTHINUS: Does he not love you?

CLEOPATRA: Love me! Pothinus: Caesar loves no one. Who are those we love. Only those whom we do not hate: all people are strangers and enemies to us except those we love. But it is not so with Caesar. He has no hatred in him: he makes friends with everyone as he does with dogs and children. His kindness to me is a wonder: neither mother, father, nor nurse have ever taken so much care for me, or thrown open their thoughts to me so freely.

POTHINUS: Well: is not this love?

CLEOPATRA: What! when he will do as much for the first girl he meets on his way back to Rome? Ask his slave, Britannus: he has been just as good to him. Nay, ask his very horse! His kindness is not for anything in m e: it is in his own nature.

POTHINUS: But how can you be sure that he does not love you as men love women?

CLEOPATRA: Because I cannot make him jealous. I have tried.

POTHINUS: Hm! Perhaps I should have asked, then, do you love h i m?

CLEOPATRA: Can one love a god? Besides, I love another Roman: one whom I saw long before Caesar—no god, but a man—one who can love and hate—one whom I can hurt and who would hurt me.

POTHINUS: Does Caesar know this?

CLEOPATRA: Yes.

POTHINUS: And he is not angry?

CLEOPATRA: He promises to send him to Egypt to please me!

POTHINUS: I do not understand this man.

CLEOPATRA (*with superb contempt*): You understand Caesar! How could you? (*Proudly.*) I do—by instinct.

POTHINUS (*deferentially, after a moment's thought*): Your Majesty caused me to be admitted today. What message has the Queen for me?

CLEOPATRA: This. You think that by making my brother king, you will rule in Egypt because you are his guardian and he is a little silly.

POTHINUS: The Queen is pleased to say so.

CLEOPATRA: The Queen is pleased to say this also. That Caesar will eat up you, and Achillas, and my brother, as a cat eats up mice; and that he will put on this land of Egypt as a shepherd puts on his garment. And when he has done that, he will return to Rome, and leave Cleopatra here as his viceroy.

POTHINUS (*breaking out wrathfully*): That he shall never do. We have a thousand men to his ten; and we will drive him and his beggarly legions into the sea.

CLEOPATRA (*with scorn, getting up to go*): You rant like any common fellow. Go, then, and marshal your thousands; and make haste; for Mithridates of Pergamos is at hand with reinforcements for Caesar. Caesar has held you at bay with two legions: we shall see what he will do with twenty.

POTHINUS: Cleopatra—

CLEOPATRA: Enough, enough: Caesar has spoiled me for talking to weak things like you. (*She goes out. Pothinus, with a gesture of rage, is following, when Ftatateeta enters and stops him.*)

POTHINUS: Let me go forth from this hateful place.

FTATATEETA: What angers you?

POTHINUS: The curse of all the gods of Egypt be upon her! She sold her country to the Roman, that she may buy it back from him with her kisses.

FTATATEETA: Fool: did she not tell you that she would have Caesar gone?

POTHINUS: You listened?

FTATATEETA: I took care that some honest woman should be at hand whilst you were with her.

POTHINUS: Now by the gods—

FTATATEETA: Enough of your gods! Caesar's gods are all powerful here. It is no use y o u coming to Cleopatra: you are only an Egyptian. She will not listen to any of her own race: she treats us all as children.

POTHINUS: May she perish for it!

FTATATEETA (*balefully*): May your tongue wither for that wish! Go! send for Lucius Septimius, the slayer of Pompey. He is a Roman: maybe she will listen to him. Begone!

POTHINUS (*darkly*): I know to whom I must go now.

FTATATEETA (*suspiciously*): To whom, then?

POTHINUS: To a greater Roman than Lucius. And mark this, mistress. You thought, before Caesar came, that Egypt should presently be ruled by you and your crew in the name of Cleopatra. I set myself against it—

FTATATEETA (*interrupting him—wrangling*): Ay; that it might be ruled by you and your crew in the name of Ptolemy.

POTHINUS: Better me, or even you, than a woman with a Roman heart; and that is what Cleopatra is now become. Whilst I live, she shall never rule. So guide yourself accordingly. (*He goes out.*)

(*It is by this time drawing on to dinner time. The table is laid on the roof of the palace; and thither Rufio is now climbing, ushered by a majestic palace official, wand of office in hand, and followed by a slave carrying an inlaid stool. After many stairs they emerge at last into a massive colonnade on the roof. Light curtains are drawn between the columns on the north and east to soften the westering sun. The official leads Rufio to one of these shaded sections. A cord for pulling the curtains apart hangs down between the pillars.*)

THE OFFICIAL (*bowing*): The Roman commander will await Caesar here.

(*The slave sets down the stool near the southernmost column, and slips out through the curtains.*)

RUFIO (*sitting down, a little blown*): Pouf! That was a climb. How high have we come?

THE OFFICIAL: We are on the palace roof, O Beloved of Victory!

RUFIO: Good! the Beloved of Victory has no more stairs to get up.

(*A second official enters from the opposite end, walking backwards.*)

THE SECOND OFFICIAL: Caesar approaches.

(*Caesar, fresh from the bath, clad in a new tunic of purple silk, comes in, beaming and festive, followed by two slaves carrying a light couch, which is hardly more than an elaborately designed bench. They place it near the northmost of the two curtained columns. When this is done they slip out through the curtains; and the two officials, formally bowing, follow them. Rufio rises to receive Caesar.*)

CAESAR (*coming over to him*): Why, Rufio! (*Surveying his dress with an air of admiring astonishment.*) A new baldrick! A new golden pommel to your sword! And you have had your hair cut! But not your beard—? impossible! (*He sniffs at Rufio's beard.*) Yes, perfumed, by Jupiter Olympus!

RUFIO (*growling*): Well: is it to please myself?

CAESAR (*affectionately*): No, my son Rufio, but to please me—
to celebrate my birthday.

RUFIO (*contemptuously*): Your birthday! You always have a
birthday when there is a pretty girl to be flattered or an
ambassador to be conciliated. We had seven of them in ten
months last year.

CAESAR (*contritely*): It is true, Rufio! I shall never break myself
of these petty deceits.

RUFIO: Who is to dine with us—besides Cleopatra?

CAESAR: Apollodorus the Sicilian.

RUFIO: That popinjay!

CAESAR: Come! the popinjay is an amusing dog—tells a story;
sings a song; and saves us the trouble of flattering the Queen.
What does she care for old politicians and camp-fed bears
like us? No, Apollodorus is good company, Rufio, good company.

RUFIO: Well, he can swim a bit and fence a bit: he might be
worse, if he only knew how to hold his tongue.

CAESAR: The gods forbid he should ever learn! Oh, this military
life! this tedious, brutal life of action! That is the worst of us
Romans: we are mere doers and drudgers: a swarm of bees
turned into men. Give me a good talker—one with wit and
imagination enough to live without continually doing something!

RUFIO: Ay! a nice time he would have of it with you when
dinner was over! Have you noticed that I am before my time?

CAESAR: Aha! I thought that meant something. What is it?

RUFIO: Can we be overheard here?

CAESAR: Our privacy invites eavesdropping. I can remedy that.
(*He claps his hands twice. The curtains are drawn, revealing
the garden with a banqueting table set across in the middle for
four persons, one at each end, and two side by side. The side
next Caesar and Rufio is blocked with golden wine vessels and
basins. A gorgeous major-domo is superintending the laying of
the table by a staff of slaves. The colonnade goes round the*

garden at both sides to the further end, where a gap in it, like a great gateway, leaves the view open to the sky beyond the western edge of the roof, except in the middle, where a life size image of Ra, seated on a huge plinth, towers up, with hawk head and crown of asp and disk. His altar, which stands at his feet, is a single white stone.) Now everybody can see us, nobody will think of listening to us. (*He sits down on the bench left by the two slaves.*)

RUFIO (*sitting down on his stool*): Pothinus wants to speak to you. I advise you to see him: there is some plotting going on here among the women.

CAESAR: Who is Pothinus?

RUFIO: The fellow with hair like squirrel's fur—the little King's bear leader, whom you kept prisoner.

CAESAR (*annoyed*): And has he not escaped?

RUFIO: No.

CAESAR (*rising imperiously*): Why not? You have been guarding this man instead of watching the enemy. Have I not told you always to let prisoners escape unless there are special orders to the contrary? Are there not enough mouths to be fed without him?

RUFIO: Yes; and if you would have a little sense and let me cut his throat, you would save his rations. Anyhow he wont escape. Three sentries have told him they would put a pilum through him if they saw him again. What more can they do? He prefers to stay and spy on us. So would I if I had to do with generals subject to fits of clemency.

CAESAR (*resuming his seat, argued down*): Hm! And so he wants to see me.

RUFIO: Ay. I have brought him with me. He is waiting there (*jerking his thumb over his shoulder*) under guard.

CAESAR: And you want me to see him?

RUFIO (*obstinately*): I dont want anything. I daresay you will do what you like. Dont put it on to me.

CAESAR (*with an air of doing it expressly to indulge Rufio*): Well, well: let us have him.

RUFIO (*calling*): Ho there, guard! Release your man and send him up. (*Beckoning.*) Come along!

(*Pothinus enters and stops mistrustfully between the two, looking from one to the other.*)

CAESAR (*graciously*): Ah, Pothinus! You are welcome. And what is the news this afternoon?

POTHINUS: Caesar: I come to warn you of a danger, and to make you an offer.

CAESAR: Never mind the danger. Make the offer.

RUFIO: Never mind the offer. Whats the danger?

POTHINUS: Caesar: you think that Cleopatra is devoted to you.

CAESAR (*gravely*): My friend: I already know what I think. Come to your offer.

POTHINUS: I will deal plainly. I know not by what strange gods you have been enabled to defend a palace and a few yards of beach against a city and an army. Since we cut you off from Lake Mareotis, and you dug wells in the salt sea sand and brought up buckets of fresh water from them, we have known that your gods are irresistible, and that you are a worker of miracles. I no longer threaten you—

RUFIO (*sarcastically*): Very handsome of you, indeed.

POTHINUS: So be it: you are the master. Our gods sent the north west winds to keep you in our hands; but you have been too strong for them.

CAESAR (*gently urging him to come to the point*): Yes, yes, my friend. But what then?

RUFIO: Spit it out, man. What have you to say?

POTHINUS: I have to say that you have a traitress in your camp. Cleopatra—

THE MAJOR-DOMO (*at the table, announcing*): The Queen! (*Caesar and Rufio rise.*)

RUFIO (*aside to Pothinus*): You should have spat it out sooner, you fool. Now it is too late.

(*Cleopatra, in gorgeous raiment, enters in state through the gap in the colonnade, and comes down past the image of Ra and past the*

table to Caesar. Her retinue, headed by Ftatateeta, joins the staff
at the table. Caesar gives Cleopatra his seat, which she takes.)

CLEOPATRA (*quickly, seeing Pothinus*): What is he doing here?

CAESAR (*seating himself beside her, in the most amiable of tempers*): Just going to tell me something about you. You shall hear it. Proceed, Pothinus.

POTHINUS (*disconcerted*): Caesar—(*he stammers*).

CAESAR: Well, out with it.

POTHINUS: What I have to say is for your ear, not for the Queen's.

CLEOPATRA (*with subdued ferocity*): There are means of making you speak. Take care.

POTHINUS (*defiantly*): Caesar does not employ those means.

CAESAR: My friend: when a man has anything to tell in this world, the difficulty is not to make him tell it, but to prevent him from telling it too often. Let me celebrate my birthday by setting you free. Farewell: we shall not meet again.

CLEOPATRA (*angrily*): Caesar: this mercy is foolish.

POTHINUS (*to Caesar*): Will you not give me a private audience? Your life may depend on it. (*Caesar rises loftily.*)

RUFIO (*aside to Pothinus*): Ass! Now we shall have some heroics.

CAESAR (*oratorically*): Pothinus—

RUFIO (*interrupting him*): Caesar: the dinner will spoil if you begin preaching your favorite sermon about life and death.

CLEOPATRA (*priggishly*): Peace, Rufio. I desire to hear Caesar.

RUFIO (*bluntly*): Your Majesty has heard it before. You repeated it to Apollodorus last week; and he thought it was all your own. (*Caesar's dignity collapses. Much tickled, he sits down again and looks roguishly at Cleopatra, who is furious. Rufio calls as before.*) Ho there, guard! Pass the prisoner out. He is released. (*To Pothinus.*) Now off with you. You have lost your chance.

POTHINUS (*his temper overcoming his prudence*): I will speak.

CAESAR (*to Cleopatra*): You see. Torture would not have wrung a word from him.

POTHINUS: Caesar: you have taught Cleopatra the arts by which the Romans govern the world.

CAESAR: Alas! they cannot even govern themselves. What then?

POTHINUS: What then? Are you so besotted with her beauty that you do not see that she is impatient to reign in Egypt alone, and that her heart is set on your departure?

CLEOPATRA (*rising*): Liar!

CAESAR (*shocked*): What! Protestations! Contradictions!

CLEOPATRA (*ashamed, but trembling with suppressed rage*): No. I do not deign to contradict. Let him talk. (*She sits down again.*)

POTHINUS: From her own lips I have heard it. You are to be her catspaw: you are to tear the crown from her brother's head and set it on her own, delivering us all into her hand —delivering yourself also. And then Caesar can return to Rome, or depart through the gate of death, which is nearer and surer.

CAESAR (*calmly*): Well, my friend; and is not this very natural?

POTHINUS (*astonished*): Natural! Then you do not resent treachery?

CAESAR: Resent! O thou foolish Egyptian, what have I to do with resentment? Do I resent the wind when it chills me, or the night when it makes me stumble in darkness? Shall I resent youth when it turns from age, and ambition when it turns from servitude? To tell me such a story as this is but to tell me that the sun will rise tomorrow.

CLEOPATRA (*unable to contain herself*): But it is false—false. I swear it.

CAESAR: It is true, though you swore it a thousand times, and believed all you swore. (*She is convulsed with emotion. To screen her, he rises and takes Pothinus to Rufio, saying:*) Come, Rufio: let us see Pothinus past the guard. I have a word to say to him. (*Aside to them.*) We must give the Queen a moment to recover herself. (*Aloud.*) Come. (*He takes Pothinus and Rufio out with him, conversing with them meanwhile.*) Tell your friends, Pothinus, that they must not think I am opposed to a reasonable settlement of the country's affairs— (*They pass out of hearing.*)

CLEOPATRA (*in a stifled whisper*): Ftatateeta, Ftatateeta.

FTATATEETA (*hurrying to her from the table and petting her*): Peace, child: be comforted—

CLEOPATRA (*interrupting her*): Can they hear us?

FTATATEETA: No, dear heart, no.

CLEOPATRA: Listen to me. If he leaves the Palace alive, never see my face again.

FTATATEETA: He? Poth—

CLEOPATRA (*striking her on the mouth*): Strike his life out as I strike his name from your lips. Dash him down from the wall. Break him on the stones. Kill, kill, kill him.

FTATATEETA (*shewing all her teeth*): The dog shall perish.

CLEOPATRA: Fail in this, and you go out from before me for ever.

FTATATEETA (*resolutely*): So be it. You shall not see my face until his eyes are darkened.

(*Caesar comes back, with Apollodorus, exquisitely dressed, and Rufio.*)

CLEOPATRA (*to Ftatateeta*): Come soon—soon. (*Ftatateeta turns her meaning eyes for a moment on her mistress; then goes grimly away past Ra and out. Cleopatra runs like a gazelle to Caesar.*) So you have come back to me, Caesar. (*Caressingly.*) I thought you were angry. Welcome, Apollodorus. (*She gives him her hand to kiss, with her other arm about Caesar.*)

APOLLODORUS: Cleopatra grows more womanly beautiful from week to week.

CLEOPATRA: Truth, Apollodorus?

APOLLODORUS: Far, far short of the truth! Friend Rufio threw a pearl into the sea: Caesar fished up a diamond.

CAESAR: Caesar fished up a touch of rheumatism, my friend. Come: to dinner! to dinner! (*They move towards the table.*)

CLEOPATRA (*skipping like a young fawn*): Yes, to dinner. I have ordered such a dinner for you, Caesar!

CAESAR: Ay? What are we to have?

CLEOPATRA: Peacocks' brains.

CAESAR (*as if his mouth watered*): Peacocks' brains, Apollodorus!

APOLLODORUS: Not for me. I prefer nightingales' tongues. (*He goes to one of the two covers set side by side.*)

CLEOPATRA: Roast boar, Rufio!

RUFIO (*gluttonously*): Good! (*He goes to the seat next Apollodorus, on his left.*)

CAESAR (*looking at his seat, which is at the end of the table, to Ra's left hand*): What has become of my leathern cushion?

CLEOPATRA (*at the opposite end*): I have got new ones for you.

THE MAJOR-DOMO: These cushions, Caesar, are of Maltese gauze, stuffed with rose leaves.

CAESAR: Rose leaves! Am I a caterpillar? (*He throws the cushions away and seats himself on the leather mattress underneath.*)

CLEOPATRA: What a shame! My new cushions!

THE MAJOR-DOMO (*at Caesar's elbow*): What shall we serve to whet Caesar's appetite?

CAESAR: What have you got?

THE MAJOR-DOMO: Sea hedgehogs, black and white sea acorns, sea nettles, beccaficoes, purple shellfish—

CAESAR: Any oysters?

THE MAJOR-DOMO: Assuredly.

CAESAR: British oysters?

THE MAJOR-DOMO (*assenting*): British oysters, Caesar.

CAESAR: Oysters, then. (*The Major-Domo signs to a slave at each order; and the slave goes out to execute it.*) I have been in Britain—that western land of romance—the last piece of earth on the edge of the ocean that surrounds the world. I went there in search of its famous pearls. The British pearl was a fable; but in searching for it I found the British oyster.

APOLLODORUS: All posterity will bless you for it. (*To the Major-Domo.*) Sea hedgehogs for me.

RUFIO: Is there nothing solid to begin with?

THE MAJOR-DOMO: Fieldfares with asparagus—

CLEOPATRA (*interrupting*): Fattened fowls! have some fattened fowls, Rufio.

RUFIO: Ay, that will do.

CLEOPATRA (*greedily*): Fieldfares for me.

THE MAJOR-DOMO: Caesar will deign to choose his wine? Sicilian, Lesbian, Chian—

RUFIO (*contemptuously*): All Greek.

APOLLODORUS: Who would drink Roman wine when he could get Greek. Try the Lesbian, Caesar.

CAESAR: Bring me my barley water.

RUFIO (*with intense disgust*): Ugh! Bring me my Falernian. (*The Falernian is presently brought to him.*)

CLEOPATRA (*pouting*): It is waste of time giving you dinners, Caesar. My scullions would not condescend to your diet.

CAESAR (*relenting*): Well, well: let us try the Lesbian. (*The Major-Domo fills Caesar's goblet; then Cleopatra's and Apollodorus'.*) But when I return to Rome, I will make laws against these extravagances. I will even get the laws carried out.

CLEOPATRA (*coaxingly*): Never mind. Today you are to be like other people: idle, luxurious, and kind. (*She stretches her hand to him along the table.*)

CAESAR: Well, for once I will sacrifice my comfort—(*kissing her hand*) there! (*He takes a draught of wine.*) Now are you satisfied?

CLEOPATRA: And you no longer believe that I long for your departure for Rome?

CAESAR: I no longer believe anything. My brains are asleep. Besides, who knows whether I shall return to Rome?

RUFIO (*alarmed*): How? Eh? What?

CAESAR: What has Rome to shew me that I have not seen already? One year of Rome is like another, except that I grow older, whilst the crowd in the Appian Way is always the same age.

APOLLODORUS: It is no better here in Egypt. The old men, when they are tired of life, say "We have seen everything except the source of the Nile."

CAESAR (*his imagination catching fire*): And why not see that? Cleopatra: will you come with me and track the flood to its cradle in the heart of the regions of mystery? Shall we leave Rome behind us—Rome, that has achieved greatness only to learn how greatness destroys nations of men who are not great! Shall I make you a new kingdom, and build you a holy city there in the great unknown?

CLEOPATRA (*rapturously*): Yes, yes. You shall.

RUFIO: Ay: now he will conquer Africa with two legions before we come to the roast boar.

APOLLODORUS: Come: no scoffing. This is a noble scheme: in it Caesar is no longer merely the conquering soldier, but the creative poet-artist. Let us name the holy city, and consecrate it with Lesbian wine.

CAESAR: Cleopatra shall name it herself.

CLEOPATRA: It shall be called Caesar's Gift to his Beloved.

APOLLODORUS: No, no. Something vaster than that—something universal, like the starry firmament.

CAESAR (*prosaically*): Why not simply The Cradle of the Nile?

CLEOPATRA: No: the Nile is my ancestor; and he is a god. Oh! I have thought of something. The Nile shall name it himself. Let us call upon him. (*To the Major-Domo.*) Send for him. (*The three men stare at one another; but the Major-Domo goes out as if he had received the most matter-of-fact order.*) And (*to the retinue*) away with you all. (*The retinue withdraws, making obeisance.*)

(*A priest enters, carrying a miniature sphinx with a tiny tripod before it. A morsel of incense is smoking in the tripod. The priest comes to the table and places the image in the middle of it. The light begins to change to the magenta purple of the Egyptian sunset, as if the god had brought a strange colored shadow with him. The three men are determined not to be impressed; but they feel curious in spite of themselves.*)

CAESAR: What hocus-pocus is this?

CLEOPATRA: You shall see. And it is not hocus-pocus. To do it properly, we should kill something to please him; but perhaps he will answer Caesar without that if we spill some wine to him.

APOLLODORUS (*turning his head to look up over his shoulder at Ra*): Why not appeal to our hawkheaded friend here?

CLEOPATRA (*nervously*): Sh! He will hear you and be angry.

RUFIO (*phlegmatically*): The source of the Nile is out of his district, I expect.

CLEOPATRA: No: I will have my city named by nobody but my dear little sphinx, because it was in its arms that Caesar found me asleep. (*She languishes at Caesar then turns curtly to the priest.*) Go. I am a priestess, and have power to take your charge from you. (*The priest makes a reverence and goes out.*) Now let us call on the Nile all together. Perhaps he will rap on the table.

CAESAR: What! table rapping! Are such superstitions still believed in this year 707 of the Republic?

CLEOPATRA: It is no superstition: our priests learn lots of things from the tables. Is it not so, Apollodorus?

APOLLODORUS: Yes: I profess myself a converted man. When Cleopatra is priestess, Apollodorus is a devotee. Propose the conjuration.

CLEOPATRA: You must say with me "Send us thy voice, Father Nile."

ALL FOUR (*holding their glasses together before the idol*): Send us thy voice, Father Nile.

(*The death cry of a man in mortal terror and agony answers them. Appalled, the men set down their glasses, and listen. Silence. The purple deepens in the sky. Caesar, glancing at Cleopatra, catches her pouring out her wine before the god, with gleaming eyes, and mute assurances of gratitude and worship. Apollodorus springs up and runs to the edge of the roof to peer down and listen.*)

CAESAR (*looking piercingly at Cleopatra*): What was that?

CLEOPATRA (*petulantly*): Nothing. They are beating some slave.

CAESAR: Nothing.

RUFIO: A man with a knife in him, I'll swear.

CAESAR (*rising*): A murder!

APOLLODORUS (*at the back, waving his hand for silence*): S-sh! Silence. Did you hear that?

CAESAR: Another cry?

APOLLODORUS (*returning to the table*): No, a thud. Something fell on the beach, I think.

RUFIO (*grimly, as he rises*): Something with bones in it, eh?

CAESAR (*shuddering*): Hush, hush, Rufio. (*He leaves the table and returns to the colonnade: Rufio following at his left elbow, and Apollodorus at the other side.*)

CLEOPATRA (*still in her place at the table*): Will you leave me, Caesar? Apollodorus: are you going?

APOLLODORUS: Faith, dearest Queen, my appetite is gone.

CAESAR: Go down to the courtyard, Apollodorus; and find out what has happened.

(*Apollodorus nods and goes out, making for the staircase by which Rufio ascended.*)

CLEOPATRA: Your soldiers have killed somebody, perhaps. What does it matter?

(*The murmur of a crowd rises from the beach below. Caesar and Rufio look at one another.*)

CAESAR: This must be seen to. (*He is about to follow Apollodorus when Rufio stops him with a hand on his arm as Ftatateeta comes back by the far end of the roof, with dragging steps, a drowsy satiety in her eyes and in the corners of the bloodhound lips. For a moment Caesar suspects that she is drunk with wine. Not so Rufio: he knows well the red vintage that has inebriated her.*)

RUFIO (*in a low tone*): There is some mischief between these two.

FTATATEETA: The Queen looks again on the face of her servant.

(*Cleopatra looks at her for a moment with an exultant reflection of her murderous expression. Then she flings her arms round her; kisses her repeatedly and savagely; and tears off her jewels and heaps them on her. The two men turn from the spectacle to look at one another. Ftatateeta drags herself sleepily to the altar; kneels before Ra; and remains there in prayer. Caesar goes to Cleopatra, leaving Rufio in the colonnade.*)

CAESAR (*with searching earnestness*): Cleopatra: what has happened?

CLEOPATRA (*in mortal dread of him, but with her utmost cajolery*): Nothing, dearest Caesar. (*With sickly sweetness, her voice almost failing.*) Nothing. I am innocent. (*She approaches him affectionately.*) Dear Caesar: are you angry with me? Why do you look at me so? I have been here with you all the time. How can I know what has happened?

CAESAR (*reflectively*): That is true.

CLEOPATRA (*greatly relieved, trying to caress him*): Of course it is true. (*He does not respond to the caress.*) You know it is true, Rufio.

(*The murmur without suddenly swells to a roar and subsides.*)

RUFIO: I shall know presently. (*He makes for the altar in the burly trot that serves him for a stride, and touches Ftatateeta on the shoulder.*) Now, mistress: I shall want you. (*He orders her, with a gesture, to go before him.*)

FTATATEETA (*rising and glowering at him*): My place is with the Queen.

CLEOPATRA: She has done no harm, Rufio.

CAESAR (*to Rufio*): Let her stay.

RUFIO (*sitting down on the altar*): Very well. Then my place is here too; and you can see what is the matter for yourself. The city is in a pretty uproar, it seems.

CAESAR (*with grave displeasure*): Rufio: there is a time for obedience.

RUFIO: And there is a time for obstinacy. (*He folds his arms doggedly.*)

CAESAR (*to Cleopatra*): Send her away.

CLEOPATRA (*whining in her eagerness to propitiate him*): Yes, I will. I will do whatever you ask me, Caesar, always, because I love you. Ftatateeta: go away.

FTATATEETA: The Queen's word is my will. I shall be at hand for the Queen's call. (*She goes out past Ra, as she came.*)

RUFIO (*following her*): Remember, Caesar, your bodyguard is also within call. (*He follows her out.*)

(*Cleopatra, presuming upon Caesar's submission to Rufio, leaves the table and sits down on the bench in the colonnade.*)

CLEOPATRA: Why do you allow Rufio to treat you so? You should teach him his place.

CAESAR: Teach him to be my enemy, and to hide his thoughts from me as you are now hiding yours?

CLEOPATRA (*her fears returning*): Why do you say that, Caesar? Indeed, indeed, I am not hiding anything. You are wrong to treat me like this. (*She stifles a sob.*) I am only a child; and you turn into stone because you think some one has been killed. I cannot bear it. (*She purposely breaks down and weeps. He looks at her with profound sadness and complete coldness. She looks up to see what effect she is producing. Seeing that he is unmoved, she sits up, pretending to struggle with her emotion and to put it bravely away.*) But there: I know you hate tears: you shall not be troubled with them. I know you are not angry, but only sad; only I am so silly, I cannot help being hurt when you speak coldly. Of course you are quite right: it is dreadful to think of anyone being killed or even hurt; and I hope nothing really serious has—(*her voice dies away under his contemptuous penetration*).

CAESAR: What has frightened you into this? What have you done? (*A trumpet sounds on the beach below.*) Aha! that sounds like the answer.

CLEOPATRA (*sinking back trembling on the bench and covering her face with her hands*): I have not betrayed you, Caesar: I swear it.

CAESAR: I know that. I have not trusted you. (*He turns from her, and is about to go out when Apollodorus and Britannus drag in Lucius Septimius to him. Rufio follows. Caesar shudders.*) Again, Pompey's murderer!

RUFIO: The town has gone mad, I think. They are for tearing the palace down and driving us into the sea straight away. We laid hold of this renegade in clearing them out of the courtyard.

CAESAR: Release him. (*They let go his arms.*) What has offended the citizens, Lucius Septimius?

LUCIUS: What did you expect, Caesar? Pothinus was a favorite of theirs.

CAESAR: What has happened to Pothinus? I set him free, here, not half an hour ago. Did they not pass him out?

LUCIUS: Ay, through the gallery arch sixty feet above ground, with three inches of steel in his ribs. He is as dead as Pompey. We are quits now, as to killing—you and I.

CAESAR (*shocked*): Assassinated!—our prisoner, our guest! (*He turns reproachfully on Rufio.*) Rufio—

RUFIO (*emphatically—anticipating the question*): Whoever did it was a wise man and a friend of yours (*Cleopatra is greatly emboldened*); but none of us had a hand in it. So it is no use to frown at me. (*Caesar turns and looks at Cleopatra.*)

CLEOPATRA (*violently—rising*): He was slain by order of the Queen of Egypt. I am not Julius Caesar the dreamer, who allows every slave to insult him. Rufio has said I did well: now the others shall judge me too. (*She turns to the others.*) This Pothinus sought to make me conspire with him to betray Caesar to Achillas and Ptolemy. I refused; and he cursed me and came privily to Caesar to accuse me of his own treachery.

I caught him in the act; and he insulted me—me, the Queen! to my face. Caesar would not avenge me: he spoke him fair and set him free. Was I right to avenge myself? Speak, Lucius.

LUCIUS: I do not gainsay it. But you will get little thanks from Caesar for it.

CLEOPATRA: Speak, Apollodorus. Was I wrong?

APOLLODORUS: I have only one word of blame, most beautiful. You should have called upon me, your knight; and in a fair duel I should have slain the slanderer.

CLEOPATRA (*passionately*): I will be judged by your very slave, Caesar. Britannus: speak. Was I wrong?

BRITANNUS: Were treachery, falsehood, and disloyalty left unpunished, society must become like an arena full of wild beasts, tearing one another to pieces. Caesar is in the wrong.

CAESAR (*with quiet bitterness*): And so the verdict is against me, it seems.

CLEOPATRA (*vehemently*): Listen to me, Caesar. If one man in all Alexandria can be found to say that I did wrong, I swear to have myself crucified on the door of the palace by my own slaves.

CAESAR: If one man in all the world can be found, now or forever, to k n o w that you did wrong, that man will have either to conquer the world as I have, or be crucified by it. (*The uproar in the streets again reaches them.*) Do you hear? These knockers at your gate are also believers in vengeance and in stabbing. You have slain their leader: it is right that they shall slay you. If you doubt it, ask your four counsellors here. And then in the name of that right (*he emphasizes the word with great scorn*) shall I not slay them for murdering their Queen, and be slain in my turn by their countrymen as the invader of their fatherland? Can Rome do less then than slay these slayers, too, to shew the world how Rome avenges her sons and her honor. And so, to the end of history, murder shall breed murder, always in the name of right and honor and peace, until the gods are tired of blood and create a race that can understand. (*Fierce uproar. Cleopatra becomes white with terror.*) Hearken, you who must not be insulted. Go near enough to catch their words: you will find them bitterer than the tongue of Pothinus. (*Loftily, wrapping himself up in an impenetrable dignity.*) Let the Queen of Egypt now give her orders for vengeance, and take her measures for defence; for she has renounced Caesar. (*He turns to go.*)

CLEOPATRA (*terrified, running to him and falling on her knees*): You will not desert me, Caesar. You will defend the palace.

CAESAR: You have taken the powers of life and death upon you. I am only a dreamer.

CLEOPATRA: But they will kill me.

CAESAR: And why not?

CLEOPATRA: In pity—

CAESAR: Pity! What! has it come to this so suddenly, that nothing can save you now but pity? Did it save Pothinus?

(*She rises, wringing her hands, and goes back to the bench in despair. Apollodorus shews his sympathy with her by quietly posting himself behind the bench. The sky has by this time become the most vivid purple, and soon begins to change to a glowing pale orange, against which the colonnade and the great image shew darklier and darklier.*)

RUFIO: Caesar: enough of preaching. The enemy is at the gate.

CAESAR (*turning on him and giving way to his wrath*): Ay; and what has held him baffled at the gate all these months? Was it my folly, as you deem it, or your wisdom? In this Egyptian Red Sea of blood, whose hand has held all your heads above the waves? (*Turning on Cleopatra.*) And yet, when Caesar says to such an one, "Friend, go free," you, clinging for your little life to my sword, dare steal out and stab him in the back? And you, soldiers and gentlemen, and honest servants as you forget that you are, applaud this assassination, and say "Caesar is in the wrong." By the gods, I am tempted to open my hand and let you all sink into the flood.

CLEOPATRA (*with a ray of cunning hope*): But, Caesar, if you do, you will perish yourself.

(*Caesar's eyes blaze.*)

RUFIO (*greatly alarmed*): Now, by great Jove, you filthy little Egyptian rat, that is the very word to make him walk out alone into the city and leave us here to be cut to pieces. (*Desperately, to Caesar.*) Will you desert us because we are a parcel of fools? I mean no harm by killing: I do it as a cat, by instinct. We are all dogs at your heels; but we have served you faithfully.

CAESAR (*relenting*): Alas, Rufio, my son, my son: as dogs we are like to perish now in the streets.

APOLLODORUS (*at his post behind Cleopatra's seat*): Caesar: what you say has an Olympian ring in it: it must be right; for it is fine art. But I am still on the side of Cleopatra. If we must die, she shall not want the devotion of a man's heart nor the strength of a man's arm.

CLEOPATRA (*sobbing*): But I dont want to die.

CAESAR (*sadly*): Oh, ignoble, ignoble!

LUCIUS (*coming forward between Caesar and Cleopatra*): Hearken to me, Caesar. It may be ignoble; but I also mean to live as long as I can.

CAESAR: Well, my friend, you are likely to outlive Caesar. Is it any magic of mine, think you, that has kept your army and this whole city at bay for so long? Yesterday, what quarrel had they with me that they should risk their lives against me? But today we have flung them down their hero, murdered; and now every man of them is set upon clearing out this nest of assassins—for such we are and no more. Take courage then; and sharpen your sword. Pompey's head has fallen; and Caesar's head is ripe.

APOLLODORUS: Does Caesar despair?

CAESAR (*with infinite pride*): He who has never hoped can never despair. Caesar, in good or bad fortune, looks his fate in the face.

LUCIUS: Look it in the face, then; and it will smile as it always has on Caesar.

CAESAR (*with involuntary haughtiness*): Do you presume to encourage me?

LUCIUS: I offer you my services. I will change sides if you will have me.

CAESAR (*suddenly coming down to earth again, and looking sharply at him, divining that there is something behind the offer*): What! At this point?

LUCIUS (*firmly*): At this point.

RUFIO: Do you suppose Caesar is mad, to trust you?

LUCIUS: I do not ask him to trust me until he is victorious. I ask for my life, and for a command in Caesar's army. And since Caesar is a fair dealer, I will pay in advance.

CAESAR: Pay! How?

LUCIUS: With a piece of good news for you.

(*Caesar divines the news in a flash.*)

RUFIO: What news?

CAESAR (*with an elate and buoyant energy which makes Cleopatra sit up and stare*): What news! What news, did you say, my son Rufio? The relief has arrived: what other news remains for us? Is it not so, Lucius Septimius? Mithridates of Pergamos is on the march.

LUCIUS: He has taken Pelusium.

CAESAR (*delighted*): Lucius Septimius: you are henceforth my officer. Rufio: the Egyptians must have sent every soldier from the city to prevent Mithridates crossing the Nile. There is nothing in the streets now but mob—mob!

LUCIUS: It is so. Mithridates is marching by the great road to Memphis to cross above the Delta. Achillas will fight him there.

CAESAR (*all audacity*): Achillas shall fight Caesar there. See, Rufio. (*He runs to the table; snatches a napkin; and draws a plan on it with his finger dipped in wine, whilst Rufio and Lucius Septimius crowd about him to watch, all looking closely, for the light is now almost gone.*) Here is the palace (*pointing to his plan*): here is the theatre. You (*to Rufio*) take twenty men and pretend to go by that street (*pointing it out*); and whilst they are stoning you, out go the cohorts by this and this. My streets are right, are they, Lucius?

LUCIUS: Ay, that is the fig market—

CAESAR (*too much excited to listen to him*): I saw them the day we arrived. Good! (*He throws the napkin on the table, and comes down again into the colonnade.*) Away, Britannus: tell Petronius that within an hour half our forces must take ship for the western lake. See to my horse and armor. (*Britannus runs out.*) With the rest, I shall march round the lake and up the Nile to meet Mithridates. Away, Lucius; and give the word. (*Lucius hurries out after Britannus.*) Apollodorus: lend me your sword and your right arm for this campaign.

APOLLODORUS: Ay, and my heart and life to boot.

CAESAR (*grasping his hand*): I accept both. (*Mighty handshake.*) Are you ready for work?

APOLLODORUS: Ready for Art—the Art of War (*he rushes out after Lucius, totally forgetting Cleopatra*).

RUFIO: Come! this is something like business.

CAESAR (*buoyantly*): Is it not, my only son? (*He claps his hands. The slaves hurry in to the table.*) No more of this mawkish revelling: away with all this stuff: shut it out of my sight and be off with you. (*The slaves begin to remove the table; and the curtains are drawn, shutting in the colonnade.*) You understand about the streets, Rufio?

RUFIO: Ay, I think I do. I will get through them, at all events.

(*The bucina sounds busily in the courtyard beneath.*)

CAESAR: Come, then: we must talk to the troops and hearten them. You down to the beach: I to the courtyard. (*He makes for the staircase.*)

CLEOPATRA (*rising from her seat, where she has been quite neglected all this time, and stretching out her hands timidly to him*): Caesar.

CAESAR (*turning*): Eh?

CLEOPATRA: Have you forgotten me?

CAESAR (*indulgently*): I am busy now, my child, busy. When I return your affairs shall be settled. Farewell; and be good and patient.

(*He goes, preoccupied and quite indifferent. She stands with clenched fists, in speechless rage and humiliation.*)

RUFIO: That game is played and lost, Cleopatra. The woman always gets the worst of it.

CLEOPATRA (*haughtily*): Go. Follow your master.

RUFIO (*in her ear, with rough familiarity*): A word first. Tell your executioner that if Pothinus had been properly killed— i n t h e t h r o a t—he would not have called out. Your man bungled his work.

CLEOPATRA (*enigmatically*): How do you know it was a man?

RUFIO (*startled, and puzzled*): It was not you: you were with us when it happened. (*She turns her back scornfully on him. He shakes his head, and draws the curtains to go out. It is now a magnificent moonlit night. The table has been removed. Ftatateeta is seen in the light of the moon and stars, again in prayer before the white altar-stone of Ra. Rufio starts; closes the curtains again softly; and says in a low voice to Cleopatra:*) Was it she? with her own hand?

CLEOPATRA (*threateningly*): Whoever it was, let my enemies beware of her. Look to it, Rufio, you who dare make the Queen of Egypt a fool before Caesar.

RUFIO (*looking grimly at her*): I will look to it, Cleopatra. (*He nods in confirmation of the promise, and slips out through the curtains, loosening his sword in its sheath as he goes.*)

ROMAN SOLDIERS (*in the courtyard below*): Hail, Caesar! Hail, hail!

(CLEOPATRA *listens. The bucina sounds again, followed by several trumpets.*)

CLEOPATRA (*wringing her hands and calling*): Ftatateeta. Ftatateeta. It is dark; and I am alone. Come to me. (*Silence.*) Ftatateeta. (*Louder.*) Ftatateeta. (*Silence. In a panic she snatches the cord and pulls the curtains apart.*)

(*Ftatateeta is lying dead on the altar of Ra, with her throat cut. Her blood deluges the white stone.*)

ACT V

High noon. Festival and military pageant on the esplanade before the palace. In the east harbor Caesar's galley, so gorgeously decorated that it seems to be rigged with flowers, is alongside the quay, close to the steps Apollodorus descended when he embarked with the carpet. A Roman guard is posted there in charge of a gangway, whence a red floorcloth is laid down the middle of the esplanade, turning off to the north opposite the central gate in the palace front, which shuts in the esplanade on the south side. The broad steps of the gate, crowded with Cleopatra's ladies, all in their gayest attire, are like a flower garden. The façade is lined by her guard, officered by the same gallants to whom Bel Affris announced the coming of Caesar six months before in the old palace on the Syrian border. The north side is lined by Roman soldiers, with the townsfolk on tiptoe behind them, peering over their heads at the cleared esplanade, in which the officers stroll about, chatting. Among these are Belzanor and the Persian; also the centurion, vinewood cudgel in hand, battle worn, thick-booted, and much outshone, both socially and decoratively, by the Egyptian officers.

Apollodorus makes his way through the townsfolk and calls to the officers from behind the Roman line.

APOLLODORUS: Hullo! May I pass?

CENTURION: Pass Apollodorus the Sicilian there! (*The soldiers let him through.*)

BELZANOR: Is Caesar at hand?

APOLLODORUS: Not yet. He is still in the market place. I could not stand any more of the roaring of the soldiers! After half an hour of the enthusiasm of an army, one feels the need of a little sea air.

PERSIAN: Tell us the news. Hath he slain the priests?

APOLLODORUS: Not he. They met him in the market place with ashes on their heads and their gods in their hands. They placed the gods at his feet. The only one that was worth looking at was Apis: a miracle of gold and ivory work. By my advice he offered the chief priest two talents for it.

BELZANOR (*appalled*): Apis the all-knowing for two talents! What said the chief priest?

APOLLODORUS: He invoked the mercy of Apis, and asked for five.

BELZANOR: There will be famine and tempest in the land for this.

PERSIAN: Pooh! Why did not Apis cause Caesar to be vanquished by Achillas? Any fresh news from the war, Apollodorus?

APOLLODORUS: The little King Ptolemy was drowned.

BELZANOR: Drowned! How?

APOLLODORUS: With the rest of them. Caesar attacked them from three sides at once and swept them into the Nile. Ptolemy's barge sank.

BELZANOR: A marvellous man, this Caesar! Will he come soon, think you?

APOLLODORUS: He was settling the Jewish question when I left.

(*A flourish of trumpets from the north, and commotion among the townsfolk, announces the approach of Caesar.*)

PERSIAN: He has made short work of them. Here he comes. (*He hurries to his post in front of the Egyptian lines.*)

BELZANOR (*following him*): Ho there! Caesar comes.

(*The soldiers stand at attention, and dress their lines. Apollodorus goes to the Egyptian line.*)

CENTURION (*hurrying to the gangway guard*): Attention there! Caesar comes.

(*Caesar arrives in state with Rufio: Britannus following. The soldiers receive him with enthusiastic shouting.*)

CAESAR: I see my ship awaits me. The hour of Caesar's farewell to Egypt has arrived. And now, Rufio, what remains to be done before I go?

RUFIO (*at his left hand*): You have not yet appointed a Roman governor for this province.

CAESAR (*looking whimsically at him, but speaking with perfect gravity*): What say you to Mithridates of Pergamos, my reliever and rescuer, the great son of Eupator?

RUFIO: Why, that you will want him elsewhere. Do you forget that you have some three or four armies to conquer on your way home?

CAESAR: Indeed! Well, what say you to yourself?

RUFIO (*incredulously*): I! I a governor! What are you dreaming of? Do you not know that I am only the son of a freedman?

CAESAR (*affectionately*): Has not Caesar called you his son? (*Calling to the whole assembly.*) Peace awhile there; and hear me.

THE ROMAN SOLDIERS: Hear Caesar.

CAESAR: Hear the service, quality, rank and name of the Roman governor. By service, Caesar's shield; by quality, Caesar's friend; by rank, a Roman soldier. (*The Roman soldiers give a triumphant shout.*) By name, Rufio. (*They shout again.*)

RUFIO (*kissing Caesar's hand*): Ay: I am Caesar's shield; but of what use shall I be when I am no longer on Caesar's arm? Well, no matter—(*He becomes husky, and turns away to recover himself.*)

CAESAR: Where is that British Islander of mine?

BRITANNUS (*coming forward on Caesar's right hand*): Here, Caesar.

CAESAR: Who bade you, pray, thrust yourself into the battle of the Delta, uttering the barbarous cries of your native land, and affirming yourself a match for any four of the Egyptians, to whom you applied unseemly epithets?

BRITANNUS: Caesar: I ask you to excuse the language that escaped me in the heat of the moment.

CAESAR: And how did you, who cannot swim, cross the canal with us when we stormed the camp?

BRITANNUS: Caesar: I clung to the tail of your horse.

CAESAR: These are not the deeds of a slave, Britannus, but of a free man.

BRITANNUS: Caesar: I was born free.

CAESAR: But they call you Caesar's slave.

BRITANNUS: Only as Caesar's slave have I found real freedom.

CAESAR (*moved*): Well said. Ungrateful that I am, I was about to set you free; but now I will not part from you for a million talents. (*He claps him friendly on the shoulder. Britannus, gratified, but a trifle shamefaced, takes his hand and kisses it sheepishly.*)

BELZANOR (*to the Persian*): This Roman knows how to make men serve him.

PERSIAN: Ay: men too humble to become dangerous rivals to him.

BELZANOR: O subtle one! O cynic!

CAESAR (*seeing Apollodorus in the Egyptian corner, and calling to him*): Apollodorus: I leave the art of Egypt in your charge. Remember: Rome loves art and will encourage it ungrudgingly.

APOLLODORUS: I understand, Caesar. Rome will produce no art itself; but it will buy up and take away whatever the other nations produce.

CAESAR: What! Rome produce no art! Is peace not an art? is war not an art? is government not an art? is civilization not an art? All these we give you in exchange for a few ornaments. You will have the best of the bargain. (*Turning to Rufio.*)

And now, what else have I to do before I embark? (*Trying to recollect.*) There is something I cannot remember: what can it be? Well, well: it must remain undone: we must not waste this favorable wind. Farewell, Rufio.

RUFIO: Caesar: I am loth to let you go to Rome without your shield. There are too many daggers there.

CAESAR: It matters not: I shall finish my life's work on my way back; and then I shall have lived long enough. Besides: I have always disliked the idea of dying: I had rather be killed. Farewell.

RUFIO (*with a sigh, raising his hands and giving Caesar up as incorrigible*): Farewell. (*They shake hands.*)

CAESAR (*waving his hand to Apollodorus*): Farewell, Apollodorus, and my friends, all of you. Aboard!

(*The gangway is run out from the quay to the ship. As Caesar moves towards it, Cleopatra, cold and tragic, cunningly dressed in black, without ornaments or decoration of any kind, and thus making a striking figure among the brilliantly dressed bevy of ladies as she passes through it, comes from the palace and stands on the steps. Caesar does not see her until she speaks.*)

CLEOPATRA: Has Cleopatra no part in this leavetaking?

CAESAR (*enlightened*): Ah, I knew there was something. (*To Rufio.*) How could you let me forget her, Rufio? (*Hastening to her.*) Had I gone without seeing you, I should never have forgiven myself. (*He takes her hands, and brings her into the middle of the esplanade. She submits stonily.*) Is this mourning for me?

CLEOPATRA: No.

CAESAR (*remorsefully*): Ah, that was thoughtless of me! It is for your brother.

CLEOPATRA: No.

CAESAR: For whom, then?

CLEOPATRA: Ask the Roman governor whom you have left us.

CAESAR: Rufio?

CLEOPATRA: Yes: Rufio. (*She points at him with deadly scorn.*) He who is to rule here in Caesar's name, in Caesar's way, according to Caesar's boasted laws of life.

CAESAR (*dubiously*): He is to rule as he can, Cleopatra. He has taken the work upon him, and will do it in his own way.

CLEOPATRA: Not in your way, then?

CAESAR (*puzzled*): What do you mean by my way?

CLEOPATRA: Without punishment. Without revenge. Without judgment.

CAESAR (*approvingly*): Ay: that is the right way, the great way, the only possible way in the end. (*To Rufio.*) Believe it, Rufio, if you can.

RUFIO: Why, I believe it, Caesar. You have convinced me of it long ago. But look you. You are sailing for Numidia today. Now tell me: if you meet a hungry lion there, you will not punish it for wanting to eat you?

CAESAR (*wondering what he is driving at*): No.

RUFIO: Nor revenge upon it the blood of those it has already eaten.

CAESAR: No.

RUFIO: Nor judge it for its guiltiness.

CAESAR: No.

RUFIO: What, then, will you do to save your life from it?

CAESAR (*promptly*): Kill it, man, without malice, just as it would kill me. What does this parable of the lion mean?

RUFIO: Why, Cleopatra had a tigress that killed men at her bidding. I thought she might bid it kill you some day. Well, had I not been Caesar's pupil, what pious things might I not have done to that tigress! I might have punished it. I might have revenged Pothinus on it.

CAESAR (*interjects*): Pothinus!

RUFIO (*continuing*): I might have judged it. But I put all these follies behind me; and, without malice, only cut its throat. And that is why Cleopatra comes to you in mourning.

CLEOPATRA (*vehemently*): He has shed the blood of my servant Ftatateeta. On your head be it as upon his, Caesar, if you hold him free of it.

CAESAR (*energetically*): On my head be it, then; for it was well done. Rufio: had you set yourself in the seat of the judge, and with hateful ceremonies and appeals to the gods handed that woman over to some hired executioner to be slain before the people in the name of justice, never again would I have touched your hand without a shudder. But this was natural slaying: I feel no horror at it.

(*Rufio, satisfied, nods at Cleopatra, mutely inviting her to mark that.*)

CLEOPATRA (*pettish and childish in her impotence*): No: not when a Roman slays an Egyptian. All the world will now see how unjust and corrupt Caesar is.

CAESAR (*taking her hands coaxingly*): Come: do not be angry with me. I am sorry for that poor Totateeta. (*She laughs in spite of herself.*) Aha! you are laughing. Does that mean reconciliation?

CLEOPATRA (*angry with herself for laughing*): No, no, NO!! But it is so ridiculous to hear you call her Totateeta.

CAESAR: What! As much a child as ever, Cleopatra! Have I not made a woman of you after all?

CLEOPATRA: Oh, it is you who are a great baby: you make me seem silly because you will not behave seriously. But you have treated me badly; and I do not forgive you.

CAESAR: Bid me farewell.

CLEOPATRA: I will not.

CAESAR (*coaxing*): I will send you a beautiful present from Rome.

CLEOPATRA (*proudly*): Beauty from Rome to Egypt indeed! What can Rome give me that Egypt cannot give me?

APOLLODORUS: That is true, Caesar. If the present is to be really beautiful, I shall have to buy it for you in Alexandria.

CAESAR: You are forgetting the treasures for which Rome is most famous, my friend. You cannot buy them in Alexandria.

APOLLODORUS: What are they, Caesar?

CAESAR: Her sons. Come, Cleopatra: forgive me and bid me farewell; and I will send you a man, Roman from head to heel and Roman of the noblest; not old and ripe for the knife; not lean in the arms and cold in the heart; not hiding a bald head under his conqueror's laurels; not stooped with the weight of the world on his shoulders; but brisk and fresh, strong and young, hoping in the morning, fighting in the day, and revelling in the evening. Will you take such an one in exchange for Caesar?

CLEOPATRA (*palpitating*): His name, his name?

CAESAR: Shall it be Mark Antony? (*She throws herself into his arms.*)

RUFIO: You are a bad hand at a bargain, mistress, if you will swop Caesar for Antony.

CAESAR: So now you are satisfied.

CLEOPATRA: You will not forget.

CAESAR: I will not forget. Farewell: I do not think we shall meet again. Farewell. (*He kisses her on the forehead. She is much affected and begins to sniff. He embarks.*)

THE ROMAN SOLDIERS (*as he sets his foot on the gangway*): Hail, Caesar; and farewell!

(*He reaches the ship and returns Rufio's wave of the hand.*)

APOLLODORUS (*to Cleopatra*): No tears, dearest Queen: they stab your servant to the heart. He will return some day.

CLEOPATRA: I hope not. But I cant help crying, all the same. (*She waves her handkerchief to Caesar; and the ship begins to move.*)

THE ROMAN SOLDIERS (*drawing their swords and raising them in the air*): Hail, Caesar!

ST. AUGUSTINE was born Aurelius Augustinus in 354 in Thagaste, a town in what is now Algeria in North Africa. Monica, the mother of Augustine, was a devout Catholic who was eventually recognized as a saint. Augustine's father, however, converted to Catholicism only a year before his death. Augustine was not baptized until he was thirty-two. As a boy, he distinguished himself at local schools, then studied and taught rhetoric in Carthage. There Augustine joined the membership of the Manicheans, a religious sect; took a mistress; and had a child with her out of wedlock. He later regarded this period of his life as one of great sins. He left Africa for Italy in 383. Due partly to the influence of St. Ambrose, who was then bishop of Milan, he was baptized a Catholic in 387, to the joy of his mother, who died soon after. Augustine returned to Africa, where he established a monastic community (his illegitimate son was among its first members), and served for the rest of his life as a priest and as bishop of the diocese of Hippo. Augustine wrote prolifically with the help of stenographers: four hundred sermons and two hundred letters remain, as well as voluminous commentary on the Psalms, *The Confessions, The City of God,* and other works. Augustine also devoted many words to the repair of doctrinal dissension in the church. He became renowned, and his influence grew after his death in 430, helping to shape the doctrines of St. Thomas Aquinas and John Calvin and, through them, the future of both the Catholic and the Protestant faiths.

From *The City of God,* translated by Marcus Dods, D.D. Publisher: The Modern Library, Random House, Inc., 1950. Pages 441–77.

The City of God

BOOK XIV

We have already stated in the preceding books that God, desiring not only that the human race might be able by their similarity of nature to associate with one another, but also that they might be bound together in harmony and peace by the ties of relationship, was pleased to derive all men from one individual, and created man with such a nature that the members of the race should not have died, had not the two first (of whom the one was created out of nothing, and the other out of him) merited this by their disobedience; for by them so great a sin was committed, that by it the human nature was altered for the worse, and was transmitted also to their posterity, liable to sin and subject to death. And the kingdom of death so reigned over men, that the deserved penalty of sin would have hurled all headlong even into the second death, of which there is no end, had not the undeserved grace of God saved some therefrom. And thus it has come to pass, that though there are very many and great nations all over the earth, whose rites and customs, speech, arms, and dress, are distinguished by marked differences, yet there are no more than two kinds of human society, which we may justly call two cities, according to the language of our Scriptures. The one consists of those who wish to live after the flesh, the other of those who wish to live after the spirit; and when they severally achieve what they wish, they live in peace, each after their kind.

171

First, we must see what it is to live after the flesh, and what to live after the spirit. For anyone who either does not recollect, or does not sufficiently weigh, the language of sacred Scripture, may, on first hearing what we have said, suppose that the Epicurean philosophers live after the flesh, because they place man's highest good in bodily pleasure; and that those others do so who have been of opinion that in some form or other bodily good is man's supreme good; and that the mass of men do so who, without dogmatizing or philosophizing on the subject, are so prone to lust that they cannot delight in any pleasure save such as they receive from bodily sensations: and he may suppose that the Stoics, who place the supreme good of men in the soul, live after the spirit; for what is man's soul, if not spirit? But in the sense of the divine Scripture both are proved to live after the flesh. For by flesh it means not only the body of a terrestrial and mortal animal . . . but uses this word in many other significations. . . .

Since, then, Scripture uses the word flesh in many ways, which there is not time to collect and investigate, if we are to ascertain what it is to live after the flesh (which is certainly evil, though the nature of flesh is not itself evil), we must carefully examine that passage of the epistle which the Apostle Paul wrote to the Galatians, in which he says, "Now the works of the flesh are manifest, which are these: adultery, fornication, uncleanness, lasciviousness, idolatry, witchcraft, hatred, variance, emulations, wrath, strife, seditions, heresies, envyings, murders, drunkenness, revellings, and such like: of the which I tell you before, as I have also told you in time past, that they which do such things shall not inherit the kingdom of God." This whole passage of the apostolic epistle being considered, so far as it bears on the matter in hand, will be sufficient to answer the question, what it is to live after the flesh. For among the works of the flesh which he said were manifest, and which he cited for condemnation, we find not only those which concern the pleasure of the flesh, as fornications, uncleanness, lasciviousness, drunkenness, revellings, but also those which, though they be remote from fleshly pleasure, reveal the vices of the soul. For who does not see that idolatries, witchcrafts, hatreds, variance, emulations, wrath, strife, heresies, envyings, are vices rather of the soul than of the flesh? . . .

But if anyone says that the flesh is the cause of all vices and ill conduct, inasmuch as the soul lives wickedly only because it is moved by the flesh, it is certain he has not carefully considered the whole nature of man. For "the corruptible body, indeed, weigheth down the soul." . . . We are then burdened with this corruptible body; but knowing that the cause of this burdensomeness is not the nature and substance of the body, but its corruption, we do not desire to be deprived of the body, but to be clothed with its immortality. For then, also, there will be a body, but it shall no longer be a burden, being no longer corruptible. . . .

For the corruption of the body, which weighs down the soul, is not the cause but the punishment of the first sin; and it was not the corruptible flesh that made the soul sinful, but the sinful soul that made the flesh corruptible. And though from this corruption of the flesh there arise certain incitements to vice, and indeed vicious desires, yet we must not attribute to the flesh all the vices of a wicked life, in case we thereby clear the devil of all these, for he has no flesh. For though we cannot call the devil a fornicator or drunkard, or ascribe to him any sensual indulgence (though he is the secret instigator and prompter of those who sin in these ways), yet he is exceedingly proud and envious. And this viciousness has so possessed him, that on account of it he is reserved in chains of darkness to everlasting punishment. Now these vices, which have dominion over the devil, the apostle attributes to the flesh, which certainly the devil has not. For he says, "hatred, variance, emulations, strife, envying" are the works of the flesh; and of all these evils pride is the origin and head, and it rules in the devil though he has no flesh. . . . For it is not by having flesh, which the devil has not, but by living according to himself—that is, according to man —that man became like the devil. For the devil, too, wished to live according to himself when he did not abide in the truth; so that when he lied, this was not of God, but of himself, who is not only a liar, but the father of lies, he being the first who lied, and the originator of lying as of sin.

When, therefore, man lives according to man, not according to God, he is like the devil. Because not even an angel might live according to an angel, but only according to God, if he was to abide in the truth, and speak God's truth and not his own lie. . . . When a man lives according to the truth, he lives not according to himself, but according to God; for He was God who said, "I am the truth." When, therefore, man lives according to himself—that is, according to man, not according to God—assuredly he lives according to a lie; not that man himself is a lie, for God is his author and creator, who is certainly not the author and creator of a lie, but because man was made upright, that he might not live according to himself, but according to Him that made him—in other words, that he might do His will and not his own; and not to live as he was made to live, that is a lie. For he certainly desires to be blessed even by not living so that he may be blessed. And what is a lie if this desire be not? Wherefore it is not without meaning said that all sin is a lie. For no sin is committed save by that desire or will by which we desire that it be well with us, and shrink from it being ill with us. That, therefore, is a lie which we do in order that it may be well with us, but which makes us more miserable than we were. And why is this, but because the source of man's happiness lies only in God, whom he abandons when he sins, and not in himself, by living according to whom he sins?

In enunciating this proposition of ours, then, that because some live according to the flesh and others according to the spirit there have arisen two diverse and conflicting cities, we might equally well have said, "because some live according to man, others according to God." . . .

There is no need, therefore, that in our sins and vices we accuse the nature of the flesh to the injury of the Creator, for in its own kind and degree the flesh is good; but to desert the Creator good, and live according to the created good, is not good, whether a man choose to live according to the flesh, or according to the soul, or according to the whole human nature, which is composed of flesh and soul, and which is therefore spoken of either by the name flesh alone, or by the name soul alone. For he who extols the nature of the soul as the chief good, and condemns the nature of the flesh as if it were evil, assuredly is fleshly both in his love of the soul and hatred of the flesh; for these his feelings arise from human fancy, not from divine truth. The Platonists, indeed, are not so foolish as, with the Manichaeans, to detest our present bodies as an evil nature; for they attribute all the elements of which this visible and tangible world is compacted, with all their qualities, to God their Creator. Nevertheless, from the death-infected members and earthly construction of the body they believe the soul is so affected, that there are thus originated in it the diseases of desires, and fears, and joy, and sorrow, under which four perturbations, as Cicero calls them, or passions, as most prefer to name them with the Greeks, is included the whole viciousness of human life. But if this be so, how is it that Aeneas in Virgil, when he had heard from his father in Hades that the souls should return to bodies, expresses surprise at this declaration, and exclaims:

"O father! and can thought conceive
That happy souls this realm would leave,
            And seek the upper sky,
With sluggish clay to reunite?
This direful longing for the light,
            Whence comes it, say, and why?"

This direful longing, then, does it still exist even in that boasted purity of the disembodied spirits, and does it still proceed from the death-infected members and earthly limbs? Does he not assert that, when they begin to long to return to the body, they have already been delivered from all these so-called pestilences of the body? From which we gather that, were this endlessly alternating purification and defilement of departing and returning souls as true as it is most certainly false, yet it could not be averred that all culpable and vicious motions of the soul originate in the earthly body; for, on their own showing, "this direful longing," to use the words of their noble exponent, is so extraneous to the body, that it moves the soul that is purged of all bodily taint, and is existing apart from any body whatever, and moves it, moreover, to be embodied again. So that even they themselves acknowledge that the soul is not only moved to desire, fear, joy, sorrow, by the flesh, but that it can also be agitated with these emotions at its own instance.

But the character of the human will is of moment; because, if it is wrong, these motions of the soul will be wrong, but if it is right, they will be not merely blameless, but even praiseworthy. For the will is in them all; yea, none of them is anything else than will. For what are desire and joy but a volition of consent to the things we wish? And what are fear and sadness but a volition of aversion from the things which we do not wish? But when consent takes the form of seeking to possess the things we wish, this is called desire; and when consent takes the form of enjoying the things we wish, this is called joy. In like manner, when we turn with aversion from that which we do not wish to happen, this volition is termed fear; and when we turn away from that which has happened against our will, this act of will is called sorrow. And generally in respect of all that we seek or shun, as a man's will is attracted or repelled, so it is changed and turned into these different affections. Wherefore the man who lives according to God, and not according to man, ought to be a lover of good, and therefore a hater of evil. And since no one is evil by nature, but whoever is evil is evil by vice, he who lives according to God ought to cherish towards evil men a perfect hatred, so that he shall neither hate the man because of his vice, nor love the vice because of the man, but hate the vice and love the man. For the vice being cursed, all that ought to be loved, and nothing that ought to be hated, will remain.

He who resolves to love God, and to love his neighbour as himself, not according to man but according to God, is on account of this love said to be of a good will; and this is in Scripture more commonly called charity, but it is also, even in the same books, called love. . . .

The right will is, therefore, well-directed love, and the wrong will is ill-directed love. Love, then, yearning to have what is loved, is desire; and having and enjoying it, is joy; fleeing what is opposed to it, is fear; and feeling what is opposed to it, when it has befallen it, is sadness. Now these motions are evil if the love is evil; good if the love is good. . . .

Those emotions which the Greeks call εὐπαθείαι, and which Cicero calls *constantiae,* the Stoics would restrict to three; and, instead of three "perturbations" in the soul of the wise man, they substituted severally, in place of desire, will; in place of joy, contentment; and for fear, caution; and as to sickness or pain, which we, to avoid ambiguity, preferred to call sorrow, they denied that it could exist in the mind of a wise man. Will, they say, seeks the good, for this the wise man does. Contentment has its object in good that is possessed, and this the wise man continually possesses. Caution avoids evil, and this the wise man ought to avoid. But sorrow arises from evil that has already happened; and as they suppose that no evil can happen to the wise man, there can be no representative of sorrow in his mind. According to them, therefore, none but the wise man wills, is contented, uses caution; and that the fool can do no more than desire, rejoice, fear, be sad. . . .

So that good and bad men alike will, are cautious, and contented; or, to say the same thing in other words, good and bad men alike desire, fear, rejoice, but the former in a good, the latter in a bad fashion, according as the will is right or wrong. Sorrow itself, too, which the Stoics would not allow to be represented in the mind of the wise man, is used in a good sense, and especially in our writings. . . . "For godly sorrow worketh repentance to salvation not to be repented of, but the sorrow of the world worketh death. For, behold, this selfsame thing that ye sorrowed after a godly sort, what carefulness it wrought in you!" [2 Corinthians.] Consequently the Stoics may defend themselves by replying, that sorrow is indeed useful for repentance of sin, but that this can have no place in the mind of the wise man, inasmuch as no sin attaches to him of which he could sorrowfully repent, nor any other evil the endurance or experience of which could make him sorrowful. For they say that Alcibiades (if my memory does not deceive me), who believed himself happy, shed tears when Socrates argued with him, and demonstrated that he was miserable because he was foolish. In his case, therefore, folly was the cause of this useful and desirable sorrow, wherewith a man mourns that he is what he ought not to be. But the Stoics maintain not that the fool, but that the wise man, cannot be sorrowful.

But so far as regards this question of mental perturbations, we have answered these philosophers in the ninth book of this work, showing that it is rather a verbal than a real dispute, and that they seek contention rather than truth. Among ourselves, according to the sacred Scriptures and sound doctrine, the citizens of the holy city of God, who live according to God in the pilgrimage of this life, both fear and desire, and grieve and rejoice. And because their love is rightly placed, all these affections of theirs are right. They fear eternal punishment, they desire eternal life; they grieve because they themselves groan within themselves, waiting for the adoption, the redemption of their body; they rejoice in hope, because there "shall be brought to pass the saying that is written, Death is swallowed up in victory." In like manner they fear to sin, they desire to persevere; they grieve in sin, they rejoice in good works. They fear to sin, because they hear that "because iniquity shall abound, the love of many shall wax cold." They desire to persevere, because they hear that it is written, "He that endureth to the end shall be saved." They grieve for sin, hearing that "If we say that we have no sin, we deceive ourselves, and the truth is not in us." They rejoice in good works, because they hear that "the Lord loveth a cheerful giver." In like manner, according as they are strong or weak, they fear or desire to be tempted, grieve or rejoice in temptation. . . .

And not only on their own account do they experience these emotions, but also on account of those whose deliverance they desire and whose perdition they fear, and whose loss or salvation affects them with grief or with joy. . . .

If these emotions and affections, arising as they do from the love of what is good and from a holy charity, are to be called vices, then let us allow these emotions which are truly vices to pass under the name of virtues. But since these affections, when they are exercised in a becoming way, follow the guidance of right reason, who will dare to say that they are diseases or vicious

passions? Wherefore even the Lord Himself, when He conde-
scended to lead a human life in the form of a slave, had no sin
whatever, and yet exercised these emotions where He judged
they should be exercised. For as there was in Him a true human
body and a true human soul, so was there also a true human
emotion. When, therefore, we read in the Gospel that the hard-
heartedness of the Jews moved Him to sorrowful indignation,
that He said, "I am glad for your sakes, to the intent ye may
believe," that when about to raise Lazarus He even shed tears,
that He earnestly desired to eat the passover with His disciples,
that as His passion drew near His soul was sorrowful, these
emotions are certainly not falsely ascribed to Him. But as He
became man when it pleased Him, so, in the grace of His definite
purpose, when it pleased Him He experienced those emotions
in His human soul.

But we must further make the admission, that even when
these affections are well regulated, and according to God's will,
they are peculiar to this life, not to that future life we look for,
and that often we yield to them against our will. And thus
sometimes we weep in spite of ourselves, being carried beyond
ourselves, not indeed by culpable desire, but by praiseworthy
charity. In us, therefore, these affections arise from human infirmity; but it was not so with the Lord Jesus, for even His
infirmity was the consequence of His power. But so long as we
wear the infirmity of this life, we are rather worse men than
better if we have none of these emotions at all. For the apostle
vituperated and abominated some who, as he said, were "without natural affection." The sacred Psalmist also found fault with
those of whom he said, "I looked for some to lament with me,
and there was none." For to be quite free from pain while we
are in this place of misery is only purchased . . . at the price of
blunted sensibilities both of mind and body. And therefore that
which the Greeks call ἀπάθεια, and what the Latins would
call, if their language would allow them, "impassibilitas," if it

be taken to mean an impassibility of spirit and not of body, or, in other words, a freedom from those emotions which are contrary to reason and disturb the mind, then it is obviously a good and most desirable quality, but it is not one which is attainable in this life. For the words of the apostle are the confession, not of the common herd, but of the eminently pious, just, and holy men: "If we say we have no sin, we deceive ourselves, and the truth is not in us." When there shall be no sin in a man, then there shall be this [impassibility]. At present it is enough if we live without crime; and he who thinks he lives without sin puts aside not sin, but pardon. And if that is to be called apathy, where the mind is the subject of no emotion, then who would not consider this insensibility to be worse than all vices? It may, indeed, reasonably be maintained that the perfect blessedness we hope for shall be free from all sting of fear or sadness; but who that is not quite lost to truth would say that neither love nor joy shall be experienced there? But if by apathy a condition be meant in which no fear terrifies nor any pain annoys, we must in this life renounce such a state if we would live according to God's will, but may hope to enjoy it in that blessedness which is promised as our eternal condition.

. . . As for that "clean fear which endureth forever," if it is to exist in the world to come (and how else can it be said to endure forever?), it is not a fear deterring us from evil which may happen, but preserving us in the good which cannot be lost. For where the love of acquired good is unchangeable, there certainly the fear that avoids evil is, if I may say so, free from anxiety. For under the name of "clean fear" David signifies that will by which we shall necessarily shrink from sin, and guard against it, not with the anxiety of weakness, which fears that we may strongly sin, but with the tranquillity of perfect love. Or if no kind of fear at all shall exist in that most imperturbable security of perpetual and blissful delights, then the expression, "The fear of the Lord is clean, enduring forever," must be taken in the same sense as that other, "The patience of the poor shall not perish forever." For patience, which is necessary only where ills are to be borne, shall not be eternal, but that which patience leads us to will be eternal. So perhaps this "clean fear" is said to endure forever, because that to which fear leads shall endure.

And since this is so—since we must live a good life in order to attain to a blessed life—a good life has all these affections right, a bad life has them wrong. But in the blessed life eternal there will be love and joy, not only right, but also assured; but fear and grief there will be none. Whence it already appears in some sort what manner of persons the citizens of the city of God must be in this their pilgrimage, who live after the spirit, not after the flesh—that is to say, according to God, not according to man—and what manner of persons they shall be also in that immortality whither they are journeying. And the city or society of the wicked, who live not according to God, but according to man, and who accept the doctrines of men or devils in the worship of a false and contempt of the true divinity, is shaken with those wicked emotions as by diseases and disturbances. And if there be some of its citizens who seem to restrain and, as it were, temper those passions, they are so elated with ungodly pride, that their disease is as much greater as their pain is less. And if some, with a vanity monstrous in proportion to its rarity, have become enamoured of themselves because they can be stimulated and excited by no emotion, moved or bent by no affection, such persons rather lose all humanity than obtain true tranquillity. For a thing is not necessarily right because it is inflexible, nor healthy because it is insensible.

But it is a fair question, whether our first parent or first parents (for there was a marriage of two), before they sinned, experienced in their animal body such emotions as we shall not experience in the spiritual body when sin has been purged and finally abolished. For if they did, then how were they blessed in that boasted place of bliss, Paradise? For who that is affected by fear or grief can be called absolutely blessed? And what could those persons fear or suffer in such affluence of blessings, where neither death nor ill-health was feared, and where nothing was wanting which a good will could desire, and nothing present which could interrupt man's mental or bodily enjoyment? Their love to God was unclouded, and their mutual affection was that of faithful and sincere marriage; and from this love flowed a wonderful delight, because they always enjoyed what was loved. Their avoidance of sin was tranquil; and, so long as it was maintained, no other ill at all could invade them and bring sorrow. Or did they perhaps desire to touch and eat the forbidden fruit, yet feared to die; and thus both fear and desire already, even in that blissful place, preyed upon those first of mankind? Away with the thought that such could be the case where there was no sin! And, indeed, this is already sin, to desire those things which the law of God forbids, and to abstain from them through fear of punishment, not through love of righteousness. Away, I say, with the thought, that before there was any sin, there should already have been committed regarding that fruit the very sin which our Lord warns us against regarding a woman: "Whosoever looketh on a woman to lust after her, hath committed adultery with her already in his heart." As happy, then, as were these our first parents, who were agitated by no mental perturbations, and annoyed by no bodily discomforts, so happy should the whole human race have been, had they not introduced that evil which they have transmitted to their posterity, and had none of their descendants committed iniquity worthy of damnation; but this original blessedness continuing until, in virtue of that benediction which said, "Increase and multiply," the number of the predestined saints should have been completed, there would then have been bestowed that higher felicity which is enjoyed by the most blessed angels—a blessedness in which there should have been a secure assurance that no one would sin, and no one die; and so should the saints have lived, after no taste of labour, pain, or death, as now they shall live in the resurrection, after they have endured all these things.

But because God foresaw all things, and was therefore not ignorant that man also would fall, we ought to consider this holy city in connection with what God foresaw and ordained, and not according to our own ideas, which do not embrace God's ordination. For man, by his sin, could not disturb the divine counsel, nor compel God to change what He had decreed; for God's foreknowledge had anticipated both—that is to say, both how evil the man whom He had created good should become, and what good He Himself should even thus derive from him. For though God is said to change His determinations (so that in a tropical [figurative] sense the Holy Scripture says even that God repented), this is said with reference to man's expectation, or the order of natural causes, and not with reference to that which the Almighty had foreknown that He would do. Accordingly God, as it is written, made man upright, and consequently with a good will. For if he had not had a good will, he could not have been upright. The good will, then, is the work of God; for God created him with it. But the first evil will, which preceded all man's evil acts, was rather a kind of falling away from the work of God to its own works than any positive work. And therefore the acts resulting were evil, not having God, but the will itself for their end; so that the will or the man himself, so far as his will is bad, was as it were the evil tree bringing forth evil fruit. Moreover, the bad will, though it be not in harmony with, but opposed to nature, inasmuch as it is a vice or blemish, yet it is true of it as of all vice, that it cannot exist except in a nature, and only in a nature created out of nothing, and not in that which the Creator has begotten of Himself, as He begot the Word, by whom all things were made. For though God formed man of the dust of the earth, yet the earth itself, and every earthly material, is absolutely created out of nothing; and man's soul, too, God created out of nothing, and joined to the body, when He made a man. But evils are so thoroughly overcome by good, that though they are permitted to exist, for the sake of demonstrating how the most righteous foresight of God can make a good use even of them, yet good can exist without evil, as in the true and supreme God Himself, and as in every invisible and visible celestial creature that exists above this murky atmosphere; but evil cannot exist without good, because the natures in which evil exists, insofar as they are natures, are good. And evil is removed, not by removing any nature, or part of a nature, which had been introduced by the evil, but by healing and correcting that which had been vitiated and depraved. The will, therefore, is then truly free, when it is not the slave of vices and sins. Such was it given us by God; and this being lost by its own fault, can only be restored by Him who was able at first to give it. And therefore the truth says, "If the Son shall make you free, ye shall be free indeed"; which is equivalent to saying, If the Son shall save you, ye shall be saved indeed. For He is our Liberator, inasmuch as He is our Saviour.

Man then lived with God for his rule in a paradise at once physical and spiritual. For neither was it a paradise only physical for the advantage of the body, and not also spiritual for the advantage of the mind; nor was it only spiritual to afford enjoyment to man by his internal sensations, and not also physical to afford him enjoyment through his external senses. But obviously it was both for both ends. But after that proud and therefore envious angel . . . preferring to rule with a kind of pomp of empire rather than to be another's subject, fell from the spiritual Paradise, and essaying to insinuate his persuasive guile into the mind of man, whose unfallen condition provoked him to envy now that himself was fallen, he chose the serpent as his mouthpiece in that bodily Paradise in which it and all

the other earthly animals were living with those two human
beings, the man and his wife, subject to them, and harmless;
and he chose the serpent because, being slippery, and moving
in tortuous windings, it was suitable for his purpose. And this
animal being subdued to his wicked ends by the presence and
superior force of his angelic nature, he abused as his instrument,
and first tried his deceit upon the woman, making his assault
upon the weaker part of that human alliance, that he might
gradually gain the whole, and not supposing that the man would
readily give ear to him, or be deceived, but that he might yield
to the error of the woman. For as Aaron was not induced to
agree with the people when they blindly wished him to make
an idol, and yet yielded to constraint; and as it is not credible
that Solomon was so blind as to suppose that idols should be
worshipped, but was drawn over to such sacrilege by the blan-
dishments of women; so we cannot believe that Adam was
deceived, and supposed the devil's word to be truth, and therefore transgressed God's law, but that he by the drawings of
kindred yielded to the woman, the husband to the wife, the
one human being to the only other human being. For not without significance did the apostle say, "And Adam was not deceived, but the woman being deceived was in the transgression";
but he speaks thus, because the woman accepted as true what
the serpent told her, but the man could not bear to be severed
from his only companion, even though this involved a part-
nership in sin. He was not on this account less culpable, but
sinned with his eyes open. And so the apostle does not say, "He
did not sin," but "He was not deceived." For he shows that
he sinned when he says, "By one man sin entered into the
world," and immediately after more distinctly, "In the likeness
of Adam's transgression." But he meant that those are deceived
who do not judge that which they do to be sin; but he knew.
Otherwise how were it true "Adam was not deceived"? But
having as yet no experience of the divine severity, he was possibly

deceived insofar as he thought his sin venial. And consequently he was not deceived as the woman was deceived, but he was deceived as to the judgment which would be passed on his apology: "The woman whom thou gavest to be with me, she gave me, and I did eat." What need of saying more? Although they were not both deceived by credulity, yet both were entangled in the snares of the devil, and taken by sin.

If anyone finds a difficulty in understanding why other sins do not alter human nature as it was altered by the transgression of those first human beings, so that on account of it this nature is subject to the great corruption we feel and see, and to death, and is distracted and tossed with so many furious and contending emotions, and is certainly far different from what it was before sin, even though it were then lodged in an animal body—if, I say, anyone is moved by this, he ought not to think that that sin was a small and light one because it was committed about food, and that not bad nor noxious, except because it was forbidden; for in that spot of singular felicity God could not have created and planted any evil thing. But by the precept He gave, God commended obedience, which is, in a sort, the mother and guardian of all the virtues in the reasonable creature, which was so created that submission is advantageous to it, while the fulfilment of its own will in preference to the Creator's is destruction. And as this commandment enjoining abstinence from one kind of food in the midst of great abundance of other kinds was so easy to keep—so light a burden to the memory—and, above all, found no resistance to its observance in lust, which only afterwards sprung up as the penal consequence of sin, the iniquity of violating it was all the greater in proportion to the ease with which it might have been kept.

Our first parents fell into open disobedience because already they were secretly corrupted; for the evil act had never been done

had not an evil will preceded it. And what is the origin of our
evil will but pride? For "pride is the beginning of sin." And
what is pride but the craving for undue exaltation? And this is
undue exaltation, when the soul abandons Him to whom it
ought to cleave as its end, and becomes a kind of end to itself.
This happens when it becomes its own satisfaction. And it does
so when it falls away from that unchangeable good which ought
to satisfy it more than itself. This falling away is spontaneous;
for if the will had remained stedfast in the love of that higher
and changeless good by which it was illumined to intelligence
and kindled into love, it would not have turned away to find
satisfaction in itself, and so become frigid and benighted; the
woman would not have believed the serpent spoke the truth,
nor would the man have preferred the request of his wife to
the command of God, nor have supposed that it was a venial
transgression to cleave to the partner of his life even in a part-
nership of sin. The wicked deed, then—that is to say, the
transgression of eating the forbidden fruit—was committed by
persons who were already wicked. That "evil fruit" could be
brought forth only by "a corrupt tree." But that the tree was
evil was not the result of nature; for certainly it could become
so only by the vice of the will, and vice is contrary to nature.
Now, nature could not have been depraved by vice had it not
been made out of nothing. Consequently, that it is a nature,
this is because it is made by God; but that it falls away from
Him, this is because it is made out of nothing. But man did
not so fall away as to become absolutely nothing; but being
turned towards himself, his being became more contracted than
it was when he clave to Him who supremely is. Accordingly,
to exist in himself, that is, to be his own satisfaction after
abandoning God, is not quite to become a nonentity, but to
approximate to that. And therefore the holy Scriptures designate
the proud by another name, "self-pleasers." For it is good to
have the heart lifted up, yet not to one's self, for this is proud,

but to the Lord, for this is obedient, and can be the act only of the humble. There is, therefore, something in humility which, strangely enough, exalts the heart, and something in pride which debases it. This seems, indeed, to be contradictory, that loftiness should debase and lowliness exalt. But pious humility enables us to submit to what is above us; and nothing is more exalted above us than God; and therefore humility, by making us subject to God, exalts us. But pride, being a defect of nature, by the very act of refusing subjection and revolting from Him who is supreme, falls to a low condition; and then comes to pass what is written: "Thou castedst them down when they lifted up themselves." For he does not say, "when they had been lifted up," as if first they were exalted, and then afterwards cast down; but "when they lifted up themselves" even then they were cast down—that is to say, the very lifting up was already a fall. And therefore it is that humility is specially recommended to the city of God as it sojourns in this world, and is specially exhibited in the city of God, and in the person of Christ its King; while the contrary vice of pride, according to the testimony of the sacred writings, specially rules his adversary the devil. And certainly this is the great difference which distinguishes the two cities of which we speak, the one being the society of the godly men, the other of the ungodly, each associated with the angels that adhere to their party, and the one guided and fashioned by love of self, the other by love of God.

The devil, then, would not have ensnared man in the open and manifest sin of doing what God had forbidden, had man not already begun to live for himself. It was this that made him listen with pleasure to the words, "Ye shall be as gods," which they would much more readily have accomplished by obediently adhering to their supreme and true end than by proudly living to themselves. For created gods are gods not by virtue of what is in themselves, but by a participation of the true God. By craving to be more, man becomes less; and by aspiring to be self-sufficing, he fell away from Him who truly suffices him. Accordingly, this wicked desire which prompts man to please himself as if he were himself light, and which thus turns him away from that light by which, had he followed it, he would himself have become light—this wicked desire, I say, already secretly existed in him, and the open sin was but its consequence. For that is true which is written, "Pride goeth before destruction, and before honour is humility"; that is to say, secret ruin precedes open ruin, while the former is not counted ruin. For who counts exaltation ruin, though no sooner is the Highest forsaken than a fall is begun? But who does not recognise it as ruin, when there occurs an evident and indubitable transgression of the commandment? And consequently, God's prohibition had reference to such an act as, when committed, could not be defended on any pretense of doing what was righteous. And I make bold to say that it is useful for the proud to fall into an open and indisputable transgression, and so displease themselves, as already, by pleasing themselves, they had fallen. For Peter was in a healthier condition when he wept and was dissatisfied with himself, than when he boldly presumed and satisfied himself. And this is averred by the sacred Psalmist when he says, "Fill their faces with shame, that they may seek Thy name, O Lord"; that is, that they who have pleased themselves in seeking their own glory may be pleased and satisfied with Thee in seeking Thy glory.

But it is a worse and more damnable pride which casts about for the shelter of an excuse even in manifest sins, as these our first parents did, of whom the woman said, "The serpent beguiled me, and I did eat"; and the man said, "The woman whom Thou gavest to be with me, she gave me of the tree, and I did eat." Here there is no word of begging pardon, no word of entreaty for healing. For though they do not, like Cain, deny that they have perpetrated the deed, yet their pride seeks to refer its wickedness to another—the woman's pride to the serpent, the man's to the woman. But where there is a plain transgression of a divine commandment, this is rather to accuse than to excuse oneself. For the fact that the woman sinned on the serpent's persuasion, and the man at the woman's offer, did not make the transgression less, as if there were anyone whom we ought rather to believe or yield to than God.

Therefore, because the sin was a despising of the authority of God—who had created man; who had made him in His own image; who had set him above the other animals; who had placed him in Paradise; who had enriched him with abundance of every kind and of safety; who had laid upon him neither many, nor great, nor difficult commandments, but, in order to make a wholesome obedience easy to him, had given him a single very brief and very light precept by which He reminded that creature whose service was to be free that He was Lord— it was just that condemnation followed, and condemnation such that man, who by keeping the commandments should have been spiritual even in his flesh, became fleshly even in his spirit; and as in his pride he had sought to be his own satisfaction, God in His justice abandoned him to himself, not to live in the absolute independence he affected, but instead of the liberty he desired, to live dissatisfied with himself in a hard and miserable bondage to him to whom by sinning he had yielded himself, doomed in spite of himself to die in body as he had willingly become dead in spirit, condemned even to eternal death (had not the grace of God delivered him) because he had forsaken eternal life. Whoever thinks such punishment either excessive or unjust shows his inability to measure the great iniquity of sinning where sin might so easily have been avoided. For as Abraham's obedience is with justice pronounced to be great, because the thing commanded, to kill his son, was very difficult, so in Paradise the disobedience was the greater, because the difficulty of that which was commanded was imperceptible. And as the obedience of the second Man was the more laudable because He became obedient even "unto death," so the disobedience of the first man was the more detestable because he became disobedient even unto death. For where the penalty annexed to disobedience is great, and the thing commanded by the Creator is easy, who can sufficiently estimate how great a wickedness it is, in a matter so easy, not to obey the authority of so great a power, even when that power deters with so terrible a penalty?

In short, to say all in a word, what but disobedience was the punishment of disobedience in that sin? For what else is man's misery but his own disobedience to himself, so that in consequence of his not being willing to do what he could do, he now wills to do what he cannot? For though he could not do all things in Paradise before he sinned, yet he wished to do only what he could do, and therefore he could do all things he wished. But now, as we recognise in his offspring, and as divine Scripture testifies, "Man is like to vanity." For who can count how many things he wishes which he cannot do, so long as he is disobedient to himself, that is, so long as his mind and his flesh do not obey his will? For in spite of himself his mind is both frequently disturbed, and his flesh suffers, and grows old, and dies; and in spite of ourselves we suffer whatever else we suffer, and which we would not suffer if our nature absolutely and in all its parts obeyed our will. But is it not the infirmities of the flesh which hamper it in its service? Yet what does it matter *how* its service is hampered, so long as the fact remains, that by the just retribution of the sovereign God whom we refused to be subject to and serve, our flesh, which was subjected to us, now torments us by insubordination, although our disobedience brought trouble on ourselves, not upon God? For He is not in need of our service as we of our body's; and therefore what we did was no punishment to Him, but what we receive is so to us. And the pains which are called bodily are pains of the soul in and from the body. For what pain or desire can the flesh feel by itself and without the soul? But when the flesh is said to desire or to suffer, it is meant, as we have explained, that the man does so, or some part of the soul which is affected by the sensation of the flesh, whether a harsh sensation causing pain, or gentle, causing pleasure. But pain in the flesh is only a discomfort of the soul arising from the flesh, and a kind of shrinking from its suffering, as the pain of the soul which is called sadness is a shrinking from those things which have happened to us in spite of ourselves. But sadness is frequently preceded by fear, which is itself in the soul, not in the flesh; while bodily pain is not preceded by any kind of fear of the flesh, which can be felt in the flesh before the pain. But pleasure is preceded by a certain appetite which is felt in the flesh like a craving, as hunger and thirst and that generative appetite which is most commonly identified with the name "lust," though this is the generic word for all desires. For anger itself was defined by the ancients as nothing else than the lust of revenge; although sometimes a man is angry even at inanimate objects which cannot feel his vengeance, as when one breaks a pen, or crushes a quill that writes badly. Yet even this, though less reasonable, is in its way a lust of revenge, and is, so to speak, a mysterious kind of shadow of [the great law of] retribution, that they who do evil should suffer evil. There is, therefore, a lust for revenge, which is called anger; there is a lust of money, which goes by the name of avarice; there is a lust of conquering, no matter by what means, which is called opinionativeness; there is a lust of applause, which is named boasting. There are many and various lusts, of which some have names of their own, while others have not. For who could readily give a name to the lust of ruling, which yet has a powerful influence in the soul of tyrants, as civil wars bear witness?

Although, therefore, lust may have many objects, yet when no object is specified, the word lust usually suggests to the mind the lustful excitement of the organs of generation. And this lust not only takes possession of the whole body and outward members, but also makes itself felt within, and moves the whole man with a passion in which mental emotion is mingled with bodily appetite, so that the pleasure which results is the greatest of all bodily pleasures. So possessing indeed is this pleasure, that at the moment of time in which it is consummated, all mental activity is suspended. What friend of wisdom and holy joys, who, being married, but knowing, as the apostle says, "how to possess his vessel in sanctification and honour, not in the disease of desire, as the Gentiles who know not God," would not prefer, if this were possible, to beget children without this lust, so that in this function of begetting offspring the members created for this purpose should not be stimulated by the heat of lust, but should be actuated by his volition, in the same way as his other members serve him for their respective ends? But even those who delight in this pleasure are not moved to it at their own will, whether they confine themselves to lawful or transgress to unlawful pleasures; but sometimes this lust importunes them in spite of themselves, and sometimes fails them when they desire to feel it, so that though lust rages in the mind, it stirs not in the body. Thus, strangely enough, this emotion not only fails to obey the legitimate desire to beget offspring, but also refuses to serve lascivious lust; and though it often opposes its whole combined energy to the soul that resists it, sometimes also it is divided against itself, and while it moves the soul, leaves the body unmoved.

Justly is shame very specially connected with this lust; justly, too, these members themselves, being moved and restrained not at our will, but by a certain independent autocracy, so to speak, are called "shameful." Their condition was different before sin.

For as it is written, "They were naked and were not ashamed" —not that their nakedness was unknown to them, but because nakedness was not yet shameful, because not yet did lust move those members without the will's consent; not yet did the flesh by its disobedience testify against the disobedience of man. For they were not created blind, as the unenlightened vulgar fancy; for Adam saw the animals to whom he gave names, and of Eve we read, "The woman saw that the tree was good for food, and that it was pleasant to the eyes." Their eyes, therefore, were open, but were not open to this, that is to say, were not observant so as to recognise what was conferred upon them by the garment of grace, for they had no consciousness of their members warring against their will. But when they were stripped of this grace, that their disobedience might be punished by fit retribution, there began in the movement of their bodily members a shameless novelty which made nakedness indecent: it at once made them observant and made them ashamed. And therefore, after they violated God's command by open transgression, it is written: "And the eyes of them both were opened, and they knew that they were naked; and they sewed fig leaves together, and made themselves aprons." "The eyes of them both were opened," not to see, for already they saw, but to discern between the good they had lost and the evil into which they had fallen. And therefore also the tree itself which they were forbidden to touch was called the tree of the knowledge of good and evil from this circumstance, that if they ate of it it would impart to them this knowledge. For the discomfort of sickness reveals the pleasure of health. "They knew," therefore, "that they were naked"— naked of that grace which prevented them from being ashamed of bodily nakedness while the law of sin offered no resistance to their mind. And thus they obtained a knowledge which they would have lived in blissful ignorance of, had they, in trustful obedience to God, declined to commit that offence which involved them in the experience of the hurtful effects of unfaithfulness and disobedience. And therefore, being ashamed of the disobedience of their own flesh, which witnessed to their disobedience while it punished it, "they sewed fig leaves together, and made themselves aprons," that is, cinctures for their privy parts. . . . Shame modestly covered that which lust disobediently moved in opposition to the will which was thus punished for its own disobedience. Consequently all nations, being propagated from that one stock, have so strong an instinct to cover the shameful parts, that some barbarians do not uncover them even in the bath, but wash with their drawers on. In the dark solitudes of India also, though some philosophers go naked, and are therefore called gymnosophists, yet they make an exception in the case of these members, and cover them.

Lust requires for its consummation darkness and secrecy; and this not only when unlawful intercourse is desired, but even such fornication as the earthly city has legalized. Where there is no fear of punishment, these permitted pleasures still shrink from the public eye. Even where provision is made for this lust, secrecy also is provided; and while lust found it easy to remove the prohibitions of law, shamelessness found it impossible to lay aside the veil of retirement. For even shameless men call this shameful; and though they love the pleasure, dare not display it. What! does not even conjugal intercourse, sanctioned as it is by law for the propagation of children, legitimate and honourable though it be, does it not seek retirement from every eye? Before the bridegroom fondles his bride, does he not exclude the attendants, and even the paranymphs, and such friends as the closest ties have admitted to the bridal chamber? The greatest master of Roman eloquence says, that all right actions wish to be set in the light, i.e., desire to be known. This right action, however, has such a desire to be known, that yet it blushes to be seen. Who does not know what passes between husband and wife that children may be born? Is it not for this purpose that wives are married with such ceremony? And yet, when this well-understood act is gone about for the procreation of children, not even the children themselves, who may already have been born to them, are suffered to be witnesses. This right action seeks the light, insofar as it seeks to be known, but yet dreads being seen. And why so, if not because that which is by nature fitting and decent is so done as to be accompanied with a shame-begetting penalty of sin?

Hence it is that even the philosophers who have approximated to the truth have avowed that anger and lust are vicious mental emotions, because, even when exercised towards objects which wisdom does not prohibit, they are moved in an ungoverned and inordinate manner, and consequently need the regulation of mind and reason. And they assert that this third part of the mind is posted as it were in a kind of citadel, to give rule to these other parts, so that, while it rules and they serve, man's righteousness is preserved without a breach. These parts, then, which they acknowledge to be vicious even in a wise and temperate man, so that the mind, by its composing and restraining influence, must bridle and recall them from those objects towards which they are unlawfully moved, and give them access to those which the law of wisdom sanctions—that anger, e.g., may be allowed for the enforcement of a just authority, and lust for the duty of propagating offspring—these parts, I say, were not vicious in Paradise before sin, for they were never moved in opposition to a holy will towards any object from which it was necessary that they should be withheld by the restraining bridle of reason. For though now they are moved in this way, and are regulated by a bridling and restraining power, which those who live temperately, justly, and godly exercise, sometimes with ease, and sometimes with greater difficulty, this is not the sound health of nature, but the weakness which results from sin. And how is it that shame does not hide the acts and words dictated by anger or other emotions, as it covers the motions of lust, unless because the members of the body which we employ for accomplishing them are moved, not by the emotions themselves, but by the authority of the consenting will? For he who in his anger rails at or even strikes someone, could not do so were not his tongue and hand moved by the authority of the will, as also they are moved when there is no anger. But the organs of generation are so subjected to the rule of lust, that they have no motion but what it communicates. It is this we are ashamed of; it is this which blushingly hides from the eyes of onlookers. And rather will a man endure a crowd of witnesses when he is unjustly venting his anger on someone, than the eye of one man when he innocently copulates with his wife.

. . . Human nature, then, is without doubt ashamed of this lust; and justly so, for the insubordination of these members, and their defiance of the will, are the clear testimony of the punishment of man's first sin. And it was fitting that this should appear specially in those parts by which is generated that nature which has been altered for the worse by that first and great sin—that sin from whose evil connection no one can escape, unless God's grace expiate in him individually that which was perpetrated to the destruction of all in common, when all were in one man, and which was avenged by God's justice.

Far be it, then, from us to suppose that our first parents in Paradise felt that lust which caused them afterwards to blush and hide their nakedness, or that by its means they should have fulfilled the benediction of God, "Increase and multiply and replenish the earth"; for it was after sin that lust began. It was after sin that our nature, having lost the power it had over the whole body, but not having lost all shame, perceived, noticed, blushed at, and covered it. But that blessing upon marriage, which encouraged them to increase and multiply and replenish the earth, though it continued even after they had sinned, was yet given before they sinned, in order that the procreation of children might be recognised as part of the glory of marriage, and not of the punishment of sin. But now, men being ignorant of the blessedness of Paradise, suppose that children could not have been begotten there in any other way than they know them to be begotten now, i.e., by lust, at which even honourable marriage blushes; some not simply rejecting, but skeptically deriding the divine Scriptures, in which we read that our first parents, after they sinned, were ashamed of their nakedness, and covered it; while others, though they accept and honour Scripture, yet conceive that this expression, "Increase and multiply," refers not to carnal fecundity, because a similar expression is used of the soul in the words, "Thou wilt multiply me with strength in my soul"; and so, too, in the words which follow in Genesis, "And replenish the earth, and subdue it," they understand by the earth the body which the soul fills with its presence, and which it rules over when it is multiplied in strength. And they hold that children could no more then than now be begotten without lust, which, after sin, was kindled, observed, blushed for, and covered; and even that children would not have been born in Paradise, but only outside of it, as in fact it turned out. For it was after they were expelled from it that they came together to beget children, and begot them.

But we, for our part, have no manner of doubt that to increase and multiply and replenish the earth in virtue of the blessing of God, is a gift of marriage as God instituted it from the beginning before man sinned, when He created them male and female—in other words, two sexes manifestly distinct. And it was this work of God on which His blessing was pronounced. For no sooner had Scripture said, "Male and female created He them," than it immediately continues, "And God blessed them, and God said unto them, Increase, and multiply, and replenish

the earth, and subdue it," etc. And though all these things may
not unsuitably be interpreted in a spiritual sense, yet "male and
female" cannot be understood of two things in one man, as if
there were in him one thing which rules, another which is ruled;
but it is quite clear that they were created male and female,
with bodies of different sexes, for the very purpose of begetting
offspring, and so increasing, multiplying, and replenishing the
earth; and it is great folly to oppose so plain a fact. It was not
of the spirit which commands and the body which obeys, nor
of the rational soul which rules and the irrational desire which
is ruled, nor of the contemplative virtue which is supreme and
the active which is subject, nor of the understanding of the mind
and the sense of the body, but plainly of the matrimonial union
by which the sexes are mutually bound together, that our Lord,
when asked whether it were lawful for any cause to put away
one's wife (for on account of the hardness of the hearts of the
Israelites Moses permitted a bill of divorcement to be given),
answered and said, "Have ye not read that He which made
them at the beginning made them male and female, and said,
For this cause shall a man leave father and mother, and shall
cleave to his wife, and they twain shall be one flesh? Wherefore
they are no more twain, but one flesh. What, therefore, God
hath joined together, let not man put asunder." It is certain,
then, that from the first men were created, as we see and know
them to be now, of two sexes, male and female, and that they
are called one, either on account of the matrimonial union, or
on account of the origin of the woman, who was created from
the side of the man. And it is by this original example, which
God Himself instituted, that the apostle admonishes all hus-
bands to love their own wives in particular.

But he who says that there should have been neither copulation
nor generation but for sin, virtually says that man's sin was
necessary to complete the number of the saints. For if these two

by not sinning should have continued to live alone, because, as is supposed, they could not have begotten children had they not sinned, then certainly sin was necessary in order that there might be not only two but many righteous men. And if this cannot be maintained without absurdity, we must rather believe that the number of the saints fit to complete this most blessed city would have been as great though no one had sinned, as it is now that the grace of God gathers its citizens out of the multitude of sinners, so long as the children of this world generate and are generated.

And therefore that marriage, worthy of the happiness of Paradise, should have had desirable fruit without the shame of lust, had there been no sin. But how that could be, there is now no example to teach us. Nevertheless, it ought not to seem incredible that one member might serve the will without lust then, since so many serve it now. Do we now move our feet and hands when we will to do the things we would by means of these members? do we meet with no resistance in them, but perceive that they are ready servants of the will, both in our own case and in that of others, and especially of artisans employed in mechanical operations, by which the weakness and clumsiness of nature become, through industrious exercise, wonderfully dexterous? and shall we not believe that, like as all those members obediently serve the will, so also should the members have discharged the function of generation, though lust, the award of disobedience, had been awanting? Did not Cicero, in discussing the difference of governments in his *De Republica,* adopt a simile from human nature, and say that we command our bodily members as children, they are so obedient; but that the vicious parts of the soul must be treated as slaves, and be coerced with a more stringent authority? And no doubt, in the order of nature, the soul is more excellent than the body; and yet the soul commands the body more easily than itself. Nevertheless this lust, of which we at present speak, is the more shameful on this account, because the soul is therein neither master of itself, so as not to lust at all, nor of the body, so as to keep the members under the control of the will; for if they were thus ruled, there should be no shame. But now the soul is ashamed that the body, which by nature is inferior and subject to it, should resist its authority. For in the resistance experienced by the soul in the other emotions there is less shame, because the resistance is from itself, and thus, when it is conquered by itself, itself is the conqueror, although the conquest is inordinate and vicious, because accomplished by those parts of the soul which ought to be subject to reason, yet, being accomplished by its own parts and energies, the conquest is, as I say, its own. For when the soul conquers itself to a due subordination, so that its unreasonable motions are controlled by reason, while it again is subject to God, this is a conquest virtuous and praise-worthy. Yet there is less shame when the soul is resisted by its own vicious parts than when its will and order are resisted by the body, which is distinct from and inferior to it, and dependent on it for life itself.

But so long as the will retains under its authority the other members, without which the members excited by lust to resist the will cannot accomplish what they seek, chastity is preserved, and the delight of sin foregone. And certainly, had not culpable disobedience been visited with penal disobedience, the marriage of Paradise should have been ignorant of this struggle and re-bellion, this quarrel between will and lust, that the will may be satisfied and lust restrained, but those members, like all the rest, should have obeyed the will. The field of generation should have been sown by the organ created for this purpose, as the earth is sown by the hand. And whereas now, as we essay to investigate this subject more exactly, modesty hinders us, and compels us to ask pardon of chaste ears, there would have been no cause to do so, but we could have discoursed freely, and without fear of seeming obscene, upon all those points which occur to one who meditates on the subject. There would not have been even words which could be called obscene, but all that might be said of these members would have been as pure as what is said of the other parts of the body. Whoever, then, comes to the perusal of these pages with unchaste mind, let him blame his disposition, not his nature; let him brand the actings of his own impurity, not the words which necessity forces us to use, and for which every pure and pious reader or hearer will very readily pardon me, while I expose the folly of that skepticism which argues solely on the ground of its own experience, and has no faith in anything beyond. He who is not scandalized at the apostle's censure of the horrible wickedness of the women who "changed the natural use into that which is against nature," will read all this without being shocked, especially as we are not, like Paul, citing and censuring a damnable uncleanness, but are explaining, so far as we can, human generation, while with Paul we avoid all obscenity of language.

The man, then, would have sown the seed, and the woman received it, as need required, the generative organs being moved by the will, not excited by lust. For we move at will not only those members which are furnished with joints of solid bone, as the hands, feet, and fingers, but we move also at will those which are composed of slack and soft nerves: we can put them in motion, or stretch them out, or bend and twist them, or contract and stiffen them, as we do with the muscles of the mouth and face. The lungs, which are the very tenderest of the viscera except the brain, and are therefore carefully sheltered in the cavity of the chest, yet for all purposes of inhaling and exhaling the breath, and of uttering and modulating the voice, are obedient to the will when we breathe, exhale, speak, shout, or sing, just as the bellows obey the smith or the organist. I will not press the fact that some animals have a natural power to move a single spot of the skin with which their whole body is covered, if they have felt on it anything they wish to drive off—a power so great, that by this shivering tremor of the skin they can not only shake off flies that have settled on them, but even spears that have fixed in their flesh. Man, it is true, has not this power; but is this any reason for supposing that God could not give it to such creatures as He wished to possess it? And therefore man himself also might very well have enjoyed absolute power over his members had he not forfeited it by his disobedience; for it was not difficult for God to form him so that what is now moved in his body only by lust should have been moved only at will.

We know, too, that some men are differently constituted from others, and have some rare and remarkable faculty of doing with their body what other men can by no effort do, and, indeed, scarcely believe when they hear of others doing. There are persons who can move their ears, either one at a time, or both together. There are some who, without moving the head, can bring the hair down upon the forehead, and move the whole scalp backwards and forwards at pleasure. Some, by lightly pressing their stomach, bring up an incredible quantity and variety of things they have swallowed, and produce whatever they please, quite whole, as if out of a bag. Some so accurately mimic the voices of birds and beasts and other men, that, unless they are seen, the difference cannot be told. Some have such command of their bowels, that they can break wind continuously at pleasure, so as to produce the effect of singing. I myself have known a man who was accustomed to sweat whenever he wished. It is well known that some weep when they please, and shed a flood of tears. But far more incredible is that which some of our brethren saw quite recently. There was a presbyter called Restitutus, in the parish of the Calamensian Church, who, as often as he pleased (and he was asked to do this by those who desired to witness so remarkable a phenomenon), on someone imitating the wailings of mourners, became so insensible, and lay in a state so like death, that not only had he no feeling when they pinched and pricked him, but even when fire was applied to him, and he was burned by it, he had no sense of pain except afterwards from the wound. And that his body remained motionless, not by reason of his self-command, but because he was insensible, was proved by the fact that he breathed no more than a dead man; and yet he said that, when anyone spoke with more than ordinary distinctness, he heard the voice, but as if it were a long way off. Seeing, then, that even in this mortal and miserable life the body serves some men by many remarkable movements and moods beyond the ordinary course of nature, what reason is there for doubting that, before man was involved by his sin in this weak and corruptible condition, his members might have served his will for the propagation of offspring without lust? Man has been given over to himself because he abandoned God, while he sought to be self-satisfying; and disobeying God, he could not obey even himself. Hence it is that he is involved in the obvious misery of being unable to live as he wishes. For if he lived as he wished, he would think himself blessed; but he could not be so if he lived wickedly.

However, if we look at this a little more closely, we see that no one lives as he wishes but the blessed, and that no one is blessed but the righteous. But even the righteous himself does not live as he wishes, until he has arrived where he cannot die, be deceived, or injured, and until he is assured that this shall be his eternal condition. For this nature demands; and nature is not fully and perfectly blessed till it attains what it seeks. But what man is at present able to live as he wishes, when it is not in his power so much as to live? He wishes to live, he is compelled to die. How, then, does he live as he wishes who does not live as long as he wishes? Or if he wishes to die, how can he live as he wishes, since he does not wish even to live? Or if he wishes to die, not because he dislikes life, but that after death he may live better, still he is not yet living as he wishes, but only has the prospect of so living when, through death, he reaches that which he wishes. But admit that he lives as he wishes, because he has done violence to himself, and forced himself not to wish what he cannot obtain, and to wish only what he can (as Terence has it, "Since you cannot do what you will, will what you can"), is he therefore blessed because he is patiently wretched? For a blessed life is possessed only by the man who loves it. If it is loved and possessed, it must necessarily be more ardently loved than all besides; for whatever else is loved must be loved for the sake of the blessed life. And if it is loved as it deserves to be—and the man is not blessed who does not love the blessed life as it deserves—then he who so loves it cannot but wish it to be eternal. Therefore it shall then only be blessed when it is eternal.

In Paradise, then, man lived as he desired so long as he desired what God had commanded. He lived in the enjoyment of God, and was good by God's goodness; he lived without any want, and had it in his power so to live eternally. He had food that he might not hunger, drink that he might not thirst, the tree of life that old age might not waste him. There was in his body no corruption, nor seed of corruption, which could produce in him any unpleasant sensation. He feared no inward disease, no outward accident. Soundest health blessed his body, absolute tranquillity his soul. As in Paradise there was no excessive heat or cold, so its inhabitants were exempt from the vicissitudes of fear and desire. No sadness of any kind was there, nor any foolish joy; true gladness ceaselessly flowed from the presence of God, who was loved "out of a pure heart, and a good conscience, and faith unfeigned." The honest love of husband and wife made a sure harmony between them. Body and spirit worked harmoniously together, and the commandment was kept without labour. No languor made their leisure wearisome; no sleepiness interrupted their desire to labour.

In such happy circumstances and general human well-being we should be far from suspecting that offspring could not have been begotten without the disease of lust, but those parts, like all the rest, would be set in motion at the command of the will; and without the seductive stimulus of passion, with calmness of mind and with no corrupting of the integrity of the body, the husband would lie upon the bosom of his wife. Nor ought we not to believe this because it cannot be proved by experiment. But rather, since no wild heat of passion would arouse those parts of the body, but a spontaneous power, according to the need, would be present, thus must we believe that the male semen could have been introduced into the womb of the wife with the integrity of the female genital organ being preserved, just as now, with that same integrity being safe, the menstrual flow of blood can be emitted from the womb of a virgin. To be sure, the seed could be introduced in the same way through which the menses can be emitted. In order that not the groans of labor-pain should relax the female organs for parturition, but rather the impulse of the fully developed foetus, thus not the eager desire of lust, but the normal exercise of the will, should join the male and female for breeding and conception.

We speak of things which are now shameful, and although we try, as well as we are able, to conceive them as they were before they became shameful, yet necessity compels us rather to limit our discussion to the bounds set by modesty than to extend it as our moderate faculty of discourse might suggest. For since that which I have been speaking of was not experienced even by those who might have experienced it—I mean our first parents (for sin and its merited banishment from Paradise anticipated this passionless generation on their part)—when sexual intercourse is spoken of now, it suggests to men's thoughts not such a placid obedience to the will as is conceivable in our first parents, but such violent acting of lust as they themselves have experienced. And therefore modesty shuts my mouth, although my mind conceives the matter clearly. But Almighty God, the supreme and supremely good Creator of all natures, who aids and rewards good wills, while He abandons and condemns the bad, and rules both, was not destitute of a plan by which He might people His city with the fixed number of citizens which His wisdom had foreordained even out of the condemned human race, discriminating them not now by merits, since the whole mass was condemned as if in a vitiated root, but by grace, and showing, not only in the case of the redeemed, but also in those who were not delivered, how much grace He has bestowed upon them. For everyone acknowledges that he has been rescued from evil, not by deserved, but by gratuitous goodness, when he is singled out from the company of those with whom he might justly have borne a common punishment, and is allowed to go scathless. Why, then, should God not have created those who He foresaw would sin, since He was able to show in and by them both what their guilt merited, and what His grace bestowed, and since, under His creating and disposing hand, even the perverse disorder of the wicked could not pervert the right order of things?

The sins of men and angels do nothing to impede the "great works of the Lord which accomplish His will." For He who by His providence and omnipotence distributes to everyone his own portion, is able to make good use not only of the good, but also of the wicked. And thus making a good use of the wicked angel, who, in punishment of his first wicked volition, was doomed to an obduracy that prevents him now from willing any good, why should not God have permitted him to tempt the first man, who had been created upright, that is to say, with a good will? For he had been so constituted, that if he looked to God for help, man's goodness should defeat the angel's wickedness;

but if by proud self-pleasing he abandoned God, his Creator and Sustainer, he should be conquered. If his will remained upright, through leaning on God's help, he should be rewarded; if it became wicked, by forsaking God, he should be punished. But even this trusting in God's help could not itself be accomplished without God's help, although man had it in his own power to relinquish the benefits of divine grace by pleasing himself. For as it is not in our power to live in this world without sustaining ourselves by food, while it is in our power to refuse this nourishment and cease to live, as those do who kill themselves, so it was not in man's power, even in Paradise, to live as he ought without God's help; but it was in his power to live wickedly, though thus he should cut short his happiness, and incur very just punishment. Since, then, God was not ignorant that man would fall, why should He not have suffered him to be tempted by an angel who hated and envied him? It was not, indeed, that He was unaware that he should be conquered, but because He foresaw that by the man's seed, aided by divine grace, this same devil himself should be conquered, to the greater glory of the saints. All was brought about in such a manner, that neither did any future event escape God's foreknowledge, nor did His foreknowledge compel anyone to sin, and so as to demonstrate in the experience of the intelligent creation, human and angelic, how great a difference there is between the private presumption of the creature and the Creator's protection. For who will dare to believe or say that it was not in God's power to prevent both angels and men from sinning? But God preferred to leave this in their power, and thus to show both what evil could be wrought by their pride, and what good by His grace.

Accordingly, two cities have been formed by two loves: the earthly by the love of self, even to the contempt of God; the heavenly by the love of God, even to the contempt of self. The

former, in a word, glories in itself, the latter in the Lord. For
the one seeks glory from men; but the greatest glory of the other
is God, the witness of conscience. The one lifts up its head in
its own glory; the other says to its God, "Thou art my glory,
and the lifter up of mine head." In the one, the princes and
the nations it subdues are ruled by the love of ruling; in the
other, the princes and the subjects serve one another in love,
the latter obeying, while the former take thought for all. The
one delights in its own strength, represented in the persons of
its rulers; the other says to its God, "I will love Thee, O Lord,
my strength." And therefore the wise men of the one city, living
according to man, have sought for profit to their own bodies or
souls, or both, and those who have known God "glorified Him
not as God, neither were thankful, but became vain in their
imaginations, and their foolish heart was darkened; professing
themselves to be wise"—that is, glorying in their own wisdom,
and being possessed by pride—"they became fools, and changed
the glory of the incorruptible God into an image made like to
corruptible man, and to birds, and four-footed beasts, and creeping things." For they were either leaders or followers of the
people in adoring images, "and worshipped and served the
creature more than the Creator, who is blessed forever." But in
the other city there is no human wisdom, but only godliness,
which offers due worship to the true God, and looks for its
reward in the society of the saints, of holy angels as well as holy
men, "that God may be all in all."

PLATO was born in Athens, Greece in about 428 B.C. One family ancestor was said to be the Greek god Poseidon, and another was Solon, the distinguished Athenian lawmaker and reformer. Plato's parents were prominent in Athenian affairs; through them he became acquainted with the philosopher Socrates. As a young man, Plato considered pursuing a political career. But the violence and corruption he observed in Athenian politics—he witnessed the destruction of the Athenian empire in the Peloponnesian War and the civil disruption that followed this—dissuaded him from his political ambitions. His association with the followers of Socrates led Plato to found the Academy, a school dedicated to philosophical and scientific research in Athens, in 387 B.C. The Academy survived for 900 years. Plato taught and officiated there—while also writing his 36 dialogues —until his death in approximately 348 B.C.

A selection from "The Symposium" translated by Michael Joyce in *The Collected Dialogues of Plato,* edited by Edith Hamilton and Huntington Cairns. Publisher: Princeton University Press, 1963.

Symposium

Characters of the Dialogue

APOLLODORUS, who narrates the story as
it was told to him by ARISTODEMUS

AGATHON, the host

SOCRATES   ERYXIMACHUS

ARISTOPHANES   PHAEDRUS

ALCIBIADES   PAUSANIAS

A troop of revelers

APOLLODORUS: Oh, if that's what you want to know, it isn't
long since I had occasion to refresh my memory. Only the day
before yesterday, as I was coming up to the city from my place
at Phalerum, a friend of mine caught sight of me from behind,
and while I was still a long way ahead he shouted after me,
Here, I say, Apollodorus! Can't you wait for me?

So I stopped and waited for him.

Apollodorus, he said as he came up, you're the very man I'm
looking for. I want to ask you about this party at Agathon's,
when Socrates and Alcibiades and the rest of them were at dinner
there. What were all these speeches they were making about
Love? I've heard something about them from a man who'd been
talking to Phoenix, but his information was rather sketchy and

213

he said I'd better come to you. So you'll have to tell me the whole story, for you know we always count on you, Apollodorus, to report your beloved Socrates. But before you begin, tell me, were you there yourself?

Well, said I, whoever was your informant I can well believe he wasn't very clear about it if you gathered it was such a recent party that I could have been there!

That was my impression, said he.

My dear Glaucon, I protested, how could it have been? Have you forgotten how long Agathon's been away from Athens? And don't you know it's only two or three years since I started spending so much of my time with Socrates, and making it my business to follow everything he says and does from day to day? Because, you know, before that I used to go dashing about all over the place, firmly convinced that I was leading a full and interesting life, when I was really as wretched as could be—much the same as you, for instance, for I know philosophy's the last thing *you'd* spend your time on.

Now don't start girding at me, said Glaucon, but tell me, when was this party, then?

It was given, I told him, when you and I were in the nursery, the day after Agathon's celebrations with the players when he'd won the prize with his first tragedy.

Yes, he admitted, that must have been a good many years ago. But who told you about it—Socrates himself?

No, no, I said. I had it from the same source as Phoenix—Aristodemus of Cydathenaeum, a little fellow who used to go about barefoot. He was there himself; indeed I fancy he was one of Socrates' most impassioned admirers at the time. As a matter of fact I did ask Socrates about one or two points later on, and he confirmed what Aristodemus had told me.

Very well, said Glaucon, then you must tell me all about it before we reach the city. I'm sure it'll pass the time most agreeably.

Well, I told him all about it as we went along, and so, as I was saying, I've got the story pretty pat, and if you want to hear it too I suppose I may as well begin. For that matter I don't know anything that gives me greater pleasure, or profit either, than talking or listening to philosophy. But when it comes to ordinary conversation, such as the stuff you talk about financiers and the money market, well, I find it pretty tiresome personally, and I feel sorry that my friends should think they're being very busy when they're really doing absolutely nothing. Of course, I know your idea of me; you think I'm just a poor unfortunate, and I shouldn't wonder if you're right. But then, I don't *think* that *you're* unfortunate—I know you are.

FRIEND: There you go again, Apollodorus! Always running down yourself and everybody else! You seem to have some extravagant idea that the whole world, with the sole exception of Socrates, is in a state of utter misery—beginning with yourself. You're always the same—perhaps that's why people think you're mad—always girding at yourself and all the rest of us, except Socrates, of course.

APOLLODORUS: My dear man, of course I am! And of course I shouldn't *dream* of thinking such things about myself or about my friends if I weren't completely crazy.

FRIEND: Oh, come now, Apollodorus! We needn't go into that. For heaven's sake, man, don't fly off at a tangent, but simply answer our question. What were these speeches about Love?

APOLLODORUS: Well then, they were something like this— but perhaps I'd better begin at the beginning and tell you in Aristodemus' own words.

I met Socrates, he told me, looking very spruce after his bath, with a nice pair of shoes on although, as you know, he generally goes about barefoot. So I asked him where he was going, cutting such a dash.

I'm going to dinner with Agathon, he said. I kept away from the public celebrations yesterday because I was afraid there'd be a crush, but I promised I'd go along this evening. And I've got myself up like this because I don't want to disgrace such a distinguished host. But what about you? he went on. How would you like to join the party uninvited?

Just as you think, I replied.

Then come along with me, he said, and we'll adapt the proverb, "Unbidden do the good frequent the tables of the good." Though, if it comes to that, Homer himself has not so much adapted that very proverb as exploded it, for after making Agamemnon extremely stout and warlike, and Menelaus a most indifferent spearman, he shows Agamemnon making merry after the sacrifice and Menelaus coming to his table uninvited—that is, the lesser man coming to supper with the greater.

I'm afraid, said I, that Homer's version is the apter so far as I'm concerned—an uninvited ignoramus going to dinner with a man of letters. So you'd better be preparing your excuses on the way, for you needn't think I'll apologize for coming without an invitation—I shall plead that you invited me.

Two heads are better than one, he said, when it comes to excuses. Well, anyway, let's be off.

Having settled this point, continued Aristodemus, we started out, and as we went along Socrates fell into a fit of abstraction and began to lag behind, but when I was going to wait for him he told me to go on ahead. So when I arrived at Agathon's, where the door was standing wide-open, I found myself in rather a curious position, for a servant immediately showed me in and announced me to the assembled company, who were already at table and just about to begin.

However, the moment Agathon saw me he cried, Ah! Here's Aristodemus—just in time for dinner, and if you've come on business it'll have to wait, that's flat. I was going to invite you yesterday, only I couldn't get hold of you. But I say, where's Socrates? Haven't you brought him with you?

I looked round, supposing that Socrates was bringing up the rear, but he was nowhere to be seen; so I explained that we'd been coming along together, and that I'd come at his invitation.

Very nice of you, said Agathon, but what on earth can have happened to the man?

He was just coming in behind me; I can't think where he can be.

Here, said Agathon to one of the servants, run along and see if you can find Socrates, and show him in. And now, my dear Aristodemus, may I put you next to Eryximachus?

And so, Aristodemus went on, I made my toilet and sat down, the servant meanwhile returning with the news that our friend Socrates had retreated into the next-door neighbor's porch.

And there he stood, said the man. And when I asked him in he wouldn't come.

This is very odd, said Agathon. You must speak to him again, and insist.

But here I broke in. I shouldn't do that, I said. You'd much better leave him to himself. It's quite a habit of his, you know; off he goes and there he stands, no matter where it is. I've no doubt he'll be with us before long, so I really don't think you'd better worry him.

Oh, very well, said Agathon. I expect you know best. We won't wait then, he said, turning to the servants. Now you understand, you fellows are to serve whatever kind of dinner you think fit; I'm leaving it entirely to you. I know it's a new idea, but you'll simply have to imagine that we've all come here as your guests. Now go ahead and show us what you can do.

Well, we started dinner, and still there was no sign of Socrates; Agathon still wanted to send for him, but I wouldn't let him. And when at last he did turn up, we weren't more than halfway through dinner, which was pretty good for him.

As he came in, Agathon, who was sitting by himself at the far end of the table, called out, Here you are, Socrates. Come and sit next to me; I want to share this great thought that's just struck you in the porch next door. I'm sure you must have mastered it, or you'd still be standing there.

My dear Agathon, Socrates replied as he took his seat beside him, I only wish that wisdom *were* the kind of thing one could share by sitting next to someone—if it flowed, for instance, from the one that was full to the one that was empty, like the water in two cups finding its level through a piece of worsted. If that were how it worked, I'm sure I'd congratulate myself on sitting next to you, for you'd soon have me brimming over with the most exquisite kind of wisdom. My own understanding is a shadowy thing at best, as equivocal as a dream, but yours, Agathon, glitters and dilates—as which of us can forget that saw you the other day, resplendent in your youth, visibly kindled before the eyes of more than thirty thousand of your fellow Greeks.

Now, Socrates, said Agathon, I know you're making fun of me; however, I shall take up this question of wisdom with you later on, and let Bacchus judge between us. In the meantime you must really show a little interest in your food.

So Socrates drew up and had his dinner with the rest of them, and then, after the libation and the usual hymn and so forth, they began to turn their attention to the wine. It was Pausanias, so far as Aristodemus could remember, who opened the conversation.

Well, gentlemen, he began, what do you say? What sort of a night shall we make of it? Speaking for myself, I'm not quite up to form. I'm still a bit the worse for what I had last night, and I don't suppose you're most of you much better—we were all in the same boat. Anyhow, what do you say? How does everybody feel about the drink?

That's a most sensible question of yours, Pausanias, said Aristophanes. We don't want to make a burden of it—I speak as one who was pretty well soaked last night.

I quite agree, observed Eryximachus, and there is just one question I should like to add. What about Agathon? Has he sufficiently recovered to feel like drinking?

Not I, said Agathon. You can count me out.

So much the better for me, then, said Eryximachus, and so much the better for Aristodemus and Phaedrus and one or two more I could mention. We never could keep up with heavy drinkers like the rest of you. I say nothing of Socrates, for we know he's equal to any occasion, drunk or sober. And now, gentlemen, since nobody seems very anxious to get drunk to-night, I may perhaps be pardoned if I take this opportunity of saying a few words on the true nature of inebriation. My own experience in medicine has entirely satisfied me that vinous excess is detrimental to the human frame. And therefore I can never be a willing party to heavy drinking, as regards either myself or my friends—especially when one is only partially recovered from the excesses of the previous night.

But here Phaedrus broke in. My·dear Eryximachus, he said, I always do what you tell me to, specially when it really is a case of "doctor's orders," and I think the others would be well advised to do the same.

Whereupon it was unanimously agreed that this was not to be a drunken party, and that the wine was to be served merely by way of refreshment.

Very well, then, said Eryximachus, since it is agreed that we need none of us drink more than we think is good for us, I also propose that we dispense with the services of the flute girl who has just come in, and let her go and play to herself or to the women inside there, whichever she prefers, while we spend our evening in discussion of a subject which, if you think fit, I am prepared to name.

It was generally agreed that he should go on with his proposal. So he continued, If I may preface my remarks by a tag from Euripides, "The tale is not my own," as Melanippe says, that

I am going to tell, but properly belongs to my friend Phaedrus here, who is continually coming to me with the following complaint. Is it not, he asks me, an extraordinary thing that, for all the hymns and anthems that have been addressed to the other deities, not one single poet has ever sung a song in praise of so ancient and so powerful a god as Love?

Take such distinguished men of letters as Prodicus, for instance, with their eulogies in prose of Heracles and all the rest of them—not that *they're* so much out of the way either, but do you know, I once came across a book which enumerated the uses of common salt and sang its praises in the most extravagant terms, and not only salt but all kinds of everyday commodities. Now isn't it, as I say, an extraordinary thing, Eryximachus, that while all these screeds have been written on such trivial subjects, the god of love has found no man bold enough to sing his praises as they should be sung—is it not, in short, amazing that there should be so little reverence shown to such a god!

This, gentlemen, is Phaedrus' complaint, and I must say I think it is justified. And, moreover, not only am I willing to oblige him with a contribution on my own account, but also I suggest that this is a most suitable occasion for each one of us to pay homage to the god. If therefore, gentlemen, this meets with your approval, I venture to think we may spend a very pleasant evening in discussion. I suppose the best way would be for each in turn from left to right to address the company and speak to the best of his ability in praise of Love. Phaedrus, I think, should open the debate, for besides being head of the table he is the real author of our discussion.

The motion is carried, Eryximachus, said Socrates, unanimously, I should think. Speaking for myself, I couldn't very well dissent when I claim that love is the one thing in the world I understand—nor could Agathon and Pausanias; neither could Aristophanes, whose whole life is devoted to Dionysus and Aphrodite; no more could any of our friends who are here with us tonight. Of course, your procedure will come very hard on us who are sitting at the bottom of the table, but if the earlier speeches are fine enough, I promise you we shan't complain. So let Phaedrus go ahead with his eulogy of Love—and good luck to him.

Then all the rest of them agreed, and told Phaedrus to begin—but before I go on I must make it quite clear that Aristodemus did not pretend to reproduce the various speeches verbatim, any more than I could repeat them word for word as I had them from him. I shall simply recount such passages as the speaker or the thought itself made, so far as I could judge, especially memorable.

As I was saying, then, Phaedrus opened with some such arguments as these—that Love was a great god, wonderful alike to the gods and to mankind, and that of all the proofs of this the greatest was his birth.

The worship of this god, he said, is of the oldest, for Love is unbegotten, nor is there mention of his parentage to be found anywhere in either prose or verse, while Hesiod tells us expressly that Chaos first appeared, and then

> From Chaos rose broad-bosomed Earth, the sure
> And everlasting seat of all that is,
> And after, Love . . .

Acusilaus agrees with Hesiod, for he holds that after Chaos were brought forth these twain, Earth and Love, and Parmenides writes of the creative principle,

> And Love she framed the first of all the gods.

Thus we find that the antiquity of Love is universally admitted, and in very truth he is the ancient source of all our highest good. . . .

In short, this, gentlemen, is my theme, that Love is the oldest and most glorious of the gods, the great giver of all goodness and happiness to men, alike to the living and to the dead.

This, to the best of Aristodemus' recollection, was Phaedrus' speech. It was followed by several more which had almost, if not quite, escaped him; so he went straight on to Pausanias, who spoke as follows.

I am afraid, my dear Phaedrus, that our arrangement won't work very well if it means that we are simply to pronounce a eulogy of Love. It would be all very well if there were only one kind of Love, but unfortunately this is not the case, and we should therefore have begun by stipulating which kind in particular was to receive our homage. In the circumstances I will try to set the matter right by first defining the Love whom we are to honor, and then singing his praises in terms not unworthy, I hope, of his divinity.

Now you will all agree, gentlemen, that without Love there could be no such goddess as Aphrodite. If, then, there were only one goddess of that name, we might suppose that there was only one kind of Love, but since in fact there are two such goddesses there must also be two kinds of Love. No one, I think, will deny that there are two goddesses of that name— one, the elder, sprung from no mother's womb but from the heavens themselves, we call the Uranian, the heavenly Aphrodite, while the younger, daughter of Zeus and Dione, we call Pandemus, the earthly Aphrodite. It follows, then, that Love should be known as earthly or as heavenly according to the goddess in whose company his work is done. And our business, gentlemen—I need hardly say that every god must command our homage—our business at the moment is to define the attributes peculiar to each of these two.

Now it may be said of any kind of action that the action itself, as such, is neither good nor bad. Take, for example, what we are doing now. Neither drinking nor singing nor talking has any virtue in itself, for the outcome of each action depends upon how it is performed. If it is done rightly and finely, the action will be good; if it is done basely, bad. And this holds good of loving, for Love is not of himself either admirable or noble, but only when he moves us to love nobly.

Well then, gentlemen, the earthly Aphrodite's Love is a very earthly Love indeed, and does his work entirely at random. It is he that governs the passions of the vulgar. For, first, they are as much attracted by women as by boys; next, whoever they may love, their desires are of the body rather than of the soul; and, finally, they make a point of courting the shallowest people they can find, looking forward to the mere act of fruition and careless whether it be a worthy or unworthy consummation. And hence they take their pleasures where they find them, good and bad alike. For this is the Love of the younger Aphrodite, whose nature partakes of both male and female.

But the heavenly Love springs from a goddess whose attributes have nothing of the female, but are altogether male, and who is also the elder of the two, and innocent of any hint of lewdness. And so those who are inspired by this other Love turn rather to the male, preferring the more vigorous and intellectual bent. One can always tell—even among the lovers of boys—the man who is wholly governed by this elder Love, for no boy can please him until he has shown the first signs of dawning intelligence, signs which generally appear with the first growth of beard. And it seems to me that the man who falls in love with a youth of such an age will be prepared to spend all his time with him, to share his whole life with him, in fact; nor will he be likely to take advantage of the lad's youth and credulity by seducing him and then turning with a laugh to some newer love.

But I cannot help thinking, gentlemen, that there should be a law to forbid the loving of mere boys, a law to prevent so much time and trouble being wasted upon an unknown quantity—for what else, after all, is the future of any boy, and who knows whether he will follow the paths of virtue or of vice, in body and in soul? Of course, your man of principle is a law unto himself, but these followers of the earthly Love should be legally compelled to observe a similar restraint—just as we prevent them, as far as possible, from making love to our own wives and daughters—for it is their behavior that has brought the name of Love into such disrepute that one has even heard it held to be degrading to yield to a lover's solicitation. Anyone who can hold such a view must surely have in mind these earthly lovers, with their offensive importunities, for there can be nothing derogatory in any conduct which is sanctioned both by decency and custom.

Then again, gentlemen, may I point out that, while in all the other states of Hellas the laws that deal with Love are so simple and well defined that they are easy enough to master, our own code is most involved. In Elis and Boeotia, for instance, and wherever else the people are naturally inarticulate, it has been definitely ruled that it is right for the lover to have his way. Nor does anyone, old or young, presume to say that it is wrong—the idea being, I suppose, to save themselves from having to plead with the young men for their favors, which is rather difficult for lovers who are practically dumb.

On the other hand, in Ionia and many other countries under Oriental rule, the very same thing is held to be disgraceful. Indeed, the Oriental thinks ill not only of Love but also of both philosophy and sport, on account of the despotism under which he lives. For I suppose it does not suit the rulers for their subjects to indulge in high thinking, or in staunch friendship and fellowship, which Love more than anything is likely to beget. And those who seized the power here in Athens learned the same lesson from bitter experience, for it was the might of Aristogiton's love and Harmodius' friendship that brought their reign to an end. Thus, wherever the law enacts that it is wrong to yield to the lover, you may be sure that the fault lies with the legislators—that is to say, it is due to the oppression of the rulers and the servility of their subjects. On the other hand, wherever you find the same thing expressly sanctioned, you may blame the legislator's mental inertia.

But in Athens, gentlemen, we have a far more admirable code—a code which, as I was saying, is not nearly so easy to understand. Take for instance our maxim that it is better to love openly than in secret, especially when the object of one's passion is eminent in nobility and virtue, and even if his personal appearance should lack the same distinction. And think how we all love to cheer the lover on, without the least idea that he is doing anything unworthy, and how we see honor in his success and shame in his defeat. And remember, gentlemen, what latitude the law offers to the lover in the prosecution of his suit, and how he may be actually applauded for conduct which, in any other circumstances or in any other cause, would call down upon him the severest censure.

Imagine what would happen to a man who wanted to get money out of someone, or a post, or powers of some kind, and who therefore thought fit to behave as the lover behaves to his beloved—urging his need with prayers and entreaties, and vowing vows, and sleeping upon doorsteps, subjecting himself, in short, to a slavery which no slave would ever endure—why, gentlemen, not only his friends, but his very enemies, would do their best to stop him, for his enemies would accuse him of the most abject servility, while his friends would take him to task because they felt ashamed of him.

But when it is a lover who does this kind of thing people only think the more of him, and the law expressly sanctions his conduct as the means to an honorable end. And, what is the most extraordinary thing of all, it is popularly supposed that the lover is the one man whom the gods will pardon for breaking his vows, for lovers' promises, they say, are made to be forsworn. And so, gentlemen, we see what complete indulgence, not only human but divine, is accorded to the lover by our Athenian code.

In view of this, one would have thought that, here if anywhere, loving and being kind to one's lover would have been
positively applauded. Yet we find in practice that if a father
discovers that someone has fallen in love with his son, he puts
the boy in charge of an attendant, with strict injunctions not to
let him have anything to do with his lover. And if the boy's
little friends and playmates see anything of that kind going on,
you may be sure they'll call him names, while their elders will
neither stop their being rude nor tell them they are talking
nonsense. So if there were no more to it than that, anyone would
think that we Athenians were really shocked at the idea of
yielding to a lover.

But I fancy we can account for the apparent contradiction if
we remember that the moral value of the act is not what one
might call a constant. We agreed that love itself, as such, was
neither good nor bad, but only insofar as it led to good or bad
behavior. It is base to indulge a vicious lover viciously, but noble
to gratify a virtuous lover virtuously. Now the vicious lover is
the follower of the earthly Love who desires the body rather
than the soul; his heart is set on what is mutable and must
therefore be inconstant. And as soon as the body he loves begins
to pass the first flower of its beauty, he "spreads his wings and
flies away," giving the lie to all his pretty speeches and dis-
honoring his vows, whereas the lover whose heart is touched by
moral beauties is constant all his life, for he has become one
with what will never fade.

Now it is the object of the Athenian law to make a firm
distinction between the lover who should be encouraged and
the lover who should be shunned. And so it enjoins pursuit in
certain cases, and flight in others, and applies various touchstones
and criteria to discriminate between the two classes of lover and
beloved. And this is why it is immoral, according to our code,
to yield too promptly to solicitation; there should first be a certain
lapse of time, which is generally considered to be the most

effective test. Secondly, it is immoral when the surrender is due to financial or political considerations, or to unmanly fear of ill-treatment; it is immoral, in short, if the youth fails to show the contempt he should for any advantage he may gain in pocket or position. For in motives such as these we can find nothing fixed or permanent, except, perhaps, the certainty that they have never been the cause of any noble friendship.

There remains, therefore, only one course open to the beloved if he is to yield to his lover without offending our ideas of decency. It is held that, just as the lover's willing and complete subjection to his beloved is neither abject nor culpable, so there is one other form of voluntary submission that shall be blameless—a submission which is made for the sake of virtue. And so, gentlemen, if anyone is prepared to devote himself to the service of another in the belief that through him he will find increase of wisdom or of any other virtue, we hold that such willing servitude is neither base nor abject.

We must therefore combine these two laws—the one that deals with the love of boys and the one that deals with the pursuit of wisdom and the other virtues—before we can agree that the youth is justified in yielding to his lover. For it is only when lover and beloved come together, each governed by his own especial law—the former lawfully enslaving himself to the youth he loves, in return for his compliance, the latter lawfully devoting his services to the friend who is helping him to become wise and good—the one sharing his wealth of wisdom and virtue, and the other drawing, in his poverty, upon his friend for a liberal education—it is then, I say, and only then, when the observance of the two laws coincides, that it is right for the lover to have his way.

There is no shame in being disappointed of such hopes as these, but any other kind of hope, whether it comes true or not, is shameful in itself. Take the case of a youth who gratifies his lover in the belief that he is wealthy and in the hope of making money. Such hopes will be nonetheless discreditable if he finds in the event that he has been the prey of a penniless seducer, for he will have shown himself for what he is, the kind of person, namely, who will do anything for money—which is nothing to be proud of. But suppose that he had yielded because he believed in his lover's virtue, and hoped to be improved by such an association; then, even if he discovered in the end that he had been duped by an unholy blackguard, there would still have been something noble in his mistake, for he, too, would have shown himself for what he was—the kind of person who will do anything for anybody for the sake of progress in the ways of virtue. And what, gentlemen, could be more admirable than that? I conclude, therefore, that it is right to let the lover have his way in the interests of virtue.

Such, then, is the Love of the heavenly Aphrodite, heavenly in himself and precious alike to cities and to men, for he constrains both lover and beloved to pay the most earnest heed to their moral welfare, but all the rest are followers of the other, the earthly Aphrodite. And this, Phaedrus, is all I have to say, extempore, on the subject of Love.

When Pausanias had paused—you see the kind of tricks we catch from our philologists, with their punning derivations— the next speaker, so Aristodemus went on to tell me, should have been Aristophanes; only as it happened, whether he'd been overeating I don't know, but he had got the hiccups so badly that he really wasn't fit to make a speech. So he said to the doctor, Eryximachus, who was sitting next below him, Eryximachus, you'll either have to cure my hiccups or take my turn and go on speaking till they've stopped.

I'm prepared to do both, said Eryximachus. I'll take your turn to speak, and then when you've recovered you can take mine. Meanwhile, you'd better try holding your breath, or if that won't stop your hiccups try gargling with a little water, or if it's particularly stubborn you'll have to get something that you can tickle your nostrils with, and sneeze, and by the time you've done that two or three times you'll find that it will stop, however bad it is.

Go ahead, then, said Aristophanes. You make your speech, and I'll be doing as you say.

Whereupon Eryximachus spoke as follows.

Well, gentlemen, since Pausanias broke off, after an excellent beginning, without having really finished, I must try to wind up his argument myself. I admit that in defining the two kinds of Love he has drawn a very useful distinction, but the science of medicine seems to me to prove that, besides attracting the souls of men to human beauty, Love has many other objects and many other subjects, and that his influence may be traced both in the brute and the vegetable creations, and I think I may say in every form of existence—so great, so wonderful, and so all-embracing is the power of Love in every activity, whether sacred or profane. . . .[1]

Well then, Eryximachus, Aristophanes began, I propose, as you suggested, to take quite a different line from you and Pausanias. I am convinced that mankind has never had any conception of the power of Love, for if we had known him as he really is, surely we should have raised the mightiest temples and altars, and offered the most splendid sacrifices, in his honor, and not—as in fact we do—have utterly neglected him. Yet he of all the gods has the best title to our service, for he, more than all the rest, is the friend of man; he is our great ally, and it is he that cures us of those ills whose relief opens the way to man's

---

[1] [Eryximachus goes on to argue that Love is an ordering principle or harmony that is necessary to the good of all things; for instance, the health of the body, which medicine tries to bring about, is the result of the harmony or concord among its various hostile and opposing elements, "hot and cold, sweet and sour, wet and dry, and so on." When he is finished, it is Aristophanes' turn.]

highest happiness. And so, gentlemen, I will do my best to acquaint you with the power of Love, and you in your turn shall pass the lesson on.

First of all I must explain the real nature of man, and the change which it has undergone—for in the beginning we were nothing like we are now. For one thing, the race was divided into three; that is to say, besides the two sexes, male and female, which we have at present, there was a third which partook of the nature of both, and for which we still have a name, though the creature itself is forgotten. For though "hermaphrodite" is only used nowadays as a term of contempt, there really was a man-woman in those days, a being which was half male and half female.

And secondly, gentlemen, each of these beings was globular in shape, with rounded back and sides, four arms and four legs, and two faces, both the same, on a cylindrical neck, and one head, with one face one side and one the other, and four ears, and two lots of privates, and all the other parts to match. They walked erect, as we do ourselves, backward or forward, whichever they pleased, but when they broke into a run they simply stuck their legs straight out and went whirling round and round like a clown turning cartwheels. And since they had eight legs, if you count their arms as well, you can imagine that they went bowling along at a pretty good speed.

The three sexes, I may say, arose as follows. The males were descended from the Sun, the females from the Earth, and the hermaphrodites from the Moon, which partakes of either sex, and they were round and they *went* round, because they took after their parents. And such, gentlemen, were their strength and energy, and such their arrogance, that they actually tried— like Ephialtes and Otus in Homer—to scale the heights of heaven and set upon the gods.

At this Zeus took counsel with the other gods as to what was to be done. They found themselves in rather an awkward position; they didn't want to blast them out of existence with thunderbolts as they did the giants, because that would be saying good-bye to all their offerings and devotions, but at the same time they couldn't let them get altogether out of hand. At last, however, after racking his brains, Zeus offered a solution.

I think I can see my way, he said, to put an end to this disturbance by weakening these people without destroying them. What I propose to do is to cut them all in half, thus killing two birds with one stone, for each one will be only half as strong, and there'll be twice as many of them, which will suit us very nicely. They can walk about, upright, on their two legs, and if, said Zeus, I have any more trouble with them, I shall split them up again, and they'll have to hop about on one.

So saying, he cut them all in half just as you or I might chop up sorb apples for pickling, or slice an egg with a hair. And as each half was ready he told Apollo to turn its face, with the half-neck that was left, toward the side that was cut away—thinking that the sight of such a gash might frighten it into keeping quiet—and then to heal the whole thing up. So Apollo turned their faces back to front, and, pulling in the skin all the way round, he stretched it over what we now call the belly—like those bags you pull together with a strong—and tied up the one remaining opening so as to form what we call the navel. As for the creases that were left, he smoothed most of them away, finishing off the chest with the sort of tool a cobbler uses to smooth down the leather on the last, but he left a few puckers round about the belly and the navel, to remind us of what we suffered long ago.

Now, when the work of bisection was complete it left each half with a desperate yearning for the other, and they ran together and flung their arms around each other's necks, and asked for nothing better than to be rolled into one. So much so, that they began to die of hunger and general inertia, for neither would do anything without the other. And whenever one half was left alone by the death of its mate, it wandered about questing and clasping in the hope of finding a spare half-woman—or a whole woman, as we should call her nowadays—or half a man. And so the race was dying out.

Fortunately, however, Zeus felt so sorry for them that he devised another scheme. He moved their privates round to the front, for of course they had originally been on the outside—which was now the back—and they had begotten and conceived not upon each other, but, like the grasshoppers, upon the earth. So now, as I say, he moved their members round to the front and made them propagate among themselves, the male begetting upon the female—the idea being that if, in all these clippings and claspings, a man should chance upon a woman, conception would take place and the race would be continued, while if man should conjugate with man, he might at least obtain such satisfaction as would allow him to turn his attention and his energies to the everyday affairs of life. So you see, gentlemen, how far back we can trace our innate love for one another, and how this love is always trying to redintegrate our former nature, to make two into one, and to bridge the gulf between one human being and another.

And so, gentlemen, we are all like pieces of the coins that children break in half for keepsakes—making two out of one, like the flatfish—and each of us is forever seeking the half that will tally with himself. The man who is a slice of the hermaphrodite sex, as it was called, will naturally be attracted by women—the adulterer, for instance—and women who run after men are of similar descent—as, for instance, the unfaithful wife. But the woman who is a slice of the original female is attracted by women rather than by men—in fact she is a Lesbian—while men who are slices of the male are followers of the male, and show their masculinity throughout their boyhood by the way they make friends with men, and the delight they take in lying beside them and being taken in their arms. And these are the most hopeful of the nation's youth, for theirs is the most virile constitution.

I know there are some people who call them shameless, but they are wrong. It is not immodesty that leads them to such pleasures, but daring, fortitude, and masculinity—the very virtues that they recognize and welcome in their lovers—which is proved by the fact that in after years they are the only men who show any real manliness in public life. And so, when they themselves have come to manhood, their love in turn is lavished upon boys. They have no natural inclination to marry and beget children. Indeed, they only do so in deference to the usage of society, for they would just as soon renounce marriage altogether and spend their lives with one another.

Such a man, then, gentlemen, is of an amorous disposition, and gives his love to boys, always clinging to his like. And so, when this boy lover—or any lover, for that matter—is fortunate enough to meet his other half, they are both so intoxicated with affection, with friendship, and with love, that they cannot bear to let each other out of sight for a single instant. It is such reunions as these that impel men to spend their lives together, although they may be hard put to it to say what they really want with one another, and indeed, the purely sexual pleasures of their friendship could hardly account for the huge delight they take in one another's company. The fact is that both their souls are longing for a something else—a something to which they can neither of them put a name, and which they can only give an inkling of in cryptic sayings and prophetic riddles.

Now, supposing Hephaestus were to come and stand over them with his tool bag as they lay there side by side, and suppose he were to ask, Tell me, my dear creatures, what do you really want with one another?

And suppose they didn't know what to say, and he went on, How would you like to be rolled into one, so that you could always be together, day and night, and never be parted again?

Because if that's what you want, I can easily weld you together, and then you can live your two lives in one, and, when the time comes, you can die a common death and still be two-in-one in the lower world. Now, what do you say? Is that what you'd like me to do? And would you be happy if I did?

We may be sure, gentlemen, that no lover on earth would dream of refusing such an offer, for not one of them could imagine a happier fate. Indeed, they would be convinced that this was just what they'd been waiting for—to be merged, that is, into an utter oneness with the beloved.

And so all this to-do is a relic of that original state of ours, when we were whole, and now, when we are longing for and following after that primeval wholeness, we say we are in love. For there was a time, I repeat, when we were one, but now, for our sins, God has scattered us abroad, as the Spartans scattered the Arcadians. Moreover, gentlemen, there is every reason to fear that, if we neglect the worship of the gods, they will split us up again, and then we shall have to go about with our noses sawed asunder, part and counterpart, like the basso-relievos on the tombstones. And therefore it is our duty one and all to inspire our friends with reverence and piety, for so we may ensure our safety and attain that blessed union by enlisting in the army of Love and marching beneath his banners.

For Love must never be withstood—as we do, if we incur the displeasure of the gods. But if we cling to him in friendship and reconciliation, we shall be among the happy few to whom it is given in these latter days to meet their other halves. Now, I don't want any coarse remarks from Eryximachus. I don't mean Pausanias and Agathon, though for all I know they may be among the lucky ones, and both be sections of the male. But what I am trying to say is this—that the happiness of the whole human race, women no less than men, is to be found in the consummation of our love, and in the healing of our dissevered nature by finding each his proper mate. And if this be a counsel of perfection, then we must do what, in our present circumstances, is next best, and bestow our love upon the natures most congenial to our own.

And so I say that Love, the god who brings all this to pass, is worthy of our hymns, for his is the inestimable and present service of conducting us to our true affinities, and it is he that offers this great hope for the future—that, if we do not fail in reverence to the gods, he will one day heal us and restore us to our old estate, and establish us in joy and blessedness.

Such, Eryximachus, is my discourse on Love—as different as could be from yours. And now I must ask you again. Will you please refrain from making fun of it, and let us hear what all the others have to say—or rather, the other two, for I see there's no one left but Agathon and Socrates.

Well, you shall have your way, said Eryximachus, and, joking apart, I enjoyed your speech immensely. Indeed, if I were not aware that Socrates and Agathon were both authorities on Love, I should be wondering what they could find to say after being treated to such a wealth and variety of eloquence. But, knowing what they are, I've no doubt we'll find them equal to the occasion. . . .[2]

Agathon took his seat, continued Aristodemus, amid a burst of applause, for we all felt that his youthful eloquence did honor to himself as well as to the god.

Then Socrates turned to Eryximachus and said, Well, Eryximachus, you laughed at my misgivings, but you see—they've been justified by the event. There's not much left for *me* to say after the wonderful speech we've just had from Agathon.

I admit, Eryximachus replied, that your prognosis was correct so far as Agathon's eloquence was concerned, but as to your own embarrassment, I'm not so sure.

---

[2] [In his speech, Agathon describes Love in the highest terms, as being tender, beautiful, wise, temperate, the "loveliest and the best" of the gods, and the "author" of virtue, peace, and friendship among men.]

My dear sir, protested Socrates, what chance have I or anyone of knowing what to say, after listening to such a flood of eloquence as that? The opening, I admit, was nothing out of the way, but when he came to his peroration, why, he held us all spellbound with the sheer beauty of his diction, while I, personally, was so mortified when I compared it with the best that I could ever hope to do, that for two pins I'd have tried to sneak away. Besides, his speech reminded me so strongly of that master of rhetoric, Gorgias, that I couldn't help thinking of Odysseus, and his fear that Medusa would rise from the lower world among the ghosts, and I was afraid that when Agathon got near the end he would arm his speech against mine with the Gorgon's head of Gorgias' eloquence, and strike me as dumb as a stone.

And then I saw what a fool I'd been to agree to take part in this eulogy of yours, and, what was worse, to claim a special knowledge of the subject, when, as it turned out, I had not the least idea how this or any other eulogy should be conducted. I had imagined in my innocence that one began by stating the facts about the matter in hand, and then proceeded to pick out the most attractive points and display them to the best advantage. And I flattered myself that my speech would be a great success, because I knew the facts. But the truth, it seems, is the last thing the successful eulogist cares about; on the contrary, what he does is simply to run through all the attributes of power and virtue, however irrelevant they may be, and the whole thing may be a pack of lies, for all it seems to matter.

I take it then that what we undertook was to flatter, rather than to praise, the god of love, and that's why you're all prepared to say the first thing about him that comes into your heads, and to claim that he either is, or is the cause of, everything that is loveliest and best. And of course the uninitiated are impressed by the beauty and grandeur of your encomiums; yet those who know will not be taken in so easily. Well then, I repeat, the whole thing was a misunderstanding, and it was only in my ignorance that I agreed to take part at all. I protest, with Euripides' Hippolytus, it was my lips that promised, not my soul, and that, gentlemen, is that. I won't have anything to do with your eulogy, and what is more, I couldn't if I tried. But I don't mind telling you the truth about Love, if you're interested; only, if I do, I must tell it in my own way, for I'm not going to make a fool of myself, at my age, trying to imitate the grand manner that sits so well on the rest of you. Now, Phaedrus, it's for you to say. Have you any use for a speaker who only cares whether his matter is correct and leaves his manner to take care of itself?

Whereupon Phaedrus and the others told him to go ahead and make whatever kind of speech he liked.

Very well, said he, but there's just one other thing. Has our chairman any objection to my asking Agathon a few simple questions? I want to make certain we're not at cross-purposes before I begin my speech.

Ask what you like, said Phaedrus. I don't mind.

Whereupon Socrates began, so far as Aristodemus could trust his memory, as follows.

I must say, my dear Agathon, that the remarks with which you prefaced your speech were very much to the point. You were quite right in saying that the first thing you had to do was to acquaint us with the nature of the god, and the second to tell us what he did. Yes, your introduction was admirable. But now that we've had the pleasure of hearing your magnificent description of Love, there's just one little point I'm not quite clear about. Tell me. Do you think it is the nature of Love to be the love of somebody, or of nobody? I don't mean, is he a mother's or a father's love? That would be a silly sort of question, but suppose I were to ask you whether a father, *as* a father, must be *somebody's* father, or not; surely the only reasonable answer would be that a father must be the father of a son or a daughter. Am I right?

Why, yes, said Agathon.

And could we say the same thing about a mother?

Yes.

Good. And now, if you don't mind answering just one or two more questions, I think you'll see what I'm driving at. Suppose I were to ask, what about a brother, *as* a brother? Must he be *somebody's* brother, or not?

Of course he must.

You mean, he must be the brother of a brother or a sister.

Precisely, said Agathon.

Well, then, Socrates went on, I want you to look at Love from the same point of view. Is he the love of something, or of nothing?

Of something, naturally.

And now, said Socrates, bearing in mind what Love is the love of, tell me this. Does he long for what he is in love with, or not?

Of course he longs for it.

And does he long for whatever it is he longs for, and is he in love with it, when he's got it, or when he hasn't?

When he hasn't got it, probably.

Then isn't it probable, said Socrates, or rather isn't it certain, that everything longs for what it lacks, and that nothing longs for what it doesn't lack? I can't help thinking, Agathon, that that's about as certain as anything could be. Don't you think so?

Yes, I suppose it is.

Good. Now, tell me. Is it likely that a big man will want to be big, or a strong man to be strong?

Not if we were right just now.

Quite, for the simple reason that neither of them would be lacking in that particular respect.

Exactly.

For if, Socrates continued, the strong were to long for strength, and the swift for swiftness, and the healthy for health—for I suppose it *might* be suggested that in such cases as these people long for the very things they have, or are, already, and so I'm trying to imagine such a case, to make quite sure we're on the right track—people in their position, Agathon, if you stop to think about them, are bound here and now to have those very qualities, whether they want them or not; so why should they trouble to want them? And so, if we heard someone saying, "I'm healthy, and I want to be healthy; I'm rich, and I want to be rich; and in fact I want just what I've got," I think we should be justified in saying, "But, my dear sir, you've *got* wealth and health and strength already, and what you want is to go on having them, for at the moment you've got them whether you want them or not. Doesn't it look as if, when you say you want these things here and now, you really mean, what you've got now, you want to go on keeping?" Don't you think, my dear Agathon, that he'd be bound to agree?

Why, of course he would, said Agathon.

Well, then, continued Socrates, desiring to secure something to oneself forever may be described as loving something which is not yet to hand.

Certainly.

And therefore, whoever feels a want is wanting something which is not yet to hand, and the object of his love and of his desire is whatever he isn't, or whatever he hasn't got—that is to say, whatever he is lacking in.

Absolutely.

And now, said Socrates, are we agreed upon the following conclusions? One, that Love is always the love of something, and two, that that something is what he lacks.

Agreed, said Agathon.

So far, so good, said Socrates. And now, do you remember what you said were the objects of Love, in your speech just now? Perhaps I'd better jog your memory. I fancy it was something like this—that the actions of the gods were governed by the love of beauty—for of course there was no such thing as the love of ugliness. Wasn't that pretty much what you said?

It was, said Agathon.

No doubt you were right, too, said Socrates. And if that's so, doesn't it follow that Love is the love of beauty, and not of ugliness?

It does.

And haven't we agreed that Love is the love of something which he hasn't got, and consequently lacks?

Yes.

Then Love has no beauty, but is lacking in it?

Yes, that must follow.

Well then, would you suggest that something which lacked beauty and had no part in it was beautiful itself?

Certainly not.

And, that being so, can you still maintain that Love is beautiful?

To which Agathon could only reply, I begin to be afraid, my dear Socrates, that I didn't know what I was talking about.

Never mind, said Socrates, it was a lovely speech, but there's just one more point. I suppose you hold that the good is also beautiful?

I do.

Then, if Love is lacking in what is beautiful, and if the good and the beautiful are the same, he must also be lacking in what is good.

Just as you say, Socrates, he replied. I'm afraid you're quite unanswerable.

No, no, dear Agathon. It's the truth you find unanswerable, not Socrates. And now I'm going to leave you in peace, because I want to talk about some lessons I was given, once upon a time, by a Mantinean woman called Diotima—a woman who was deeply versed in this and many other fields of knowledge. It was she who brought about a ten years' postponement of the great plague of Athens on the occasion of a certain sacrifice, and it was she who taught me the philosophy of Love. And now I am going to try to connect her teaching—as well as I can without her help—with the conclusions that Agathon and I have just arrived at. Like him, I shall begin by stating who and what Love is, and go on to describe his functions, and I think the easiest way will be to adopt Diotima's own method of inquiry by question and answer. I'd been telling her pretty much what Agathon has just been telling me—how Love was a great god, and how he was the love of what is beautiful, and she used the same arguments on me that I've just brought to bear on Agathon to prove that, on my own showing, Love was neither beautiful nor good.

Whereupon, My dear Diotima, I asked, are you trying to make me believe that Love is bad and ugly?

Heaven forbid, she said. But do you really think that if a thing isn't beautiful it's therefore bound to be ugly?

Why, naturally.

And that what isn't learned must be ignorant? Have you never heard of something which comes between the two?

And what's that?

Don't you know, she asked, that holding an opinion which is in fact correct, without being able to give a reason for it, is neither true knowledge—how can it be knowledge without a reason?—nor ignorance—for how can we call it ignorance when it happens to be true? So may we not say that a correct opinion comes midway between knowledge and ignorance?

Yes, I admitted, that's perfectly true.

Very well, then, she went on, why must you insist that what isn't beautiful is ugly, and that what isn't good is bad? Now, coming back to Love, you've been forced to agree that he is neither good nor beautiful, but that's no reason for thinking that he must be bad and ugly. The fact is that he's between the two.

And yet, I said, it's generally agreed that he's a great god.

It all depends, she said, on what you mean by "generally." Do you mean simply people that don't know anything about it, or do you include the people that do?

I meant everybody.

At which she laughed, and said, Then can you tell me, my dear Socrates, how people can agree that he's a great god when they deny that he's a god at all?

What people do you mean? I asked her.

You for one, and I for another.

What on earth do you mean by that?

Oh, it's simple enough, she answered. Tell me, wouldn't you say that all the gods were happy and beautiful? Or would you suggest that any of them were neither?

Good heavens, no! said I.

And don't you call people happy when they possess the beautiful and the good?

Why, of course.

And yet you agreed just now that Love lacks, and consequently longs for, those very qualities?

Yes, so I did.

Then, if he has no part in either goodness or beauty, how can he be a god?

I suppose he can't be, I admitted.

And now, she said, haven't I proved that you're one of the people who don't believe in the divinity of Love?

Yes, but what can he be, then? I asked her. A mortal?

Not by any means.

Well, what then?

What I told you before—halfway between mortal and immortal.

And what do you mean by that, Diotima?

A very powerful spirit, Socrates, and spirits, you know, are halfway between god and man.

What powers have they, then? I asked.

They are the envoys and interpreters that ply between heaven and earth, flying upward with our worship and our prayers, and descending with the heavenly answers and commandments, and since they are between the two estates they weld both sides together and merge them into one great whole. They form the medium of the prophetic arts, of the priestly rites of sacrifice, initiation, and incantation, of divination and of sorcery, for the divine will not mingle directly with the human, and it is only through the mediation of the spirit world that man can have any intercourse, whether waking or sleeping, with the gods. And the man who is versed in such matters is said to have spiritual powers, as opposed to the mechanical powers of the man who is expert in the more mundane arts. There are many spirits, and many kinds of spirits, too, and Love is one of them.

Then who were his parents? I asked.

I'll tell you, she said, though it's rather a long story.

On the day of Aphrodite's birth the gods were making merry, and among them was Resource, the son of Craft. And when they had supped, Need came begging at the door because there was good cheer inside. Now, it happened that Resource, having drunk deeply of the heavenly nectar—for this was before the days of wine—wandered out into the garden of Zeus and sank into a heavy sleep, and Need, thinking that to get a child by Resource would mitigate her penury, lay down beside him and in time was brought to the bed of Love. So Love became the follower and servant of Aphrodite because he was begotten on the same day that she was born, and further, he was born to love the beautiful since Aphrodite is beautiful herself.

Then again, as the son of Resource and Need, it has been his fate to be always needy; nor is he delicate and lovely as most of us believe, but harsh and arid, barefoot and homeless, sleeping on the naked earth, in doorways, or in the very streets beneath the stars of heaven, and always partaking of his mother's poverty. But, secondly, he brings his father's resourcefulness to his designs upon the beautiful and the good, for he is gallant, impetuous, and energetic, a mighty hunter, and a master of device and artifice—at once desirous and full of wisdom, a life-long seeker after truth, and adept in sorcery, enchantment, and seduction.

He is neither mortal nor immortal, for in the space of a day he will be now, when all goes well with him, alive and blooming, and now dying, to be born again by virtue of his father's nature, while what he gains will always ebb away as fast. So Love is never altogether in or out of need, and stands, moreover, midway between ignorance and wisdom. You must understand that none of the gods are seekers after truth. They do not long for wisdom, because they are wise—and why should the wise be seeking the wisdom that is already theirs? Nor, for that matter, do the ignorant seek the truth or crave to be made wise. And indeed, what makes their cause so hopeless is that, having neither beauty, nor goodness, nor intelligence, they are satisfied with what they are, and do not long for the virtues they have never missed.

Then tell me, Diotima, I said, who are these seekers after truth, if they are neither the wise nor the ignorant?

Why, a schoolboy, she replied, could have told you that, after what I've just been saying. They are those that come between the two, and one of them is Love. For wisdom is concerned with the loveliest of things, and Love is the love of what is lovely. And so it follows that Love is a lover of wisdom, and, being such, he is placed between wisdom and ignorance—for which his parentage also is responsible, in that his father is full of wisdom and resource, while his mother is devoid of either.

Such, my dear Socrates, is the spirit of Love, and yet I'm not altogether surprised at your idea of him, which was, judging by what you said, that Love was the beloved rather than the lover. So naturally you thought of Love as utterly beautiful, for the beloved is, in fact, beautiful, perfect, delicate, and prosperous—very different from the lover, as I have described him.

Very well, dear lady, I replied, no doubt you're right. But in that case, what good can Love be to humanity?

That's just what I'm coming to, Socrates, she said. So much, then, for the nature and the origin of Love. You were right in thinking that he was the love of what is beautiful. But suppose someone were to say, Yes, my dear Socrates. Quite so, my dear Diotima. But what do you mean by the love of what is beautiful? Or, to put the question more precisely, what is it that the lover of the beautiful is longing for?

He is longing to make the beautiful his own, I said.

Very well, she replied, but your answer leads to another question. What will he gain by making the beautiful his own?

This, as I had to admit, was more than I could answer on the spur of the moment.

Well then, she went on, suppose that, instead of the beautiful, you were being asked about the good. I put it to you, Socrates. What is it that the lover of the good is longing for?

To make the good his own.

Then what will he gain by making it his own?

I can make a better shot at answering that, I said. He'll gain happiness.

Right, said she, for the happy are happy inasmuch as they possess the good, and since there's no need for us to ask why men should want to be happy, I think your answer is conclusive.

Absolutely, I agreed.

This longing, then, she went on, this love—is it common to all mankind? What do you think, do we all long to make the good our own?

Yes, I said, as far as that goes we're all alike.

Well then, Socrates, if we say that everybody always loves the same thing, does that mean that everybody is in love? Or do we mean that some of us are in love, while some of us are not?

I was a little worried about that myself, I confessed.

Oh, it's nothing to worry about, she assured me. You see, what we've been doing is to give the name of Love to what is only one single aspect of it; we make just the same mistake, you know, with a lot of other names.

For instance. . . ?

For instance, poetry. You'll agree that there is more than one kind of poetry in the true sense of the word—that is to say, calling something into existence that was not there before, so that every kind of artistic creation is poetry, and every artist is a poet.

True.

But all the same, she said, we don't call them all poets, do we? We give various names to the various arts, and only call the one particular art that deals with music and meter by the name that should be given to them all. And that's the only art that we call poetry, while those who practice it are known as poets.

Quite.

And that's how it is with Love. For "Love, that renowned and all-beguiling power," includes every kind of longing for happiness and for the good. Yet those of us who are subject to this longing in the various fields of business, athletics, philosophy, and so on, are never said to be in love, and are never known as lovers, while the man who devotes himself to what is only one of Love's many activities is given the name that should apply to all the rest as well.

Yes, I said, I suppose you must be right.

I know it has been suggested, she continued, that lovers are people who are looking for their other halves, but as I see it, Socrates, Love never longs for either the half or the whole of anything except the good. For men will even have their hands and feet cut off if they are once convinced that those members are bad for them. Indeed I think we only prize our own belongings insofar as we say that the good belongs to us, and the bad to someone else, for what we love is the good and nothing but the good. Or do you disagree?

Good heavens, no! I said.

Then may we state categorically that men are lovers of the good?

Yes, I said, we may.

And shouldn't we add that they long for the good to be their own?

We should.

And not merely to be their own but to be their own forever?

Yes, that must follow.

In short, that Love longs for the good to be his own forever?

Yes, I said, that's absolutely true.

Very well, then. And that being so, what course will Love's followers pursue, and in what particular field will eagerness and exertion be known as Love? In fact, what *is* this activity? Can you tell me that, Socrates?

If I could, my dear Diotima, I retorted, I shouldn't be so much amazed at *your* grasp of the subject, and I shouldn't be coming to you to learn the answer to that very question.

Well, I'll tell you, then, she said. To love is to bring forth upon the beautiful, both in body and in soul.

I'm afraid that's too deep, I said, for my poor wits to fathom.

I'll try to speak more plainly, then. We are all of us prolific, Socrates, in body and in soul, and when we reach a certain age our nature urges us to procreation. Nor can we be quickened by ugliness, but only by the beautiful. Conception, we know, takes place when man and woman come together, but there's a divinity in human propagation, an immortal something in the midst of man's mortality which is incompatible with any kind of discord. And ugliness is at odds with the divine, while beauty is in perfect harmony. In propagation, then, Beauty is the goddess of both fate and travail, and so when procreancy draws near the beautiful it grows genial and blithe, and birth follows swiftly on conception. But when it meets with ugliness it is overcome with heaviness and gloom, and turning away it shrinks into itself and is not brought to bed, but still labors under its painful burden. And so, when the procreant is big with child, he is strangely stirred by the beautiful, because he knows that Beauty's tenant will bring his travail to an end. So you see, Socrates, that Love is not exactly a longing for the beautiful, as you suggested.

Well, what is it, then?

A longing not for the beautiful itself, but for the conception and generation that the beautiful effects.

Yes. No doubt you're right.

Of course I'm right, she said. And why all this longing for propagation? Because this is the one deathless and eternal element in our mortality. And since we have agreed that the lover longs for the good to be his own forever, it follows that we are bound to long for immortality as well as for the good—which is to say that Love is a longing for immortality.

So much I gathered, gentlemen, at one time and another from Diotima's dissertations upon Love.

And then one day she asked me, Well, Socrates, and what do you suppose is the cause of all this longing and all this love? Haven't you noticed what an extraordinary effect the breeding instinct has upon both animals and birds, and how obsessed they are with the desire, first to mate, and then to rear their litters and their broods, and how the weakest of them are ready to stand up to the strongest in defense of their young, and even die for them, and how they are content to bear the pinch of hunger and every kind of hardship, so long as they can rear their offspring?

With men, she went on, you might put it down to the power of reason, but how can you account for Love's having such remarkable effects upon the brutes? What do you say to that, Socrates?

Again I had to confess my ignorance.

Well, she said, I don't know how you can hope to master the philosophy of Love, if *that's* too much for you to understand.

But, my dear Diotima, I protested, as I said before, that's just why I'm asking you to teach me—because I realize how ignorant I am. And I'd be more than grateful if you'd enlighten me as to the cause not only of this, but of all the various effects of Love.

Well, she said, it's simple enough, so long as you bear in mind what we agreed was the object of Love. For here, too, the principle holds good that the mortal does all it can to put on immortality. And how can it do that except by breeding, and thus ensuring that there will always be a younger generation to take the place of the old?

Now, although we speak of an individual as being the same so long as he continues to exist in the same form, and therefore assume that a man is the same person in his dotage as in his infancy, yet, for all we call him the same, every bit of him is different, and every day he is becoming a new man, while the old man is ceasing to exist, as you can see from his hair, his flesh, his bones, his blood, and all the rest of his body. And not only his body, for the same thing happens to his soul. And neither his manners, nor his disposition, nor his thoughts, nor his desires, nor his pleasures, nor his sufferings, nor his fears are the same throughout his life, for some of them grow, while others disappear.

And the application of this principle to human knowledge is even more remarkable, for not only do some of the things we know increase, while some of them are lost, so that even in our knowledge we are not always the same, but the principle applies as well to every single branch of knowledge. When we say we are studying, we really mean that our knowledge is ebbing away. We forget, because our knowledge disappears, and we have to study so as to replace what we are losing, so that the state of our knowledge may seem, at any rate, to be the same as it was before.

This is how every mortal creature perpetuates itself. It cannot, like the divine, be still the same throughout eternity; it can only leave behind new life to fill the vacancy that is left in its species by obsolescence. This, my dear Socrates, is how the body and all else that is temporal partakes of the eternal; there is no other way. And so it is no wonder that every creature prizes its own issue, since the whole creation is inspired by this love, this passion for immortality.

Well, Diotima, I said, when she had done, that's a most impressive argument. I wonder if you're right.

Of course I am, she said with an air of authority that was almost professorial. Think of the ambitions of your fellow men, and though at first they may strike you as upsetting my argument, you'll see how right I am if you only bear in mind that men's great incentive is the love of glory, and that their one idea is, "To win eternal mention in the deathless roll of fame."

For the sake of fame they will dare greater dangers, even, than for their children; they are ready to spend their money like water and to wear their fingers to the bone, and, if it comes to that, to die.

Do you think, she went on, that Alcestis would have laid down her life to save Admetus, or that Achilles would have died for the love he bore Patroclus, or that Codrus, the Athenian king, would have sacrificed himself for the seed of his royal consort, if they had not hoped to win "the deathless name for valor," which, in fact, posterity has granted them? No, Socrates, no. Every one of us, no matter what he does, is longing for the endless fame, the incomparable glory that is theirs, and the nobler he is, the greater his ambition, because he is in love with the eternal.

Well then, she went on, those whose procreancy is of the body turn to woman as the object of their love, and raise a family, in the blessed hope that by doing so they will keep their memory green, "through time and through eternity." But those whose procreancy is of the spirit rather than of the flesh—and they are not unknown, Socrates—conceive and bear the things of the spirit. And what are they? you ask. Wisdom and all her sister virtues; it is the office of every poet to beget them, and of every artist whom we may call creative.

Now, by far the most important kind of wisdom, she went on, is that which governs the ordering of society, and which goes by the names of justice and moderation. And if any man is so closely allied to the divine as to be teeming with these virtues even in his youth, and if, when he comes to manhood, his first ambition is to be begetting, he too, you may be sure, will go about in search of the loveliness—and never of the ugliness—on which he may beget. And hence his procreant nature is attracted by a comely body rather than an ill-favored one, and if, besides, he happens on a soul which is at once beautiful, distinguished, and agreeable, he is charmed to find so welcome an alliance. It will be easy for him to talk of virtue to such a listener, and to discuss what human goodness is and how the virtuous should live—in short, to undertake the other's education.

And, as I believe, by constant association with so much beauty, and by thinking of his friend when he is present and when he is away, he will be delivered of the burden he has labored under all these years. And what is more, he and his friend will help each other rear the issue of their friendship—and so the bond between them will be more binding, and their communion even more complete, than that which comes of bringing children up, because they have created something lovelier and less mortal than human seed.

And I ask you, who would not prefer such fatherhood to merely human propagation, if he stopped to think of Homer, and Hesiod, and all the greatest of our poets? Who would not envy them their immortal progeny, their claim upon the admiration of posterity?

Or think of Lycurgus, she went on, and what offspring he left behind him in his laws, which proved to be the saviors of Sparta and, perhaps, the whole of Hellas. Or think of the fame of Solon, the father of Athenian law, and think of all the other names that are remembered in Grecian cities and in lands beyond the sea for the noble deeds they did before the eyes of all the world, and for all the diverse virtues that they fathered. And think of all the shrines that have been dedicated to them in memory of their immortal issue, and tell me if you can of *anyone* whose mortal children have brought him so much fame.

Well now, my dear Socrates, I have no doubt that even you might be initiated into these, the more elementary mysteries of Love. But I don't know whether you could apprehend the final revelation, for so far, you know, we are only at the bottom of the true scale of perfection.

Never mind, she went on, I will do all I can to help you understand, and you must strain every nerve to follow what I'm saying.

Well then, she began, the candidate for this initiation cannot, if his efforts are to be rewarded, begin too early to devote himself to the beauties of the body. First of all, if his preceptor instructs him as he should, he will fall in love with the beauty of one individual body, so that his passion may give life to noble discourse. Next he must consider how nearly related the beauty of any one body is to the beauty of any other, when he will see that if he is to devote himself to loveliness of form it will be absurd to deny that the beauty of each and every body is the same. Having reached this point, he must set himself to be the lover of every lovely body, and bring his passion for the one into due proportion by deeming it of little or of no importance.

Next he must grasp that the beauties of the body are as nothing to the beauties of the soul, so that wherever he meets with spiritual loveliness, even in the husk of an unlovely body, he will find it beautiful enough to fall in love with and to cherish—and beautiful enough to quicken in his heart a longing for such discourse as tends toward the building of a noble nature. And from this he will be led to contemplate the beauty of laws and institutions. And when he discovers how nearly every kind of beauty is akin to every other he will conclude that the beauty of the body is not, after all, of so great moment.

And next, his attention should be diverted from institutions to the sciences, so that he may know the beauty of every kind of knowledge. And thus, by scanning beauty's wide horizon, he will be saved from a slavish and illiberal devotion to the individual loveliness of a single boy, a single man, or a single institution. And, turning his eyes toward the open sea of beauty, he will find in such contemplation the seed of the most fruitful discourse and the loftiest thought, and reap a golden harvest of philosophy, until, confirmed and strengthened, he will come upon one single form of knowledge, the knowledge of the beauty I am about to speak of.

And here, she said, you must follow me as closely as you can.

Whoever has been initiated so far in the mysteries of Love and has viewed all these aspects of the beautiful in due succession, is at last drawing near the final revelation. And now, Socrates, there bursts upon him that wondrous vision which is the very soul of the beauty he has toiled so long for. It is an everlasting loveliness which neither comes nor goes, which neither flowers nor fades, for such beauty is the same on every hand, the same then as now, here as there, this way as that way, the same to every worshiper as it is to every other.

Nor will his vision of the beautiful take the form of a face, or of hands, or of anything that is of the flesh. It will be neither words, nor knowledge, nor a something that exists in something else, such as a living creature, or the earth, or the heavens, or anything that is—but subsisting of itself and by itself in an eternal oneness, while every lovely thing partakes of it in such sort that, however much the parts may wax and wane, it will be neither more nor less, but still the same inviolable whole.

And so, when his prescribed devotion to boyish beauties has carried our candidate so far that the universal beauty dawns upon his inward sight, he is almost within reach of the final revelation. And this is the way, the only way, he must approach, or be led toward, the sanctuary of Love. Starting from individual beauties, the quest for the universal beauty must find him ever mounting the heavenly ladder, stepping from rung to rung— that is, from one to two, and from two to *every* lovely body, from bodily beauty to the beauty of institutions, from institutions to learning, and from learning in general to the special lore that pertains to nothing but the beautiful itself—until at last he comes to know what beauty is.

And if, my dear Socrates, Diotima went on, man's life is ever worth the living, it is when he has attained this vision of the very soul of beauty. And once you have seen it, you will never be seduced again by the charm of gold, of dress, of comely boys, or lads just ripening to manhood; you will care nothing for the beauties that used to take your breath away and kindle such a longing in you, and many others like you, Socrates, to be always at the side of the beloved and feasting your eyes upon him, so that you would be content, if it were possible, to deny yourself the grosser necessities of meat and drink, so long as you were with him.

But if it were given to man to gaze on beauty's very self— unsullied, unalloyed, and freed from the mortal taint that haunts the frailer loveliness of flesh and blood—if, I say, it were given to man to see the heavenly beauty face to face, would you call *his,* she asked me, an unenviable life, whose eyes had been opened to the vision, and who had gazed upon it in true contemplation until it had become his own forever?

And remember, she said, that it is only when he discerns beauty itself through what makes it visible that a man will be quickened with the true, and not the seeming, virtue—for it is virtue's self that quickens him, not virtue's semblance. And when he has brought forth and reared this perfect virtue, he shall be called the friend of god, and if ever it is given to man to put on immortality, it shall be given to him.

This, Phaedrus—this, gentlemen—was the doctrine of Diotima. I was convinced, and in that conviction I try to bring others to the same creed, and to convince them that, if we are to make this gift our own, Love will help our mortal nature more than all the world. And this is why I say that every man of us should worship the god of love, and this is why I cultivate and worship all the elements of Love myself, and bid others do the same. And all my life I shall pay the power and the might of Love such homage as I can. So you may call this my eulogy of Love, Phaedrus, if you choose; if not, well, call it what you like.

Socrates took his seat amid applause from everyone but Aristophanes, who was just going to take up the reference Socrates had made to his own theories, when suddenly there came a knocking at the outer door, followed by the notes of a flute and the sound of festive brawling in the street.

Go and see who it is, said Agathon to the servants. If it's one of our particular friends you can ask him in, but if not, you'd better say the party's over and there's nothing left to drink.

Well, it wasn't long before they could hear Alcibiades shouting in the courtyard, evidently very drunk, and demanding where Agathon was, because he *must* see Agathon at once. So the flute girl and some of his other followers helped him stagger in, and there he stood in the doorway, with a mass of ribbons and an enormous wreath of ivy and violets sprouting on his head, and addressed the company.

Good evening, gentlemen, he said. I'm pretty well bottled already, so if you'd rather I didn't join the party, only say the word and I'll go away, as soon as I've hung this wreath on Agathon's head—which is what I really came for. I couldn't get along yesterday, so here I am tonight, with a bunch of ribbons on my head, all ready to take them off and put them on the head of the cleverest, the most attractive, and, I may say—well, anyway, I'm going to crown him. And now I suppose you're laughing at me, just because I'm drunk. Go on, have your laugh out, don't mind me. I'm not so drunk that I don't know what I'm saying, and you can't deny it's true. Well, what do you say, gentlemen? Can I come in on that footing? And shall we all have a drink together, or shan't we?

At that they all cheered and told him to come in and make himself at home, while Agathon gave him a more formal invitation. And while his people helped him in he started pulling off the ribbons, so that he could transfer them to Agathon's head as soon as he was near enough. As it happened, the wreath slipped over his eyes and he didn't notice Socrates, although he sat down on the same couch, between him and Agathon—for Socrates had made room for him as soon as he came in. So down he sat, with a "How d' you do!" to Agathon, and began to tie the ribbons round his head.

Then Agathon said to the servants, Here, take off Alcibiades' shoes, so that we can all three make ourselves comfortable.

Yes, do, said Alcibiades. But just a minute, who's the third?

And when he turned round and saw who it was, he leaped out of his seat and cried, Well I'll be damned! You again, Socrates! So that's what you're up to, is it?—The same old game of lying in wait and popping out at me when I least expect you. Well, what's in the wind tonight? And what do you mean by sitting *here,* and not by Aristophanes or one of these other humorists? Why make such a point of sitting next to the handsomest man in the room?

I say, Agathon, said Socrates, I'll have to ask you to protect me. You know, it's a dreadful thing to be in love with Alcibiades. It's been the same ever since I fell in love with him; I've only got to look at anyone who's in the least attractive, or say a single word to him, and he flies into a fit of jealous fury, and calls me the most dreadful names, and behaves as if it was all he could do to keep his hands off me. So I hope you'll keep an eye on him, in case he tries to do me an injury. If you can get him to be friends, so much the better, but if you can't, and if he gets violent, you'll really have to protect me—for I shudder to think what lengths he might go to in his amorous transports.

Friends with *you?* said Alcibiades. Not on your life! I'll be getting my own back on you one of these days, but at the moment—Agathon, give me back some of those ribbons, will you? I want to crown Socrates' head as well—and a most extraordinary head it is. I don't want him to say I wreathed a garland for Agathon and none for him, when *his* words have been too much for all the world—and all his life too, Agathon, not just the other day, like yours.

So saying, he crowned Socrates' head with a bunch of ribbons, and took his seat again.

And now, gentlemen, he said, as he settled himself on the couch, can I be right in thinking that you're sober? I say, you know, we can't have this! Come on, drink up! You promised to have a drink with me. Now, I'll tell you, there's no one fit to take the chair at this meeting—until you've all got reasonably drunk—but me. Come on, Agathon, tell them to bring out something that's worth drinking out of.

No, never mind, he went on. Here, you, just bring me that wine cooler, will you?

He saw it would hold a couple of quarts or so. He made them fill it up, and took the first drink himself, after which he told them to fill it again for Socrates, and remarked to the others, But I shan't get any change out of *him.* It doesn't matter *how* much you make him drink, it never makes him drunk.

Meanwhile the servant had filled the wine cooler up for Socrates and he had his drink.

But here Eryximachus broke in, Is this the way to do things, Alcibiades? he asked. Is there to be no grace before we drink? Are we to pour the wine down our throats like a lot of thirsty savages?

Why, there's Eryximachus, said Alcibiades, the noblest, soberest father's soberest, noblest son, what? Hallo, Eryximachus!

Hallo yourself, said Eryximachus. Well, what do you say?

What do *you* say? retorted Alcibiades. We have to take *your* orders, you know. What's the tag?—"A good physician's more than all the world." So let's have your prescription.

Here it is, then, said Eryximachus. Before you came in we had arranged for each of us in turn, going round from left to right, to make the best speech he could in praise of Love. Well, we've all had our turn; so since you've had your drink without having made a speech I think it's only right that you should make it now. And then, when you've finished, you can tell Socrates to do whatever you like and he can do the same to the next man on his right, and so on all the way round.

That's a very good idea, Eryximachus, said Alcibiades. Only you know it's hardly fair to ask a man that's more than half cut already to compete with a lot of fellows who are practically sober. And another thing, my dear Eryximachus. You mustn't believe a word of what Socrates has just been telling you. Don't you see that it's just the other way round? It's him that can't keep his hands off *me* if he hears me say a good word for anyone—god or man—but him.

Oh, do be quiet, said Socrates.

You can't deny it, retorted Alcibiades. God knows I've never been able to praise anyone else in front of you.

Now there's a good idea, said Eryximachus. Why don't you give us a eulogy of Socrates?

Do you really mean that? asked Alcibiades. Do you think I ought to, Eryximachus? Shall I go for him, and let you all hear me get my own back?

Here, I say, protested Socrates. What are you up to now? Do you want to make me look a fool with this eulogy, or what?

I'm simply going to tell the truth—you won't mind that, will you?

Oh, of course, said Socrates, you may tell the truth; in fact I'll go so far as to say you must.

Then here goes, said Alcibiades. There's one thing, though. If I say a word that's not the solemn truth I want you to stop me right away and tell me I'm a liar—but I promise you it won't be my fault if I do. On the other hand, you mustn't be surprised if I tell them about you just as it comes into my head, and jump from one thing to another. You can't expect anyone that's as drunk as I am to give a clear and systematic account of all *your* eccentricities.

Well, gentlemen, I propose to begin my eulogy of Socrates with a simile. I expect he'll think I'm making fun of him, but, as it happens, I'm using this particular simile not because it's funny, but because it's true. What he reminds me of more than anything is one of those little sileni that you see on the statuaries' stalls; you know the ones I mean—they're modeled with pipes or flutes in their hands, and when you open them down the middle there are little figures of the gods inside. And then again, he reminds me of Marsyas the satyr.

Now I don't think even you, Socrates, will have the face to deny that you *look* like them, but the resemblance goes deeper than that, as I'm going to show. You're quite as impudent as a satyr, aren't you? If you plead not guilty I can call witnesses to prove it. And aren't you a piper as well? I should think you were—and a far more wonderful piper than Marsyas, who had only to put his flute to his lips to bewitch mankind. It can still be done, too, by anyone who can play the tunes he used to play. Why, there wasn't a note of Olympus' melodies that he hadn't learned from Marsyas. And whoever plays them, from an absolute virtuoso to a twopenny-halfpenny flute girl, the tunes will still have a magic power, and by virtue of their own divinity they will show which of us are fit subjects for divine initiation.

Now the only difference, Socrates, between you and Marsyas is that you can get just the same effect without any instrument at all—with nothing but a few simple words, not even poetry. Besides, when we listen to anyone else talking, however eloquent he is, we don't really care a damn what he says. But when we listen to you, or to someone else repeating what you've said, even if he puts it ever so badly, and never mind whether the person who's listening is man, woman, or child, we're absolutely staggered and bewitched. And speaking for myself, gentlemen, if I wasn't afraid you'd tell me I was completely bottled, I'd swear on oath what an extraordinary effect his words have had on me—and still do, if it comes to that. For the moment I hear him speak I am smitten with a kind of sacred rage, worse than any Corybant, and my heart jumps into my mouth and the tears start into my eyes—oh, and not only me, but lots of other men.

Yes, I've heard Pericles and all the other great orators, and very eloquent I thought they were, but they never affected me like that; they never turned my whole soul upside down and left me feeling as if I were the lowest of the low. But this latter-day Marsyas, here, has often left me in such a state of mind that I've felt I simply couldn't go on living the way I did—now, Socrates, you can't say that isn't true—and I'm convinced that if I were to listen to him at this very moment I'd feel just the same again. I simply couldn't help it. He makes me admit that while I'm spending my time on politics I am neglecting all the things that are crying for attention in myself. So I just refuse to listen to him—as if he were one of those Sirens, you know—and get out of earshot as quick as I can, for fear he keep me sitting listening till I'm positively senile.

And there's one thing I've never felt with anybody else—not the kind of thing you'd expect to find in me, either—and that is a sense of shame. Socrates is the only man in the world that

can make me feel ashamed. Because there's no getting away
from it, I know I ought to do the things he tells me to, and
yet the moment I'm out of his sight I don't care what I do to
keep in with the mob. So I dash off like a runaway slave, and
keep out of his way as long as I can, and then next time I meet
him I remember all that I had to admit the time before, and
naturally I feel ashamed. There are times when I'd honestly be
glad to hear that he was dead, and yet I know that if he did
die I'd be more upset than ever—so I ask you, what is a man
to do?

Well, that's what this satyr does for me, and plenty like me,
with his pipings. And now let me show you how apt my comparison was in other ways, and what extraordinary powers he
has got. Take my word for it, there's not one of you that really
knows him. But now I've started on him, I'll show him up.
Notice, for instance, how Socrates is attracted by good-looking
people, and how he hangs around them, positively gaping with
admiration. Then again, he loves to appear utterly uninformed
and ignorant—isn't that like Silenus? Of course it is. Don't you
see that it's just his outer casing, like those little figures I was
telling you about? But believe me, friends and fellow drunks,
you've only got to open him up and you'll find him so full of
temperance and sobriety that you'll hardly believe your eyes.
Because, you know, he doesn't really care a row of pins about
good looks—on the contrary, you can't think how much he
looks down on them—or money, or any of the honors that most
people care about. He doesn't care a curse for anything of that
kind, or for any of us either—yes, I'm telling you—and he
spends his whole life playing his little game of irony, and laughing up his sleeve at all the world.

I don't know whether anybody else has ever opened him up
when he's been being serious, and seen the little images inside,
but I saw them once, and they looked so godlike, so golden, so
beautiful, and so utterly amazing that there was nothing for it

but to do exactly what he told me. I used to flatter myself that he was smitten with my youthful charms, and I thought this was an extraordinary piece of luck because I'd only got to be a bit accommodating and I'd hear everything he had to say—I tell you, I'd a pretty high opinion of my own attractions. Well, I thought it over, and then, instead of taking a servant with me as I always used to, I got rid of the man, and went to meet Socrates by myself. Remember, I'm bound to tell you the whole truth and nothing but the truth; so you'd all better listen very carefully, and Socrates must pull me up if I begin telling lies.

Well, gentlemen, as I was saying, I used to go and meet him, and then, when we were by ourselves, I quite expected to hear some of those sweet nothings that lovers whisper to their darlings when they get them alone—and I liked the idea of that. But not a bit of it! He'd go on talking just the same as usual till it was time for him to go, and then he said good-bye and went.

So then I suggested we should go along to the gymnasium and take a bit of exercise together, thinking that something was bound to happen there. And, would you believe it, we did our exercises together and wrestled with each other time and again, with not a soul in sight, and still I got no further. Well, I realized that there was nothing to be gained in *that* direction, but having put my hand to the plow I wasn't going to look back till I was absolutely certain how I stood; so I decided to make a frontal attack. I asked him to dinner, just as if I were the lover trying to seduce his beloved, instead of the other way round. It wasn't easy, either, to get him to accept, but in the end I managed to.

Well, the first time he came he thought he ought to go as soon as we'd finished dinner, and I was too shy to stop him. But next time, I contrived to keep him talking after dinner, and went on far into the night, and then, when he said he must be going, I told him it was much too late and pressed him to stay the night with me. So he turned in on the couch beside me—where he'd sat at dinner—and the two of us had the room to ourselves.

So far I've said nothing I need blush to repeat in any company, but you'd never have heard what I'm going to tell you now if there wasn't something in the proverb, "Drunkards and children tell the truth"—drunkards anyway. Besides, having once embarked on my eulogy of Socrates it wouldn't be fair not to tell you about the arrogant way he treated me. People say, you know, that when a man's been bitten by a snake he won't tell anybody what it feels like except a fellow sufferer, because no one else would sympathize with him if the pain drove him into making a fool of himself. Well, that's just how I feel, only I've been bitten by something much more poisonous than a snake; in fact, mine is the most painful kind of bite there is. I've been bitten in the heart, or the mind, or whatever you like to call it, by Socrates' philosophy, which clings like an adder to any young and gifted mind it can get hold of, and does exactly what it likes with it. And looking round me, gentlemen, I see Phaedrus, and Agathon, and Eryximachus, and Pausanias, and Aristodemus, and Aristophanes, and all the rest of them—to say nothing of Socrates himself—and every one of you has had his taste of this philosophical frenzy, this sacred rage; so I don't mind telling *you* about it because I know you'll make allowances for me—both for the way I behaved with Socrates and for what I'm saying now. But the servants must put their fingers in their ears, and so must anybody else who's liable to be at all profane or beastly.

Well then, gentlemen, when the lights were out and the servants had all gone, I made up my mind to stop beating about the bush and tell him what I thought point-blank.

So I nudged him and said, Are you asleep, Socrates?

No, I'm not, he said.

Then do you know what I think? I asked.

Well, what?

I think, I said, you're the only lover I've ever had who's been really worthy of me. Only you're too shy to talk about it. Well, this is how I look at it. I think it'd be just as absurd to refuse you *this* as anything else you wanted that belonged to me or any of my friends. If there's one thing I'm keen on it's to make the best of myself, and I think you're more likely to help me there than anybody else, and I'm sure I'd find it harder to justify myself to men of sense for refusing to accommodate a friend of that sort than to defend myself to the vulgar if I *had* been kind to him.

He heard me out, and then said with that ironical simplicity of his, My dear Alcibiades, I've no doubt there's a lot in what you say, if you're right in thinking that I have some kind of power that would make a better man of you, because in that case you must find me so extraordinarily beautiful that your own attractions must be quite eclipsed. And if you're trying to barter your own beauty for the beauty you have found in me, you're driving a very hard bargain, let me tell you. You're trying to exchange the semblance of beauty for the thing itself—like Diomede and Glaucus swapping bronze for gold. But you know, my dear fellow, you really must be careful. Suppose you're making a mistake, and I'm not worth anything at all. The mind's eye begins to see clearly when the outer eyes grow dim—and I fancy yours are still pretty keen.

To which I replied, Well, I've told you exactly how I feel about it, and now it's for you to settle what's best for us both.

That sounds reasonable enough, he said. We must think it over one of these days, and do whatever seems best for the two of us—about this and everything else.

Well, by this time I felt that I had shot my bolt, and I'd a pretty shrewd idea that I'd registered a hit. So I got up, and, without giving him a chance to say a word, I wrapped my own cloak round him—for this was in the winter—and, creeping under his shabby old mantle, I took him in my arms and lay there all night with this godlike and extraordinary man—you can't deny that, either, Socrates. And after *that* he had the insolence, the infernal arrogance, to laugh at my youthful beauty and jeer at the one thing I was really proud of, gentlemen of the jury—I say "jury" because that's what you're here for, to try the man Socrates on the charge of arrogance—and believe it, gentlemen, or believe it not, when I got up the next morning I had no more *slept* with Socrates, within the meaning of the act, than if he'd been my father or an elder brother.

You can guess what I felt like after *that*. I was torn between my natural humiliation and my admiration for his manliness and self-control, for this was strength of mind such as I had never hoped to meet. And so I couldn't take offense and cut myself off from his society, but neither was there any way I could think of to attract him. I knew very well that I'd no more chance of getting at him with money than I had of getting at Ajax with a spear, and the one thing I'd made sure would catch him had already failed. So I was at my wits' end, and went about in a state of such utter subjection to the man as was never seen before.

It was after all this, you must understand, that we were both sent on active service to Potidaea, where we messed together. Well, to begin with, he stood the hardships of the campaign far better than I did, or anyone else, for that matter. And if— and it's always liable to happen when there's fighting going on—we were cut off from our supplies, there was no one who put such a good face on it as he. But on the other hand, when there was plenty to eat he was the one man who really seemed to enjoy it, and though he didn't drink for choice, if we ever pressed him to he'd beat the lot of us. And, what's the most extraordinary thing of all, there's not a man living that's ever seen Socrates drunk. And I dare say he'll have a chance to show what he's made of before *this* party's over.

Then again, the way he got through that winter was most impressive, and the winters over there are pretty shocking. There was one time when the frost was harder than ever, and all the rest of us stayed inside, or if we did go out we wrapped ourselves up to the eyes and tied bits of felt and sheepskins over our shoes, but Socrates went out in the same old coat he'd always worn, and made less fuss about walking on the ice in his bare feet than we did in our shoes. So much so, that the men began to look at him with some suspicion and actually took his toughness as a personal insult to themselves.

Well, so much for that. And now I must tell you about another thing "our valiant hero dared and did" in the course of the same campaign. He started wrestling with some problem or other about sunrise one morning, and stood there lost in thought, and when the answer wouldn't come he still stood there thinking and refused to give it up. Time went on, and by about midday the troops noticed what was happening, and naturally they were rather surprised and began telling each other how Socrates had been standing there thinking ever since daybreak. And at last, toward nightfall, some of the Ionians brought out their bedding after supper—this was in the summer, of course—partly because it was cooler in the open air, and partly to see whether he was going to stay there all night. Well, there he stood till morning, and then at sunrise he said his prayers to the sun and went away.

And now I expect you'd like to hear what kind of a show he made when we went into action, and I certainly think you ought to know. They gave me a decoration after one engagement, and do you know, Socrates had saved my life, absolutely singlehanded. I'd been wounded and he refused to leave me, and he got me out of it, too, armor and all. And as you know, Socrates, I went straight to the general staff and told them *you* ought to have the decoration, and you can neither deny that nor blame me for doing it. But the authorities thought they'd rather give it to me, because of my family connections and so forth, and you were even keener than they were that I should have it instead of you.

And then, gentlemen, you should have seen him when we were in retreat from Delium. I happened to be in the cavalry, while he was serving with the line. Our people were falling back in great disorder and he was retreating with Laches when I happened to catch sight of them. I shouted to them not to be downhearted and promised to stand by them. And this time I'd a better chance of watching Socrates than I'd had at Potidaea—you see, being mounted, I wasn't quite so frightened. And I noticed for one thing how much cooler he was than Laches, and for another how—to borrow from a line of yours, Aristophanes—he was walking about with the same "lofty strut and sideways glance" that he goes about with here in Athens. His "sideways glance" was just as unconcerned whether he was looking at his own friends or at the enemy, and you could see from half a mile away that if you tackled *him* you'd get as good as you gave—with the result that he and Laches both got clean away. For you're generally pretty safe if that's the way you look when you're in action; it's the man whose one idea it is to get away that the other fellow goes for.

Well, there's a lot more to be said about Socrates, all very peculiar and all very much to his credit. No doubt there's just as much to be said about any of his little ways, but personally I think the most amazing thing about him is the fact that he is absolutely unique; there's no one like him, and I don't believe there ever was. You could point to some likeness to Achilles in Brasidas and the rest of them; you might compare Nestor and Antenor, and so on, with Pericles. There are plenty of such parallels in history, but you'll never find anyone like Socrates, or any ideas like his ideas, in our own times or in the past— unless, of course, you take a leaf out of my book and compare him, not with human beings, but with sileni and satyrs—and the same with his ideas.

Which reminds me of a point I missed at the beginning; I should have explained how his arguments, too, were exactly like those sileni that open down the middle. Anyone listening to Socrates for the first time would find his arguments simply laughable; he wraps them up in just the kind of expressions you'd expect of such an insufferable satyr. He talks about pack asses and blacksmiths and shoemakers and tanners, and he always seems to be saying the same old thing in just the same old way, so that anyone who wasn't used to his style and wasn't very quick on the uptake would naturally take it for the most utter nonsense. But if you open up his arguments, and really get into the skin of them, you'll find that they're the only arguments in the world that have any sense at all, and that nobody else's are so godlike, so rich in images of virtue, or so peculiarly, so entirely, pertinent to those inquiries that help the seeker on his way to the goal of true nobility.

And there, gentlemen, you have my eulogy of Socrates, with a few complaints thrown in about the unspeakable way he's treated me. I'm not the only one, either; there's Charmides, and Euthydemus, and ever so many more. He's made fools of them all, just as if he were the beloved, not the lover. Now, Agathon, I'm telling you this for your own good, so that you'll know what to look out for, and I hope you'll learn from our misfortunes, and not wait for your own to bring it home to you, like the poor fool in the adage.

As Alcibiades took his seat there was a good deal of laughter at his frankness—especially as he seemed to be still in love with Socrates. But the latter said, I don't believe you're as drunk as you make out, Alcibiades, or you'd never have given the argument such a subtle twist and obscured the real issue. What you were really after—though you only slipped it in casually toward the end—was to make trouble between me and Agathon, so that I as your lover, and he as your beloved, should both belong to you and nobody else. But you can't humbug me; I can see what you're getting at with all this satyr and silenus business. I only hope, Agathon, my dear, that he won't succeed, and I hope you'll be very careful not to let anybody come between us.

I'm inclined to think you're right, Socrates, said Agathon. Remember how he sat down in the middle so as to keep us apart. But I'll come round and sit next to you, so that won't help him very much.

Yes, do, said Socrates. Come round the other side.

Oh, God! cried Alcibiades. Look what I have to put up with! He's determined to drive me off the field. All the same, Socrates, I think you might let Agathon sit in the middle.

Oh, no, said Socrates, that would never do. Now you've finished singing my praises, I've got to do the same by the next man on my right. So you see, if he sat next to you, he'd have to start eulogizing me before he'd had my eulogy of him. So be a good chap and let the boy alone; you mustn't grudge him the praise I'm going to give him, because I'm dying to start my eulogy.

Aha! cried Agathon. You don't catch me staying *here* much longer, Alcibiades. I shall certainly change places if it means a tribute from Socrates.

Oh, it's always the same, said Alcibiades bitterly. No one else gets a look in with the beauties when Socrates is there. Look how easily he trumped up an excuse for Agathon to sit beside him.

And then, all of a sudden, just as Agathon was getting up to go and sit by Socrates, a whole crowd of revelers came to the door, and finding it open, as someone was just going out, they marched straight in and joined the party. No sooner had they sat down than the whole place was in an uproar; decency and order went by the board, and everybody had to drink the most enormous quantities of wine. By this time Eryximachus and Phaedrus and some of the others were beginning to leave, so Aristodemus told me, while he himself fell off to sleep.

He slept on for some time, for this was in the winter and the nights were long, and when at last he woke it was near daybreak and the cocks were crowing. He noticed that all the others had either gone home or fallen asleep, except Agathon and Aristophanes and Socrates, who were still awake and drinking out of an enormous bowl which they kept passing round from left to right. Socrates was arguing with the others—not that Aristodemus could remember very much of what he said, for, besides having missed the beginning, he was still more than half asleep. But the gist of it was that Socrates was forcing them to admit that the same man might be capable of writing both comedy and tragedy—that the tragic poet might be a comedian as well.

But as he clinched the argument, which the other two were scarcely in a state to follow, they began to nod, and first Aristophanes fell off to sleep and then Agathon, as day was breaking. Whereupon Socrates tucked them up comfortably and went away, followed, of course, by Aristodemus. And after calling at the Lyceum for a bath, he spent the rest of the day as usual, and then, toward evening, made his way home to rest.